Measuring Educational Progress

A STUDY OF THE NATIONAL ASSESSMENT

Measuring Educational Progress

WILLIAM GREENBAUM
Harvard University

with MICHAEL S. GARET, M.I.T.

and ELLEN R. SOLOMON, Harvard University

including
a response from
the Staff of the National Assessment of Educational Progress

McGRAW-HILL BOOK COMPANY

New York   St. Louis   San Francisco   Düsseldorf
London   Mexico   Sydney   Toronto

Library of Congress Cataloging in Publication Data

Greenbaum, William.
Measuring educational progress.
Bibliography: p.
Includes index.
1. National Assessment of Educational Progress
(Project)   2.   Educational surveys.   3.   Education—United
States.   I.   Garet, Michael S., joint author.   II.   Solomon, Ellen R.,
joint author.   III.   Title.
LB2823.G73   379'.151'0973   76-25986
ISBN 0-07-024285-2

1 2 3 4 5 6 7 8 9   RRDRRD   7 5 4 3 2 1 0 8 7

The editors for this book were Thomas Quinn and Cheryl Hanks, the designer
was Ellen Seham, and the production supervisor was Milton Heiberg. It was set
in Baskerville with display lines in Bookman by National ShareGraphics, Inc.

Printed and bound by R. R. Donnelly & Sons Company.

CONTENTS

FOREWORD

The 1867 Act establishing the U.S. Department of Education specified that its purpose should include collecting information which would "show the condition and progress of education in the several states and territories."

In 1963, in the interest of a fuller implementation of this provision of the law, the then Commissioner of Education, Francis Keppel asked John Gardner, the president of Carnegie Corporation, whether the Corporation might be willing to support consideration of the feasibility of establishing some kind of system to measure the educational level of the United States population, presumably on a recurrent basis. The Corporation responded favorably and in December 1963 and January 1964 sponsored two meetings of educators, test experts, officials, and lay persons to explore the questions of whether, and if so how, some kind of national testing program should be established. The meetings led to the creation of the Exploratory Committee on Assessing the Progress of Education (ECAPE), chaired by Dr. Ralph Tyler, Director of the Center for Advanced Study in the Behavioral Sciences. As the plans for implementing the assessment proceeded, ECAPE became CAPE, and then in 1969 CAPE was adopted as a project of the Education Commission of the States and became the National Assessment of Educational Progress (NAEP).

Support for the development of the Assessment came in a series of grants from the Corporation, from the Fund for the Advancement of Education, the Ford Foundation, and from the U.S. Office of Education. The current operating expenses of NAEP are funded by the federal government (originally by the Office of Education and now by the National Center for Educational Statistics, which has become a separate branch of the Department of Health, Education, and Welfare). Carnegie Corporation's total contributions to the development of NAEP amounted to $2,432,900.

Given that amount, coupled with the degree of Corporation participation in the planning and development of NAEP and the potential importance of the project itself, the National Assessment was a logical first choice for evaluation when the Corporation's trustees decided in 1971 to establish a special fund to be used to sponsor independent evaluations of some of the major projects the Corporation had supported. In April 1972 the Corporation commissioned the Center for Educational Policy Research of the Harvard Graduate School of Education, directed by Professor David K. Cohen, to undertake a review and evaluation of the National Assessment—particularly of the period during which the Corporation was involved. Since the evaluators were concerned with learning about the value of their own processes as well as about the Assessment, their broad charge left room to consider what might have been as well as what was. The evaluation was to take about half a year, and $23,984 was allocated for this purpose. The evaluation was carried out by William Greenbaum and his associates, Michael Garet and Ellen Solomon. They had the assistance of consultants where necessary.

The evaluation was completed early in 1973. Although a good deal of attention is given to the quality of the exercises and to the nature and implications of the sampling design NAEP decided to use, the evaluation is not a detailed technical consideration of the Assessment. Instead it is primarily a thoughtful analysis of the expectations and choices which lay behind the basic design of the Assessment and an evaluation of the implications of that design for what can be expected of the Assessment. The evidence is mainly the written record of some of the discussions leading up to the creation of the Assessment and documentation from NAEP itself. The argument is therefore more accessible to the informed layperson—and its central points seem to stand or fall primarily on matters of logic and judgment. The evaluation is an individual product, not the considered outcome of a committee's deliberation, and the reader has a chance of forming his or her opinion of the case made.

The evaluation does make a number of criticisms of the Assessment and of its conceptions, and it therefore is necessarily controversial. The evaluators are rightly impressed by the difficulty of launching such an enterprise in this society, but they are also concerned about a mismatch between some of the expectations for NAEP and what, given the Assessment's design, it can reasonably deliver. The evaluators caution that either the expectations, or the design, or perhaps both, should change if this mismatch is not to become increasingly troublesome.

This study was commissioned as a report to the Corporation, and it therefore had the responsibility of deciding how it was to be used and to whom it should be made available. It felt as a matter of principle and of foundation accountability that the products of its support should be open to public scrutiny.

An evaluation, however, both by definition and by intention should not be a neutral document. It has to take a stand, to make judgments. If it is an evaluation of any real life enterprise, those judgments can have an impact on other peoples' real interests. While NAEP had its origins in the Corporation's support, it was the product of the serious efforts of a great many people not connected with the foundation. Other foundations and the government had given it support. By the time of this study, NAEP was fully supported by the government. This evaluation nevertheless had the full cooperation of the NAEP staff and of the other funding sources. I would like to commend them warmly for their willingness to be hospitable to a process in which they would not be participants and yet which could subject them to possible criticism. The Corporation felt that the report should be made available immediately to NAEP and to its other sponsors so that they would have a chance to take advantage of any suggestions they found to be constructive and so that they would have an opportunity to respond, to agree or disagree, and to correct.

The report was sent to the Corporation's trustees, and for their April 1973 meeting Ralph Tyler, who had played the leading role in developing NAEP and who then headed its Analysis and Advisory Committee, was invited to join William Greenbaum in leading a discussion of the report. It was clear that there was disagreement on a number of matters, and the Corporation encouraged NAEP to prepare a written response. The Corporation felt that the report should be made available to the interested public, but we also felt in fairness to the serious issues and interests involved that a response from NAEP should accompany it. A first draft of NAEP's reaction was prepared in 1973, and we received a revised version in 1974. The package was then made available to see whether there might be commercial interest in publishing it. McGraw-Hill expressed such an interest in February 1975, and after a series of negotiations this publication resulted.

The National Assessment is an important development in the history of American education. The Corporation is proud to be associated with it. As one of the first attempts truly to take stock nationally of "the progress of education," it is itself an evaluation, and it is inherently controversial. Its future directions—and the future of other expressions of our national desire to know how we are doing and how we could do better—are matters of continuing debate. I hope that this publication will make an interesting and constructive contribution to that debate.

Finally, I hope that the report may prove interesting and useful not just as a contribution to our understanding of assessment and of the Assessment but also as an example of a foundation's willingness to subject itself and, perforce, its grantees to scrutiny. We already have learned a good deal from the report about the role of the interplay between expectations and reality in the launching of a major enterprise, and about the processes of evaluation itself. I expect that we will learn still more from the ways in which this report and the response are received.

Alan Pifer
President
Carnegie Corporation

PREFACE

Evaluation seems to spawn further evaluation, but so long as essential actions are not forestalled by the process, it seems a healthy one. The National Assessment of Educational Progress (NAEP) was created to evaluate the progress of education in the United States; then we were asked to conduct a small-scale assessment of the Assessment; and now there may well be others who will evaluate the purposes, methods, evidence, and conclusions of our evaluation. Redundant as such a process might at first appear, such evaluation (and hopefully self-evaluation as well) may be prerequisite to a more complete understanding of social policies and social indicators.

Several aspects of this evaluation deserve mention here. First, as is described in more detail in the Introduction, it seemed proper to evaluate the National Assessment on the basis of several quite different criteria. Most significantly, we have examined the Assessment's purposes, methods, and conclusions not only in terms of the Assessment's own definitions but also in terms of other possible and reasonable approaches to defining and measuring the nation's educational progress. Both these sets of criteria seemed necessary to a full evaluation. In the report we have tried to be explicit about when we are measuring NAEP against its own definitions of its purposes, methods, and conclusions and when we are measuring it against approaches which it never considered or adopted. For instance, the list of the Assessment's objectives and subobjectives which appears in Chapter 2 includes only NAEP's purposes as they appear in its early planning documents.

A second aspect of this evaluation concerns methodology. Efforts were made to approach the evaluation through as many information sources as possible. All early correspondence and transcripts of planning meetings relating to the development of the Assessment were reviewed. All available documents produced by NAEP between 1968 and 1974, including statements of purpose, objectives, booklets in subject matter areas, test exercises, reports on results, and public relations efforts were reviewed. Similarly, outside commentaries on the validity and utility of Assessment results were examined. Extensive interviews were conducted with NAEP policy advisors, administrators, and research staff in Denver during the spring and late summer of 1972. Interviews were also conducted at the National Center for Educational Statistics, the branch of the United States Office of Education (USOE) responsible for monitoring the National Assessment's activities. In late 1972 and early 1973 our preliminary findings were presented to both NAEP officials and the related personnel at USOE for criticism. Finally, the National Assessment was invited to respond to the evaluation report within the pages of this book, a procedure which we feel is in the interests of fairness and complexity.

Third, there is the issue of the timing of the publication of this book. It is apparent from recent experience with policy and program evaluations that no matter how accurate and useful any particular evaluation might be, the intent, findings, and recommendations of the evaluation will undergo varying distortions depending on how and when the evaluation is disseminated. It was our judgment that this evaluation would prove most useful if NAEP and the pertinent staff at USOE had an extended period of time to debate and perhaps act upon the substantive aspects of this report before its publication. We assumed that broader political debates about the efficacy of the Assessment would and should later occur, and that our report would be made available to help inform those debates. Privately sponsored evaluations such as ours obviously have more flexibility with regard to publication methods and schedules than the great majority of evaluations that are publicly sponsored. But even in the case of "private" studies of public programs, there are obligations regarding the diffusion of research and the distribution of detailed information to conflicting political and educational groups. These obligations must constantly be weighed against the question of whether the chances of constructive changes in social policies will be enhanced by deliberately staged separations of the more substantive and more political aspects of policy debates. In this case we believe that USOE has made extensive use of the report which might well have been impossible in an atmosphere of constant and contemporaneous charges from Congress; but at the same time, while NAEP has had to respond to numerous hard questions and criticisms from USOE in the last two years, the relative lack of direct Congressional criticism may have delayed a serious NAEP response to the larger questions raised by the report. The main issues raised in the report remain as crucial to the Assessment today as they were when the first draft was circulated some two years ago. Where there may have been changes in operational details or the goals of the Assessment, the inclusion of a response, provided in 1975, allows NAEP to mention them and to take issue with any or all aspects of our study.

Fourth, we would like to congratulate the Carnegie Corporation for its openness in making available all of its internal records regarding the early development of the Assessment. We believe this to be a precedent, and one which other project-initiating agencies, both private and public might follow. Without Carnegie's in-house documents, the evaluation of the Assessment might well have been restricted to measuring its results against its own statement of purposes at the start of operations in 1968. But as is evident in the report itself, the use of virtually all documentation increases our understanding of the range of possibilities and expectations that surrounded the creation of the Assessment from 1963 to 1968, and greatly enhances our knowledge of decision-making processes in general as well as of the Assessment in particular.

Finally, if our evaluation occasionally seems quite critical of the Assessment, it should be remembered that the criticisms are offered in a constructive spirit and that they are comments on substantive and technical issues, not individual people. We must stress that we conducted the evaluation with a more than usually generous advantage of hindsight, almost a decade having passed between the first meetings regarding the Assessment and the beginning of our study. It is essential to note that the last decade produced vast changes in our conventional wisdoms about education and educational research. The task for the Assessment is much less to defend itself against anyone's criticism of its original conception and design than to internalize the changes in education and educational research in the last decade, as well as its own knowledge about its limitations and possibilities—and to act boldly upon this knowledge in the future.

William Greenbaum

Cambridge
December 1975

ACKNOWLEDGMENTS

This evaluation of the National Assessment of Educational Progress was supported by a grant from the Carnegie Corporation. The Corporation's willingness to support an outside evaluation of one of its own major projects is commendable, as is its making available to us virtually all significant documentation relevant to the life of the Assessment. We acknowledge too the cooperation of both the leaders and staff of the National Assessment and its administrative sponsor, the Education Commission of the States. And we are grateful for the aid we received from the staff at USOE's National Center for Educational Statistics, the federal agency responsible for financing and monitoring the National Assessment.

In preparing our evaluation, we were given important help by several people; this report was strengthened by their suggestions, but of course, they are not responsible for its limitations: Nikki Smith, of Harvard University, and Elizabeth Nardine performed the analysis of the Reading and Literature objectives and the item analysis of the exercises in those subject areas. David K. Cohen, chairman of the Education and Social Policy Program at the Harvard Graduate School of Education, participated in crucial early discussions of approaches to such an evaluation. Stan Bolster, professor in Learning Environments, Harvard Graduate School of Education, contributed to our understanding of the historical context of curriculum development during the last two decades.

Measuring Educational Progress

PART ONE

A STUDY OF
THE NATIONAL ASSESSMENT

1

INTRODUCTION

In recent decades there has been increased interest in establishing systems of social accounting and evaluation to measure progress, or its lack, in policy areas such as education and health. If society is to become more self-aware and improve itself through use of social accounting and evaluation, however, it must first become more self-conscious about these processes themselves. The potential, limits, and negative side effects of these processes must be more fully understood, for the sake of both those who engage in such work and those who enjoy or suffer its consequences. It is essential to explore the conceptual and political limits of seeking change through improved information, recognizing the tension that emerges from the interplay between the "softness" of reality and the social sciences and our urgent need for "hard" information on which to base decisions. It is also necessary to think more deeply about the effects of raising or lowering expectations for what can be accomplished through social accounting and evaluation, and therefore for the society in general. Social scientists must avoid raising societal expectations for systematic change too far beyond those that can be fulfilled, or lowering expectations to such a point of "realism" that sight of society's ideals is unwittingly lost. Moreover, serious consideration must be given to the differences between evaluations which can produce relatively immediate and *real* improvements versus those that can produce meaningful symbols which might lead to progress only in the future, versus those which have little direct utility or positive symbolic value but which become excuses for existing inadequate conditions.

The authors of this book hope to make a contribution to this larger effort of our society to become more self-aware about the processes of evaluation and change. And yet our contribution necessarily will be limited, given the contexts of this study: First, this inquiry is in the field, or rather the quagmire, of education—a public policy area that has been ravaged by dramatic societal changes, bureaucratization, conflicting and ambiguous goals, and rapid cycles of overdramatized social-scientific promises and cynicisms. Second, the task is complicated, as would be the analysis of almost any area of public policy in America, by the decentralized nature of our political system which exercises a profound effect not only on the character of the educational system, but also on our capacity to conduct meaningful evaluations of that system. *Our primary task in this Report is to evaluate the performance and utility of one particular effort at social accounting, the National Assessment of Educational Progress (NAEP),* now a $6 million per year project of the United States Office of Education. We were initially commissioned to perform this particular evaluation rather than undertake a broader analysis of the general processes of social accounting and evaluation. Yet we have approached our task with these larger aspects firmly in mind. In fact, as the Report demonstrates, the two inquiries are inextricably intertwined. It is at the intersection of American education, politics, and social science methodology that NAEP evolved its purposes, and it is at that same intersection that we are likely to develop deeper insights into the challenges encountered by NAEP, as well as those which will be encountered by any future efforts to measure levels of functional literacy in society.

THE ASSESSMENT'S CURRENT SCOPE AND MANDATE

The history of the National Assessment of Educational Progress falls into four distinct periods: the conception of the Assessment and discussions leading to a decision to move ahead with it (late 1963–early 1964), the design period (1964–1968), the formal announcement of its purposes and the start of Assessment operations (1968), and the present period of evaluation and redesign.

For the moment, in briefly describing the scope and primary mandate of the Assessment, we cite NAEP's formal objectives as published in 1968, at the start of its operations. This statement contains enough ambiguities so that although emphases and expectations have shifted noticeably since then, the description of NAEP's intent remains accurate in an overall sense.

National Assessment is a plan for a systematic, census-like survey of knowledges, skills, understandings, and attitudes designed to sample four age levels in ten different subject areas. National Assessment is an information-gathering program designed to provide both the educational community and the lay public with information about some of the direct outcomes of education as they are exhibited by our students and young adults. The ultimate goal of National Assessment is to provide information that can be used to improve the educational process, to improve education at any and all levels where knowledge will be useful about what students know, what skills they have developed, or what their attitudes are. In brief, then, National Assessment aims at providing information in one of the many areas in education where more information is needed, the area of knowledges, skills, understandings and attitudes.[1]

During 1969–70 the Assessment administered exercises in three subject areas—Science, Citizenship, and Writing—to a national sample of approximately 80,000 respondents, subdivided into four age groups: nine-year-olds, thirteen-year-olds, seventeen-year-olds, and a young-adult group (ages twenty-six to thirty-five). During 1970–71 exercises in two more areas were added, Reading and Literature, and during 1971–72 the exercises in Social Studies and Music. The long-term plan is to readminister the exercises in each of ten subject areas—the above seven plus Math, Art, and Career and Occupational Development—every few years so that trends in the knowledge, attitudes, skills, and understandings of American youth can be traced over time. A combination of NAEP's purposes, the size and quality of its sample population, and its multimillion-dollar annual budget makes it the most sizable continuing effort to evaluate the educational attainments of American youth.

Outside NAEP's immediate circle, few critics have responded in strong positive terms to the actual Assessment results, although, as we shall see, various of its subobjectives have become of substantial interest to particular constituencies. The responses have ranged from "This is just the first benchmark so it is hard to say what the trends and uses of the Assessment will be over time" to "The Assessment has produced no significant and directly usable information about educational outcomes that was not already known, and the large expenditure is so far unjustified." One objective of the present study is to put into perspective these conflicting calls for patience and pessimism in order to produce a more sophisticated understanding of what can

---

[1] Frank Womer, *What Is National Assessment?* (Denver: Education Commission of the States [hereinafter cited as ECS], 1968, reprinted 1970), p. 1.

and cannot be expected of the Assessment. One central issue throughout this Report is the meaning of the word "ultimate" in the quotation cited above: "The ultimate goal of National Assessment is to provide information that can be used to improve the educational process. . . ." Or more directly, How long will the society in general and Congress in particular spend several million dollars per year, or more, without demanding some more direct usefulness of the Assessment results?

THIS EVALUATION'S APPROACH

To fulfill our charge of evaluating the performance and utility of the National Assessment of Educational Progress, we first had to choose from a wide range of possible criteria. For example, the Assessment could be evaluated in terms of its very earliest objectives, if any could be discerned; its formal objectives as they were presented in 1968–69 when the Assessment actually began functioning; its operational subobjectives and means, some of which can now be deemed ends in themselves; its unintended consequences; the extent to which its objectives might have been reached either more successfully or less expensively by other means; the conceptual and political factors that helped determine its objectives; or, finally, in terms of fundamentally different approaches that might have been taken in deciding *why* and *how* educational progress in America should be evaluated. For the sake of fairness and in deference to the subject's essential complexity, we decided to take all these criteria into account. The attempt here to use several kinds of criteria simultaneously forces clearer awareness of the ambiguities inherent in the Assessment's purposes and methods.

Two limitations of this Report must be mentioned. First, some of the details concerning NAEP's testing materials and procedures are bound to be inaccurate at times because NAEP frequently changes its materials and procedures. However, the kinds of incremental changes that have been typical of the past few years and that are planned for the foreseeable future do not essentially alter the basic characteristics which this study describes and analyzes.

Second, and more importantly, while the study can evaluate *decisions* made and *actions* taken, it cannot as readily elucidate the *intentions* of those who first conceived the Assessment. We have interviewed many key individuals, and we have read literally thousands of pages of verbatim transcripts of all the early planning meetings; in addition, all available in-house memoranda and correspondence have been examined. And yet, no doubt, some intentions will be interpreted differently from the way they were experienced.

The purposes of this inquiry require an effort to ascertain not only the Assessment's present efficacy but also factors that might increase or limit its efficacy in the future. This latter has necessitated a special concern with the Assessment's past, and thus we have given attention to both its history and many of its technical aspects. Macroanalysis of the past illuminates the broader conceptual and political realities that will help shape the Assessment's future, and microanalysis provides a detailed picture of what would have to be done, and what can be done, to increase its overall utilization. At the same time, however, we also hope that several sections, particularly Chapters 3–8 and the Epilogue, Chapter 10, will be independently useful within the specialized areas they address.

2

NAEP'S OBJECTIVES AND ORGANIZATIONAL DEVELOPMENT

The recorded history of the National Assessment of Educational Progress began September 5, 1963, when Francis Keppel, the U.S. Commissioner of Education, contacted John Gardner, then president of the Carnegie Corporation, seeking foundation support to develop the Assessment. On September 16, a $12,500 discretionary grant was awarded to sponsor two conferences to "discuss the means of ascertaining the educational level attained through American public education." Ralph W. Tyler, director of the Center for Advanced Study in the Behavioral Sciences, was approached by the Carnegie Corporation to begin planning.

The first indication that the Assessment was an inevitability appeared in the wording of the original discretionary grant: The conferences were to discuss the *means* of developing an assessment, rather than the *value* or *utility* of such an undertaking. One staff member of the Carnegie Corporation picked up this indication of inevitability and in an in-house memo suggested that the conference time be devoted to discussing the larger questions of the potential worth and feasibility of such a project. The response was to retain plans for the one-day conference on developing the Assessment, but to precede the conference with an evening dinner meeting to deal with and presumably answer affirmatively the utility questions, so that planning could begin the next day. In addition, the intent of the planning session was qualified somewhat: The conference finally was called "to explore whether developments in testing and in methods of sampling now enable a fair assessment of the level of national educational attainment." However, this more detailed objective, still emphasizing technology rather than utility, did not really encourage serious discussion of the project's potential worth.

The first conference took place December 18–19, 1963, in New York under the chairmanship of John Gardner. Many of the most capable and influential figures in American education and social science attended: From the foundations—John Gardner, Lloyd Morrisett, and Alan Pifer of the Carnegie Corporation, Frank Bowles of Ford, and Orville G. Brim and David Goslin of Russell Sage; from institutions of higher education—Lee J. Cronbach of Stanford, John Fischer of Columbia Teachers College, and John Tukey of Princeton; from the testing services and research institutes—John Flanagan of the American Institute for Research, Henry Dyer of Educational Testing Service, John Holland of National Merit Scholarship Corporation, Peter Rossi of the National Opinion Research Center, and Ralph Tyler; and from government organizations—Francis Keppel, the United States Commissioner of Education, Ralph Flynt and David Seeley of the United States Office of Education, and William Firman of the New York State Department of Education.

At the dinner meeting on December 18, following several humorous exchanges between Gardner and Keppel, the latter outlined his interest in the project.[1] He noted that in four years the Office of Education would be 100 years old and that in that time little had been done to honor the mandate of the Act of 1867 which created the Office and asked it to report on the "condition and progress of American education."[2] Keppel briefly mentioned that the Assessment idea arose because he had found it difficult to go before Congress "without evidence that is clear, clear and dependable on what you really mean by lack of opportunity. . . ." Keppel also stated that he had brought the idea before the Carnegie Corporation because of his "family

---

[1] The history in this chapter is based largely on transcripts of the *Proceedings of the National Testing Project Conference*, December 18–19, 1963, Carnegie files. Keppel was quite familiar with Carnegie and its officials; his father, Frederick P. Keppel, was president of the corporation for nineteen years, beginning in 1923.

[2] The act provides that the Office is to "collect statistics and facts showing the condition and progress of education in the several states and territories and to diffuse such information respecting the organization and management of schools and school systems and otherwise promote the cause of education throughout the country."

connections and affilial connection with Gardner," remarking that he came with both "filial and disrespectful affection."[3]

A few moments later, Ralph Tyler assumed what can only be regarded as his continuing public chairmanship of the Assessment. He observed that he and John Tukey had already met and begun exploring ways of evaluating the nation's educational progress. During the course of the next few hours of dialogue, it became clear that Tyler had already formulated strong notions of how he would go about developing the Assessment. To summarize his presentation, he emphasized that (1) the Assessment would test *general* levels of knowledge, "what people have learned, not necessarily all within the school system," (2) the tests would not be aimed at discriminating among individuals, unlike most educational tests, (3) there would be an attempt to assess more accurately the levels of learning of the least educated, average, and most educated groups in the society, (4) some sort of matrix sampling system would test individuals only on a small number of questions but results could be aggregated to reflect the knowledge of particular subgroups in the population, (5) adults might be included in the sample, (6) stages, such as the end of elementary school, the end of intermediate school, and the end of high school, should be used in connection with specific testing ages rather than at specific grade levels, and (7) the effects of the tests themselves would have to be carefully considered because they might become standards for educational curricula and might also reflect on the status of particular communities.[4]

The transcript of the first conference covers some two hundred pages; for the moment, the deliberations can be characterized as follows. First, it was generally assumed that more information about educational achievement would be useful per se. Yet, given this assumption, and the general thrust of the agenda and tone of the meeting, there was no sustained consideration of how the Assessment could be useful *specifically*. Second, numerous penetrating questions were raised about the various objectives of the Assessment and how they would be achieved, but almost none of these questions were resolved during this meeting, nor have they been in subsequent years. Finally, although some individuals dissented on certain aspects of the general proposal, the group as a whole gave its prestigious consent to the idea, and, more importantly, to Tyler and Tukey's specific conception of the idea. Indeed, Tyler's first six proposals made during that first meeting have guided and dominated the Assessment from that time until the present.

---

[3] *Proceedings of the National Testing Project Conference,* p. 6.
[4] *Proceedings of the National Testing Project Conference,* pp. 8–10.

Within another month, three more major elements of NAEP's design were formulated. A second major conference took place on January 27–28, 1964, and while most of the participants had also been present at the first conference, they were joined by several additional educational leaders: James Allen, New York State Commissioner of Education; William Carr, of the National Education Association; Harold Howe, then superintendent of schools, Scarsdale, New York; Leon Minear, superintendent of public instruction, Salem, Oregon; Logan Wilson, president of the American Council on Education; Robert Wyatt, president of the National Education Association; Edward Meade, the Ford Foundation; William Golden, member of various boards of directors; John Corson, Princeton University; George Stoddard, New York University; and Robert Thorndike, Columbia Teachers College.

The brief invitation that went out to participants in this second conference suggested, among other things, that the "outlines of the initial assessment might be as follows":

> Tests will cover all the main areas of the curriculum, reading, language, mathematics, science, and social studies.
>
> *Testing will be limited to two or three hours in length.* The basic concern is with the achievement of groups of students. As a result, single tests can be short and breadth of coverage obtained by giving different forms of tests to different individuals. (Emphasis added.)[5]

In addition, during the early part of the meeting, in summarizing the first meeting, it was stated that the Assessment would "be broad enough to fairly reflect the aims of education in the United States."

When these three extra proposals were added to Tyler's original list, essentially all the most important aspects of the National Assessment were already known. The complete list of guidelines includes: (1) assessing general knowledge, not just what people learn in schools, (2) moving away from norm-referencing, which ranks individuals against each other, toward a system of measurement ranking individuals in terms of what they actually know about specific things, (3) testing at different levels of difficulty to discern what is known by the least educated, average, and most educated groups in the country, (4) employing a matrix sampling system, (5) including adults, (6) testing school-age children by age near the end of elementary, intermediate, and high school, (7) testing

---

[5] Jan. 4, 1964, Carnegie files.

for knowledge of specific subject areas, (8) using a short testing period and concentrating on measuring the achievement of groups, not individuals, and (9) being broad enough to reflect the aims of American education and to avoid distorting educational curricula and making invidious comparisons among communities.

We repeat this list because within it are contained practically all the major strengths, limitations, and contradictions of the ultimate Assessment design. We also repeat the list to express our surprise: In the next five years (1964–1968) there were dozens of conferences and many heated debates about what the Assessment should be and how it should be designed. But in essence, when all the participatory processes were done, virtually all the most important decisions that had been made were basically unaltered versions of those made by Tyler and Tukey from September 1963 to January 1964.

THE EARLIEST OBJECTIVES OF THE ASSESSMENT

The January conference was quite similar in main emphasis and style to the first conference. The general assumption about more information being useful per se was still widely accepted. But, despite the lack of consideration of specifically whether or how the assessment would achieve its objectives, from the transcripts of the first two conferences we can draw some conclusions about what the original objectives of the Assessment were.[6] Examination of the transcripts of these two meetings and of all the related in-house memoranda reveals five different *types* of objectives for the Assessment. No single objective can be fairly evaluated until we have at least tried to define its relation to others. First, and of greatest importance, were the *major short-term objectives*. Second were *major long-term objectives*. Third were *subordinate objectives,* proposed partly because they might themselves be useful in secondary ways and partly because of political expediency. Fourth were important but understated testing objectives which can be viewed as *major low-profile objectives.* Finally, there were *operational objectives,* which had to be met if the Assessment was to be implemented in the first place.

Below we list these original objectives of the Assessment, placing them in what the available evidence suggests are the most appropriate categories.

---

[6] While the objectives are drawn from all documents regarding the early planning meetings, they rely primarily on the *Summary Report: Two Conferences on a National Assessment of Educational Attainment,* prepared by David Goslin at Russell Sage Foundation, Carnegie files.

The Earliest Objectives of the Assessment

A. Major Short-Term Objectives
    1. To obtain *meaningful* national data on the strengths and weaknesses of American education (by locating deficiencies and inequalities in particular subject areas and particular subgroups of the population).
    2. To provide this data to Congress, the lay public, and educational decision makers so that they could make more informed decisions on new programs, bond issues, new curricula, steps to reduce inequalities, and so on.
    3. To provide this data to researchers working on various teaching and learning problems, either to answer research questions or to identify specific problems which would generate research hypotheses.

B. Major Long-Term Objectives
    4. To continue collecting the national data at regular intervals so that comparisons could be made over time concerning national levels of achievement, performance in various subject areas, and performance in various subgroups, vis-a-vis themselves and other subgroups. This would provide a census of educational progress in America.
    5. To forestall the development of "less effective or misdirected" attempts at assessment. Some backers of the Assessment disapproved of plans for a California assessment and the national proposals of Admiral Hyman Rickover, both of which were less interested in reducing inequality than in separating elites from the average population so "excellence" could be pursued efficiently.[7]
    6. To make international comparisons possible once sampling and testing problems could be resolved.

C. Subordinate Objectives
    7. To promote concern about more meaningfully defining the nation's educational objectives.
    8. To provide comparative data to stimulate competition among the states and local communities (without encouraging invidious comparisons).

D. Major Low-Profile Objectives
    9. To lead a movement away from relying solely on norm-referenced testing, which discriminates among individuals, and toward some form of objective- or criterion-

---

[7] See H. G. Rickover, *American Education: A National Failure* (New York: Dutton, 1963).

referenced tests that assess how much an individual or group actually knows about a particular area of knowledge.

10. To lead a movement away from current testing which relies largely on measuring knowledge in ways that overemphasize memorization and that underemphasize actual skills, understandings, and attitudes.

11. To encourage new modes of testing that are better fitted to the kinds of information being gathered and the particular characteristics of the respondents.

E. Operational Objectives

12. To create an independent committee to manage the development of the Assessment.

13. To develop widespread acceptance among the educational establishment so that the Assessment could gain access to school systems.

14. To develop widespread political support so that the federal government would take over the funding of the Assessment, while at the same time assuring that representatives of state and local governments would not be too uneasy about the project being federally funded.

15. To develop lists of educational objectives that would "fairly reflect the aims of American education" and serve as guides for the exercise writers.

Each of these objectives is considered later in detail, but a few comments must be made at this point concerning the interrelationships among these objectives and the development of the Assessment. Between 1964 and 1968 a very high proportion of time was spent trying to achieve objectives 12–15, the operational objectives. While this prevented leaders from pursuing the broader objectives, it was an understandable preoccupation since organizational and political support had to be stimulated, and the lists of educational objectives developed. This indicates one of the several ways in which the politics of American education limited the Assessment.

And yet there is a much more basic point to be emphasized here. *The preoccupation with operational objectives helped prevent the Assessment's original leaders from recognizing the extent of their own differences with each other. These were not so much differences in priorities as to what the Assessment should be, as they were differences in expectations as to what the Assessment could be.* But, of course, in turn, diverse expectations led to diverse priorities.

In examining the first four major objectives and the transcripts and correspondence relating to these, it seems clear that Keppel, Gardner, and Tyler assigned similar top priorities to objectives 1 and 4, the immediate and long-term collection of censuslike data on the strengths and weaknesses of American education. The priorities with regard to objectives 2 and 3 were also strong and fairly close, at least between Keppel and Gardner, although, given their respective positions in the government and in the foundation, it is not surprising that Keppel showed a greater desire for politically useful data (objective 2) and that Gardner showed a slightly stronger desire for data helpful to researchers (objective 3).

The truly significant differences occur, however, with regard to expectations. While Keppel and Gardner believed that Tyler's concept of a census might be useful and feasible, Tyler never really reciprocated by agreeing the Assessment could actually produce data in the short run that would be directly applicable either in policymaking or in research. The point is not to suggest that Tyler did not care about producing short-term data for direct use in policy or research; rather, it is that as an active social scientist he had a strong sense that such data *could not* be gathered in the short run. Given his low expectations in this regard, it is not surprising that Tyler gave relatively little priority to objectives 2 and 3, to provide useful data for policy makers and researchers.

At first reading this may seem to be a relatively minor matter, but it is not. Keppel and Gardner surely expected some relatively quick and substantial returns in terms of objectives 2 and 3; and certainly Congress and USOE expect such returns now. Thus, the matter of differences in expectations for the Assessment is crucial. And so is the fact that Tyler has consistently promised no more than the Assessment realistically can produce, while refusing overtly to contradict other NAEP officials who claim that the Assessment can fulfill objectives 2 and 3. Tyler's stance is understandable since the federal government might not as generously support a long-term descriptive census, but nonetheless the continuing gap between societal expectations for the Assessment and its real potential creates intense conceptual, organizational, and political strains.

THE ORGANIZATIONAL DEVELOPMENT
OF THE ASSESSMENT

Following the second planning conference in January 1964, John Corson of Princeton University was asked to prepare a paper on alternative organizational plans for the Assessment. Early in that memorandum dated April 14,

1964, Corson noted that the Assessment idea had not really been tested with many representatives of the education establishment and that he expected major opposition from school administrators and other organized interest groups. Indeed, he noted that developing "greater consensus among opinion-influencing groups that a periodic assessment is feasible and desirable" might be *the* major task before the project could be launched.[8]

Other tasks for the developmental period included: identifying the educational purposes and objectives toward which progress is to be measured; developing the instruments for assessing the status of education; and planning how the periodic assessment shall be administered. Corson's paper assumed that eventually the United States Office of Education (USOE) would take over responsibility for the Assessment and would contract to have it administered by some nongovernmental agency or nonprofit corporation. During the interim he recommended that a temporary committee be appointed to do the initial work, especially to meet with educational interest groups to test their opinions and convince them of the Assessment's feasibility and desirability. He also recommended that approximately one year later a presidential commission on the progress of education be delegated to carry on the Assessment's development.

In June 1964 the Carnegie Corporation made a $100,000 grant to establish the interim committee, which met for the first time in August 1964 and chose the name the Exploratory Committee on Assessing the Progress of Education, which became known as ECAPE. Ralph Tyler served as chairman.[9] The committee's life expectancy was five months, and its mandate was to:

> Develop a greater consensus among influential educational groups that a periodic national assessment of education is feasible and desirable
>
> Develop the instruments for assessing the status of education

---

[8] "Launching a National Educational Assessment," Carnegie files, p. 4.

[9] The other members of the committee included Melvin W. Barnes, Superintendent of Schools, Portland, Oregon; John J. Corson, Princeton University; Paul F. Johnson, State Superintendent of Public Instruction, Iowa; Devereaux C. Josephs, New York Life Insurance; Roy E. Larsen, Time, Incorporated; Katherine E. McBride, president, Bryn Mawr College; The Reverend Paul C. Reinert, president, St. Louis University; Mabel Smythe, principal, New Lincoln School, New York City. The staff director was Stephen B. Withey of the Survey Research Center, University of Michigan, Ann Arbor.

Plan how the assessment could be administered and monitored in the public interest

ECAPE held a series of conferences throughout the nation with various groups of school superintendents, administrators, and curriculum personnel. While considerable interest in the hypothetical value of an assessment was demonstrated at these conferences, it was made very clear that opposition to federal control of such an undertaking was substantial. This was an important factor leading to the conclusion that it was premature to appoint a presidential commission on the progress of education, and so ECAPE's life was extended and actually lasted through most of the development period, or until July 1, 1968.

Between 1964 and 1968 ECAPE was responsible for coordinating, overseeing, and evaluating the work of the various contractors chosen to perform specific tasks essential to implement the Assessment. In addition, a great deal more time and energy was spent kindling support among politicians and the educational interest groups. Public-relations articles about the Assessment were published and key school people were included in various conferences and as members of the many review panels used in establishing the subject-matter objectives and exercises. Developing the testing instruments and political support thus occurred simultaneously. During its four-year existence virtually all ECAPE's funding, amounting to approximately $2 million, came from the Carnegie Corporation and the Ford Foundation's Fund for the Advancement of Education. The only exception was a $100,000 grant from USOE to the University of Minnesota, to support lay review conferences to consider whether any of the Assessment exercises might be in any way offensive.

On July 1, 1968, ECAPE dropped the "Exploratory" and became CAPE, the Committee on Assessing the Progress of Education. As the Assessment moved into its operational phase, between 1968 and 1970, it spent another $3 million, again using Carnegie Corporation and Ford Foundation moneys, but also receiving two direct grants from USOE. Since that time the federal government has taken complete responsibility for funding the Assessment, which, as noted earlier, now has an annual budget of approximately $6 million. (Until late 1968, the ECAPE estimate was that the project would cost approximately $1 million per year.)

When ECAPE became CAPE its membership was more than doubled. All the new members were recruited from educational interest groups, including the American Association of School Administrators, the Chief State School Officers, the National Association of Secondary School Principals, the Department of Elementary School Principals, the National Education Association, the American Federation of Teachers, the National Congress of Parents and Teachers, the National Association of State Boards of Education, and the National School Boards Association.

The search for an appropriate permanent administrative sponsoring agency began in earnest in the summer of 1967 but was not concluded until the steering committee of the Denver-based Education Commission of the States (ECS) voted to accept governance of the Assessment in June 1969. It was clear from the outset that the project would have to be administered by some group that explicitly represented the interests of the education groups opposed to initiation of the Assessment. The decision to ask ECS to take over clearly was designed to convince the states and others that they would in no way be hurt by the project. In fact, when ECS was first approached in 1967, its steering committee voted 7 to 6 *against* assuming governance, largely because it was felt that the ECS interstate COMPACT, which was intended to promote harmonious relations among states and between educational and political leaders, was just building its membership and any cooperation with a program that might embarrass or offend some states might be injurious for the COMPACT itself. After considerable negotiating, involving reassurances that very little about the Assessment would prove objectionable, ECS voted to accept governance of the project.

One of the many ironies concerning the Assessment's evolution is that one of the ECS steering committee members who opposed administering it in 1967 did so not out of fear that it would be too strong, but precisely because it was being designed so that there would be nothing objectionable in it. Leroy Greene stated:

> . . . we are being told . . . that since some people have diabetes, we can't have any sugar in this report, and since others of us are prone toward heartburn we had better watch out for spices, so unless this turns out to be pablum it is not going to be satisfactory.
>
> We are told by some of those who have gotten up here, "We support this program. However—" and then the "however" went on to indicate that it had to be satisfactory to the point of view that they were representing, and I would suggest, then, we have a great difficulty here because, among other things, we are concerned that perhaps some will misinterpret this information.
>
> Now, "a fact is a fact is a fact," to quote Gertrude Stein, and if

we can present facts and then they are misinterpreted, it seems to me one of the prime requisites of an educator is to educate, and if we can't straighten out misinterpretations we are in pretty bad shape, particularly those among us who are educators. If they cannot defend their own positions, perhaps it is because they are not defensible.

I would suggest if we are compelled to accept the limitations that are being suggested here, then I, for one, would move that we have nothing to do with it whatever.[10]

Despite all the problems of building support and all the debates about what the Assessment should and should not be, when operations actually began in 1969–70, the nine guidelines laid down by Ralph Tyler and other key backers in 1963 and 1964 were still the dominant guiding principles. Similarly, objectives 1 through 4 (see page 13) were still intact, although by this time the importance of differing expectations had increased among various groups who thought they knew how the project might benefit them. As the following chapters indicate, some of these expectations were in direct conflict with each other, while others were in sharp contrast with Tyler's relatively humble sense of what the Assessment could accomplish.

---

[10] *Proceedings of ECS Steering Committee,* Denver, Sept. 29, 1967, pp. 82–83.

3

DIVIDING KNOWLEDGE
INTO SUBJECT AREAS

Once the National Assessment was a reality, ECAPE's next concern became the question of precisely what would be assessed. This question was potentially a complex one, given Ralph Tyler's early insistence that in order to measure general levels of knowledge, the Assessment would measure what the American people learned outside the schools as well as within them. From this broad recognition that institutions other than the schools are critical educators, it would have been possible for the Assessment to define knowledge in relatively broad terms and to focus on units of measure other than the conventional subject-matter areas taught in most schools. That it did not and instead assesses ten distinct school subjects is a matter of considerable interest.

Examination of the early transcripts of policy meetings and ECAPE discussions gives no exact picture of when and by whom it was decided to address primarily school subject-matter areas. Perhaps it is misleading to think of this as a *decision* at all. The subject areas were inevitably present and attractive from the beginning. Yet the transcripts reveal many more imaginative and searching conceptions of what constitutes the "knowledge" of the American people.

Though it may be impossible to say that a decision to neglect these conceptions in favor of the simpler scheme of subject areas was ever individually or collectively made, the deliberations in these early meetings reveal a process that seems to have played an important part in other ECAPE decisions. This process involves whittling away at more complex conceptualizations until simpler, sometimes simplistic categories are reached. It involves, too, an inevitable foreshortening of historical perspective in favor of the more immediately expedient.

In examining some of the deliberations about what was to be assessed, we can also see the context of political and educational issues within which the deliberations took place, a context which had implications for all important aspects of the Assessment: the relationship between the definition of knowledge and actual school curricula; the varieties of curricula and their purposes throughout the nation; the hope held by many national educators that the Assessment would help remediate educational inequities and the fear by local school officials that national norms would arise; the question of where responsibility lies for different aspects of education for the nation's children—in the home, the schools, and other arenas within the community.

While specification of the ten subject-matter areas may seem to be the most efficient way to define the knowledge to be assessed, the procedure brought with it numerous problems—political and methodological as well as theoretical—many of which the Assessment still is struggling with today.

THE DEFINITION OF KNOWLEDGE
AS SCHOOL-RELATED SUBJECTS

Tyler's original statement concerning a census of knowledge in the country was not logically wedded to the subject-matter divisions or even to the notion of institutionalized schooling. For instance, to use an analogy, it is clear that the information conveyed by the GNP is not limited to the *terms of reference* of existing economic institutions, although it certainly includes them. Similarly, a national index of knowledge or even imparted knowledge need not be construed exclusively in the schools' terms of reference.

In an early ECAPE memo, written in April 1964, John Flanagan of the American Institute for Research stressed the possibility that a national assessment should begin from a broader conception.

> The evaluation of any system requires a precise statement of what the system is intended to accomplish. Thus, to evaluate the adequacy or effectiveness of any educational program it is necessary to have a comprehensive statement of its objectives. The statements prepared by many national committees and commissions in

recent years have shown substantial agreement on the broad general objectives of elementary and secondary education. Although the terminology varies from one report to another, the general aims are usually stated as developing the individual's maximum potentials and producing *free and responsible citizens.* In accordance with most recent thinking in regard to public education these statements refer to individuals and not to fields of knowledge or disciplines. . . .[1]

Moreover, the division into subject-matter areas did not *necessarily* follow from the original 1867 mandate of the Office of Education—to make an annual report to Congress on the state of American education. As has been noted, it was the existence of this mandate, long unfulfilled, which Commissioner Keppel used as the justification for asking Carnegie to begin to consider a national assessment. As we shall see, many voices were raised during the early planning meetings convened by Carnegie and then by ECAPE against using subject-matter divisions. These voices presented a range of suggestions, from urging the project to view education as a means of developing functionally literate citizens to warning of the difficulties the Assessment would encounter if, in choosing some subjects and omitting others, it provoked the lobbies of excluded-subject-matter teachers and curriculum specialists.

Records of all the preliminary meetings indicate that these arguments were reviewed and that considerable time was spent discussing the inclusion of extra-subject-matter items—such as students' self-concept, general problem-solving ability, moral attitudes, and more general conceptions of knowledge. But these issues never became part of the Assessment. Why this was so will be considered later. First, it is important to understand that Keppel and Gardner originally began to think of the Assessment within a context that had considerable consequences for the division into subject areas.

THE ASSESSMENT AS A MEANS TO REDUCE EDUCATIONAL INEQUITIES

Although Tyler continually spoke of the Assessment as a census, it seems that he never really conceived of it as a device to gather information in the relatively disinterested or indirect way that "census" implies. From the out-

---

[1] "Evaluating the Effectiveness of Elementary and Secondary Education," Carnegie files, p. 1.

set, he made analogies between the Assessment and those indices that show the existence of unemployment and typhoid. It seems clear that as he construed it, the Assessment would be a means for locating areas of unequal educational achievement, similar to the pockets of unemployment that can be isolated through Department of Labor statistical surveys. A census of knowledge as Flanagan viewed it—one through which the society would *self-consciously examine its values and goals* through assessing the knowledge, skills, and attitudes held by its citizens—was evidently subordinated from the start, although several participants supported it throughout the meetings.

Perhaps such a conception as Flanagan's would be seen as fanciful and luxurious at any time in history—including the present. Certainly in the early sixties it would have been considered impractical in light of what were then perceived as the urgent needs of American education. Powerful and conflicting pressures were being brought to bear to redirect greater resources to the education of elites and to equalize educational opportunity for the masses. Admiral Rickover's campaign to sustain and "increase the amount of cream at the top of the educational milk bottle" was followed by the Kennedy administration's commitment to "churn the pale milk at the bottom to at least the consistency of the middle."

For those concerned with educational inequities, improving the quality of schooling was the obvious task at hand. In those days before the Coleman Report, comparing levels of achievement by schoolchildren was the most meaningful way to prove to the country and to Congress in particular how much inequity existed and where funds should be channeled to remedy the deficiencies. The following discussion from the first meeting illustrates Commissioner Keppel's insistence on the constructive role the comparisons—by states and even by cities—would play in promoting positive educational policy:

> *MR. HENRY S. DYER* [Vice-President for College Board Program, Educational Testing Service, Princeton, New Jersey]: May I ask a question of Frank? In this appraisal, do you think of state-by-state comparisons, or are you thinking of just one national index?
> *MR. KEPPEL:* Probably more the former than the latter. . . . I think my response would be that we still do believe in centers of initiative, quite widely diffused; that it is, in that sense, a competitive enterprise; that, inevitably, somebody is going to fuss around with a national standard. Inevitably, it will turn out to be somewhere in Missouri.

> *MR. TYLER:* The types of questions you raised would involve some other types of breakdown.
> *MR. KEPPEL:* Of course it would—the breakdowns of the cities. You can cut this one a half a dozen different ways.
> *MR. DYER:* But you'd have comparative data.
> *MR. KEPPEL:* My enthusiasm for having a national mean can be restrained. I am more interested in using the national competitive quality of it, you see, if this can be used that way to push the whole damned thing up. . . . [2]

Keppel's enthusiasm for such a strategy led him to encourage the others present to do their best to develop a good method for uncovering specific areas of educational malaise while he took care of the politics of gaining acceptance for the Assessment, a more difficult task if schoolpeople felt threatened by pressure for "a national mean" or by the possibility that their own failures would be exposed.

It was within this context of avoiding antagonistic relations with schoolpeople that the accomplishments of the *schools* became the Assessment's focus of measurement. Participants throughout this first meeting expressed concern for distinguishing between what is learned in school and what is learned elsewhere so that "inadequate" school systems could receive more aid. Nowhere is this better illustrated than in the following exchange:

> *MR. JOHN W. TUKEY* [Princeton University]: I would like to say, I don't see why we have to fail to regard the television commercials as part of the educational system in the country, if we are to be realistic. We may not like it as a part of the educational system but, if this is what educates people, I think we need to be concerned with it.
> *MR. FISCHER* [Columbia Teachers College]: Don't we need to distinguish between what they learn from the commercials and what they learn from the teachers?
> *MR. TUKEY:* Why?
> *MR. TYLER:* For some purposes, but not so as to say that this country has a relatively low educational level.
> *MR. FISCHER:* If we want to blame it on somebody, we'd need to distinguish.
> *MR. TUKEY:* What is this responsibility to report—on the status and progress of education, or on the school system?
> *MR. KEPPEL:* "Education," I think, is the word used.

---

[2] *Proceedings of the National Testing Project Conference,* Dec. 18–19, 1963, Carnegie files, pp. 12–13.

MR. FLYNT [USOE]: ". . . in order to improve the school system."

MR. FISCHER: If you looked at the intent of the Congress in the year the Office was set up, they meant the school system.[3]

Thus the perceived major uses of the Assessment to some extent dictated its nature. Although it might not be possible to isolate the effects of schooling completely, the Assessment was to be useful to school systems and its content was to be primarily school-related. However, the selection of discrete school-defined subject-matter divisions did not, even then, necessarily follow. Many persons present, including Tyler, recognized that *education* included much that was imparted by media other than the schools—television, for example—and were interested in evaluating such knowledge as well. Partly they had a genuine desire to develop a comprehensive definition of "knowledge"; partly they simply recognized the difficulty in separating out what was learned in school from what was learned in other ways.

It was not until late in the meeting that the division into specific subjects was broached. This occurred when Gardner, who had, perhaps, assumed such an approach all along, said the following:

> Since you have brought up the subject of the kinds of tests in terms of subject matter, I'd be interested to get an idea of the range of subject matter that ought to be covered. If we are talking about the schools, now, what subjects should be dealt with in these tests—every subject covered by the schools?[4]

It is interesting that Flanagan, who had just been describing the approach of Project TALENT, was indeed talking about "subjects" but not *school* subjects. In fact, he was describing the ferment in the schools over what was involved in teaching a discipline such as science or mathematics, and pointed out the difficulty of distinguishing among the "mixtures of various skill processes—knowledge, concepts, application of principles"—if the Assessment were to work within traditional subject areas.[5]

But after Gardner's question, the issue seems to have been somewhat settled, at least in the minds of the Assessment founders. Whenever subjects or content-areas are spoken of during the rest of the meeting, they are considered only as school-defined areas. Whether the Assessment should simply

---

[3] Ibid., p. 18.
[4] Ibid., p. 102.
[5] Ibid., pp. 100–102.

stick to the more basic subject areas or include a wider spectrum of curriculum offerings, some of which would not be available in all schools, was vigorously discussed. A decision on this matter would raise the issue of the Assessment's impact on the schools' conceptions of which subjects were important. If only the basics were evaluated, programs such as those in art or music might be seen as less important and might receive less local support. But if the Assessment included only *some* of the nonbasic subjects, the lobbying from curriculum specialists in excluded areas might become fierce.[6]

Discussion turned likewise to the Assessment's impact on the ways in which subject areas would be construed by the schools. In fields such as social studies, mathematics, and language, considerably different approaches prevailed throughout the country. Whatever approach the Assessment used as the basis for its tests would influence the schools and might provoke great controversy.

After the initial meetings, these issues were broken down into five major points for those in the Assessment to keep in mind as they decided on strategies for classifying subject-matter areas.[7]

Content of Tests

A. Range of subjects to be covered: The tests should fairly reflect the aims of education in the United States, including both the traditional and modern curriculum.
    1. Greater coverage of subject matter would reduce the impact of the program on any one field.
    2. Greater coverage of subject matter might stimulate schools to venture into areas covered by the test, but which would be new to the school.
    3. Greater coverage of subject matter might give more schools an opportunity to excel in something, thereby reducing the possibility of invidious comparisons.
    4. Greater coverage of subject matter would lead to a greater danger of harmful impact (or possible lack of local cooperation) in those fields (for example, social studies) about which there is less agreement among schoolpeople regarding content or approach.

---

[6] Flanagan's approach in Project TALENT was to test items of "general information." During the discussion of the lobbying that might accompany the Assessment's choices of subject-matter areas, he pointed out that if it followed his format, the National Assessment could avoid such problems.

[7] "Summary Report: Two Conferences on a National Assessment of Educational Attainment," prepared by David Goslin of the Russell Sage Foundation, Carnegie files, p. 4.

5. At the individual level, greater coverage might lead to more frustration whenever children have not received instruction in a subject covered by the test.

Thus, in its effort to measure educational inequalities, the Assessment would focus on learning that occurred in the schools. Subject-matter divisions were the most obvious means for making comparisons, and future decisions on choosing those subject areas or on choosing among disparate approaches within a subject area would depend upon possible impact on the schools themselves.

MORALITY, FEELINGS, AND ATTITUDES: THE "INTANGIBLES"

Even though school subjects were generally agreed upon as the primary unit of dividing the educational pie, another general area was suggested for the Assessment to take seriously. John Holland, of the American College Testing Program, proposed that attitudes concerning schooling, educational aspirations, and self-concept be included:

> I'd like to go back to what Lee Cronbach talked about, and we have been talking about, generally—the fact of doing the assessment of the 1870 curriculum. I think one thing that we might do would be to ask for things which would offset this—not necessarily subject matter—that would suggest the school has some other function than teaching people that they should know such-and-such which really I have some doubt about how useful this is. For example, the sort of item I think you might ask would be attitude toward school, the degree to which they like school.
> Do they read on their own time? There are lots of students who simply don't read except when they are in school. Well, school can enhance at a particular level the amount of reading done. I think this is a reasonable sort of thing. What are the levels of educational plan, how far do they plan to go in school, when you control for the background.
> Another notion which is a kind of personality item but which might be something you might be able to get away with is students' self-conceptions as to how they rate themselves on their abilities, and so-forth and so-on. There are schools which crush kids; it would be of considerable interest whether kids in "School A" see themselves positively or not. We have done a recent study which suggests that kids of high talent who go to certain kinds of

schools do less than we have expected them to do, and these are the very schools which everybody thinks are the finest in the world. I am sure it happens at other levels.

Well, I think it's possible; I have been daydreaming on the side, here, to find some simple, crude, nonsensitive items which would take the heat off the subject matter.[8]

Holland's proposal that the Assessment might measure areas that went beyond school subjects was expressed in terms of what such inclusions might do for the Assessment, e.g., make it more modern than critics might say, help it pass through the controversy that might be aroused if school subjects were the only focus. In later meetings, when the matter was raised by educators consulted by ECAPE, the tone was very different. These educators did not champion the inclusion of such areas because they would help the Assessment become a reality but instead justified their inclusion because the educators regarded them as the most important outcomes of education. The areas involved such qualities as creative thinking, critical thinking, curiosity, lifelong interest in reading, respect for the rights of others and for the law, the development of risk-taking behavior, and positive self-concept.

As the participating educators discussed these attributes, habits, and values, they stressed the increasingly important role of the schools in fulfilling what once was considered the moral function of the home and other community institutions. Tyler seems to have been reluctant to acquiesce to the schools' responsibility for transmitting, and especially for changing, students' values; in addition, he emphasized the difficulty of measuring the achievement of such "intangibles," even if agreement could be reached on their importance. The educators concurred that "objective" standards would be difficult to formulate, but insisted that it would be more useful to provide unfinished instruments that could be improved than to leave out the intangibles entirely. The tenor of the educators' concerns and Tyler's responses are well illustrated in the following exchanges:

> *FATHER CURTIN:* . . . I think it's tremendously important we begin with the difficult things to measure which are important to society. It doesn't make any difference, it seems to me, whether a child can learn the mathematical computations with great accuracy, almost by rote, if he uses it to steal.
>
> I think society is more concerned about whether he uses that correctly and intellectually and as a citizen in a community rath-

---

[8] *Proceedings of the National Testing Project Conference,* pp. 128–129.

er than just as an intellectual gimmick, and then, in trying to line up the attitude, the set of values, the ideals that the school is supposed to teach, how much did the school teach, how much did the home teach, how much did the community teach? What is the relative contribution of each of these agencies to the development or lack of development of these attributes?

The school may do a tremendous job of teaching these values which are completely abrogated at home, or by the community. . . . I certainly feel that we should get to the difficult things first. It's easy to get achievement in the content subjects; it's a matter of a test and a good, scientific sampling—but, to get at the intangible outcomes which build our community is an important factor. *MRS. GREENFIELD:* I'd like to see us begin to tackle these because I believe that the public school system is being called upon, more and more, particularly in the large cities of the United States, to assume the responsibilities that once were thought to be solely the responsibilities of the home. Certainly this is true in the inner city, and I think—if we really could go to a discussion of whether or not as people interested in education we think this is something that, one, is desirable and, two, will be continued, whether it is desirable or not—[we should ask] how, then, do you measure some of these. . . . Should these be part of the output that you expect in a school, that a child is taught to be honest, in its simplest terms, if he doesn't learn it in his home?

I'd like to see us discuss, list and discuss some of these things because—well, I don't think I have to argue why, in this room! *FATHER BEHRENS:* Do you think the Carnegie study in process right now. . . .

CHAIRMAN TYLER: The study of Catholic education? *FATHER BEHRENS:* Right! Do you think that some of the instruments we have used here in the Duke studies of parental expectations might lead us in our consideration of structuring an instrument to be used for this group?

FATHER CURTIN: Well, it's part of the reason I raised this question. My understanding of the study at this time is that Educational Testing Service is having a very difficult time trying to evaluate the outcomes; first of all, to get a correct measure of value; secondly, to determine whether or not the value was learned or not learned because of the school or because of the home or because of the community. Does the community make a great contribution to the value system? If the child lives downtown, he gets one value system; if he lives in a very fancy suburb, he gets another value system, and the one in the fancy suburb might be worse than the one downtown! It can go that way.

But I think that we've then got to find out . . . since the school is the only instrument that we have in formal education. . . .

CHAIRMAN TYLER: I am sort of puzzled, because it's certainly true from what we know about the acquisition of values that the school can become part of a consistent system of the home and community in helping to use the anthropological phase to socialize youngsters to develop moral values, how you behave in a social group, the responsibility for others, and so forth. But when the home and the community set up quite contrary values, is the school an effective agency? Do they really try? Can they do much in that regard? This is one of the questions.

FATHER CURTIN: That's the question I raise, Ralph, right at this point.

CHAIRMAN TYLER: "All the things you have been learning at school is sissy stuff. We don't act that way!"

FATHER CURTIN: The peer group doesn't act that way.

MR. CARROLL: Respect for law, for example!

CHAIRMAN TYLER: And, if the schools are actually undertaking this responsibility, Bill, how do they do it in a way that enables them to transcend the influence of home and community, and the church and school would seem to be about the only ones in some communities where these are going to be taught.

MR. SPEARS: We'd like to have some instruments to play around with, rather than somebody just develop them and not show them to us, and then make us take the test and then have us have to defend ourselves. We'd rather be a party to it.

MRS. GREENFIELD: We do it in broad, general terms when we say "good citizenship," but it's the kind of thing that is accepted, I think, in the country as one of the goals of the school. But a school that taught good English and math and didn't teach a child to be a good citizen in a democratic society hasn't succeeded, and certainly it's something that they ought not to leave to chance, in my view. We ought to know whether we are doing it or not.

MR. ROGIN: We have greater difficulty getting consensus on what that term means than we do about successful reading.

CHAIRMAN TYLER: And I am also raising the additional question, "If we got consensus, is it proper to say that this is a function of the school, alone, if the community is really concerned with it, and doesn't it have some responsibility to do something about it, the community, roundabout?"

MR. SPEARS: We can use the test to reflect the community back to the community. They won't expect us to be doing all that and, if we can show them up a little in their public relations, I think it might help.

CHAIRMAN TYLER: First of all, if I recall some of the data from the Catholic education study, the parental aspirations and the youngster's achievement are fairly well correlated.

FATHER BEHRENS: Yes.

CHAIRMAN TYLER: So, what the adults do expect and expect for their children does have an influence, apparently. But this means that, if we are going to do that for education generally, we have to get some measures of what the community atmosphere is. . . . what we call "good" citizenship" in a negative community has quite a different meaning from . . . where all of the citizens are consistent with it.

MR. KIERNAN: Take the concept of self-image, say, in the ghetto—

CHAIRMAN TYLER: Our committee might recommend, if you felt it was important, that one of the early studies to be sponsored and supported would be one with some intensive students, and you can come into these where students would be happy to have this done. But it's by no means an easy job, and I am really raising the prior question to what extent do you school people think that your responsibility is to change the moral climate of the communities in which your schools are located, because that's really what you are asking when you talk about having the youngsters different from the parents or the places outside the school in that community.

MRS. GREENFIELD: I serve on the school board in Philadelphia, and I must say that I think any large-city school board has to face this problem, and most of them are facing it and making the decision they must enter into this field, which has not been a conventional educational field in the past. But I happen to believe that the future of the country depends on intervening, so I don't think you have much choice.

CHAIRMAN TYLER: I would think there's another alternative, Mrs. Greenfield, which is to develop other community resources, including or in addition to the school.

MRS. GREENFIELD: Oh, I don't think the school should do it alone.

CHAIRMAN TYLER: The mobilization of youth, not just the school.

MRS. GREENFIELD: I didn't mean to imply the school was the only agency, but—

MR. SPEARS: Aren't we getting back to the point of the danger listed in here, in your sheet you sent out to us, the danger you get into the areas that are easier to operate in and that we won't get the total and won't get the measurement of the total objective of the school?

CHAIRMAN TYLER: Well, that is a danger, but my own talk was to be sure you seriously meant that this is one of the objectives you work on, and how do you work with your teachers on it and what do you do about it. I am sure how you work some of the things you do in reading, arithmetic, and science, but what do you do in connection with the development of moral value if the community has quite different moral values?

MR. SPEARS: You will come out with it in your input as a part of a standard of what the school, after all, should be putting in, but you don't tell what it is and let the schools see themselves a little better, and you go as far as you can, giving us instruments to help. That's all you do.

I don't think there is going to be anything totally objective about the whole operation. You just can't leave those areas out, because they are difficult. We are struggling with it, all the time—attitudes of children toward other children, their feelings toward other human beings.

CHAIRMAN TYLER: I understand that, but am also conscious of the time when I was Dean of Chicago, of the quite proper question raised by the schools, "Why should they be blamed for the delinquency of the community, where the whole community setup was teaching it?" The school wasn't teaching it. So, can you expect them to teach morality in a delinquent community?

MR. SPEARS: We had six hundred teachers in a course last semester, with an office and an assistant superintendent in charge of it, and we've got all compensatory education put under his office, as curriculum. He is in the area of curriculum, whether he goes on the high school assembly stages for panels with superintendents or somebody else. We are in the field right now and, unless a movement such as this is coming at the national level and will appreciate these things that we are in by making an effort, we are just going to be out there floundering by ourselves, as individual school systems.

CHAIRMAN TYLER: If this group agrees this is an important part of it, there are certainly indices of behavior for a community, for a sample of children, youth, and adults, that can be applied, that can be improved as time goes on. But, certainly, we know better how to do it and assess it than we apparently now know how to teach it.[9]

Tyler continued in the course of this meeting to articulate the principle that the schools should not be held accountable for changing the moral climates of communities or for transmitting values that were not transmitted through the total life of a community. But many participants firmly maintained that their school systems were now involved in teaching civic and moral values and were being held answerable for achievement in this arena.

---

[9] *Proceedings of ECAPE Conference with Superintendents and Administrators,* Sept. 22, 1964, pp. 63–68.

In taking his position about the limited role of schools in affecting values, Tyler introduced another point which he mentioned only in passing—the relationship of the community's aspirations for its children and its socioeconomic makeup to the achievement of even the *tangible* items, such as reading and mathematics. Although the Coleman Report had not then been published, similar conclusions about the importance of socioeconomic background pervaded the meeting if only as hunches. But these hunches took a strange direction: While many participants mentioned the importance of the family's and community's influence on the school's outcomes, what they stressed was the school's responsibility for changing the community's values by educating children into "better" social values. This was not merely an indication of the hubris of these particular educators but a reflection of the fact that, at least at this point in history, many educators saw themselves as educators of the whole child, *in loco communitas,* as it were.

Tyler did at least give the appearance of seeming responsive to measuring some of the more difficult intangibles, if enough educators agreed they were important.

> *FATHER CURTIN:* I'd like to raise a question. . . . It has to do with the committee's own attitude toward the possibility of getting at certain outcomes with some validity and reliability. For instance, you mentioned attitudes. There are certain values to an educational system which are not outputs to be measured—social values, which involve a racial question. There are certain other outcomes that are highly intangible—creative thinking, critical thinking, such things as an interest in reading, not just reading achievement but an interest in reading that matures as the person grows older, through the grades.
>
> These and other intangibles, in the estimation of the committee, can these be measured sufficiently well to warrant the measuring instrument we are discussing?
>
> *CHAIRMAN TYLER:* What our committee has planned to do is to get from people like yourselves a notion of what you think ought to be appraised; then to contract with individuals or groups who seem to have a good deal of competence in these areas—like, for example, Educational Testing Service; like Science Research Associates; like Lundquist of Iowa; like Bloom of Chicago, and others—wherever we can find competence and interest, to see what they can come up with as kinds of devices that could be used.
>
> Now, for example, let's take some of those that you illustrated. Some of those are more easily assessed and with less sense of invasion of privacy than others. For example, to find out whether

youngsters are interested in reading and whether they are actually doing reading beyond that which is actually required for the
school. It's much easier to find out without invasion of privacy
than the question of "How do you feel about persons of other
races or of other religions or other groups?" things of that sort. So
I am sure that the questions you raise are different in the degree
to which the kind of assessment is easy or difficult.

But, if you say, "We think you should include these things,"
then our next step is to try to find out from what then we would
call pilot contracts the possibility of getting the devices, and I
mentioned test people but we also planned to explore with persons
like the Survey Research Center at Michigan and the National
Opinion Research Center in Chicago and the Bureau of Applied
Social Research at Columbia and the Survey Research Center at
California, kinds of devices that could be used. . . . You'd not
take lightly the business but would try to see how far they could
be measured before making any recommendation to any ongoing
project after this exploratory committee is over.

MR. JOHNSON: I feel very strongly that such an index should be
developed and should explore new areas, insofar as possible—
perhaps the chief among them curiosity and an inquiring mind. I
think there is no greater prerequisite to success in any field than
an inquiring mind so as to improve procedures. . . .

MRS. GREENFIELD: In that particular context, if there were a
way of finding out what influence a school had on a particular
inquiring mind—in other words, is that mind encouraged by his
school experience or does it forget about it and stop asking questions, because of the kind of teaching he has, because of the climate of the school. These are the kinds of elements we think are
just as critical, as I said before.[10]

THE "INTANGIBLES" BECOME CITIZENSHIP

While many of the complex questions raised by these educators might have
mired the Assessment in irresolvable difficulties, at least two of their concerns
might have led to clarification of what the Assessment was trying to accomplish. The first was their point that in evaluating important personal qualities, such as honesty and respect for others, the Assessment would inevitably
be involved in measuring the values of the general social community. Taken
to its logical conclusion, this can be extended to show the inevitable interrelationships between certain "intangible" qualities, such as intellectual curiosity
and attitude toward school, and more tangible outcomes of achievement in

---

[10] Ibid., pp. 78–79.

school subjects. In other words, even if the Assessment measured only achievement in school subjects, it would by definition be investigating community values, because of the interconnection between socioeconomic factors, values, and educational achievement. Secondly, the educators took seriously the Assessment's intention to measure attributes of the adult population and therefore pointed out that many of the qualities considered to be crucial for success as an adult were not necessarily related to school subjects.

These issues do not seem to have been raised seriously in subsequent meetings of ECAPE members; the momentum was great to go directly about the business of measuring. Since contractors were to be hired to produce the instruments, the terms of assessment had to be manageable; since the schools were seen as both the means and the constituency for the Assessment, their terms of reference were predominant. Eventually, instead of really dealing with the possible interrelationships among the intangibles and conventional subject areas, the committee created the nonsubject area of "citizenship" as an umbrella under which some, though not all, of the intangibles could be included.

Tyler summed up for the members of ECAPE the fields discussed in the various discussions with schoolpeople:

> *CHAIRMAN TYLER:* Well, let's consider, first, all the fields that have been discussed in these two previous conferences. They have been reading; the language arts, more generally; mathematics; science; the several social studies—history and the like; health and whether or not it is treated with, as part of science; vocational education; the fine arts—music and the graphic arts under that; and either treated alone or as viewed as part of social studies, citizenship, which refers to such matters as respect for law and order, concern for the rights of others and that type of thing; and then for a moment considering any one of these or all these fields as involving one or more types of knowledge or understanding, ability to use this knowledge or understanding in problem solving or thinking through, analyzing, recognizing problems, interest in activities and learning in this field—in many cases, attitudes toward phenomena or people. This would vary with the field; in some cases, attitudes are less important . . . in some cases, habits or practices are important, as in health.
>
> If we leave this last column as being something that is understanding, interests and attitudes, and so forth, as something that would be applied where relevant for each of these fields, then let's look at these nine fields and see which six or seven you think it important to work on first.
> *MR. WITHEY:* I have eight.
> *MR. JOSEPHS:* I have eight.

MR. WITHEY: Reading, mathematics, science. . . .

CHAIRMAN TYLER: If you put "language arts" as reading, under it, then you have eight. Actually, in the elementary school, somewhat I think unwisely, perhaps, but because reading is considered so important a problem, they tend to be separated, and language arts, involving writing, speaking, and so forth, is usually treated separately. . . .

MRS. SMYTHE: Where do you put the intangibles that came up, such as the moral values, honesty, the self-image the child has, regard for scholarship?

CHAIRMAN TYLER: I'd put them under the heading of "citizenship," broadly defined, but that's just a catchall at the moment. Perhaps the best way to start out is, which of these would you leave out?

MR. BARNES: I suspect the contractors would have some rather strong notions about which were preferable to include, wouldn't they?

CHAIRMAN TYLER: They would find "citizenship" most difficult to deal with.

MR. JOHNSTON: The whole area of social studies!

MRS. SMYTHE: This is why I felt so strongly, this is the kind of decision we can't contract out, that we've got to make, even if it takes extra staff to do it, to do the necessary work.[11]

The discussion continued until it was agreed that all the major fields of the school curriculum were to be assessed.[12] Steve Withey of the Survey Research Center, University of Michigan, was commissioned to prepare a document for a later meeting, which would list all these areas and the controversial aspects of the objectives in each.

WHO SHOULD CONTROL DECISIONS ON WHAT TO MEASURE?

The difficulties of choosing among certain conflicting points of view within each subject area were argued at length before adjourning in September, and Mabel Smythe, principal, New Lincoln School, New York City, continued to urge that ECAPE itself take on the responsibility of making most decisions rather than leaving them to contractors. Yet, by the time that Withey's sum-

---

[11] *Proceedings of ECAPE,* Sept. 23–24, 1964, pp. 325–327.
[12] Ibid., p. 331.

mary was presented at a December 6, 1964, meeting, there seemed to be little desire by ECAPE members to become directly involved in selecting subjects and defining objectives.

Tyler spoke about the necessity of including actual teachers in the formulation process and now emphasized the fact that there were common objectives within each subject on which it would be possible to reach eventual agreement. The problems involved in testing the intangibles were taken up in some detail, and again Tyler stressed only assessing understandings and attitudes which could then be measured. But Mrs. Smythe continued to object to giving control to the contractors, who might "be tempted to choose those areas where the instruments are easier to come by, simply because the job is so big." [13] Tyler continued to insist that participants at future conferences—members of the teaching profession, curriculum specialists, and potential contractors—would resolve whatever conflicts existed. If the contracting organizations "see this as something that is desirable, that they have a part to play in; that it can be a real contribution to their own development . . . they will be anxious to involve their ablest people and not to feel that . . . it would be done, as somebody suggested, by second-rate people and only viewed as a minor part of their main job." [14]

Mrs. Smythe persisted in pressing her point that the contractors might be making crucial definitional decisions on the nature and content of the subject areas—decisions which ECAPE itself should control:

MRS. SMYTHE: I am a little confused. We are—we are asking people to develop instruments for us without really telling them what our objectives are except in the most general sense.
CHAIRMAN TYLER: Well, if you call "reading interests" a most general term, of course, that's a fairly specific thing, but that's the level at which I think we'd be ready to proceed after the seminar.
MRS. SMYTHE: What are we going to hand them as a summary of our objectives? Have we a summary of objectives yet, is what I am really saying, I think.
CHAIRMAN TYLER: You mean, in addition to having broken down reading into areas like skills, comprehension, interests, and so forth, how much beyond that?
MRS. SMYTHE: No. Perhaps I am misinterpreting merely the materials which we have, but my understanding was that while

---

[13] *Proceedings of ECAPE,* Denver, Dec. 6, 1964, p. 160.
[14] Ibid., p. 165.

we had a summary of the literature, the literature is not unanimous in agreement as to what education is attempting to do.[15]

Tyler tried to reassure Mrs. Smythe that the elaborate process he envisioned would involve himself and other ECAPE members from its inception to its end. But she persevered:

MRS. SMYTHE: What I was groping toward was the basis on which we would evaluate the instruments after they'd been developed. We would want to look at these things brought to us next July and say, "Now this one better meets our objectives than that one," and, in order to do this, we would have to have some reasonably clear consensus of what objectives they were expected to meet. . . . Perhaps I am asking for more direction for the test developers than is necessary, but I was thinking, if we hand it to someone, this document, and say, "In general, these represent a consensus; they're all interesting and reasonable approaches; see what you can do to fulfill them all . . ."
CHAIRMAN TYLER: They wouldn't be able to find their way around, that way.
MRS. SMYTHE: Yes, it would be too much for them.
CHAIRMAN TYLER: I think of one that summarizes down to outlining the content areas and the actual habit and participation [that] evidences they are really doing these things outside the school class room . . . and then working with teachers would spell these out still further. Then it would come back to us for further criticism.
MRS. SMYTHE: I think if they had you at their elbow, they'd be in no difficulty. I just wanted to be sure when they get away from you, they will have something to refer to.
CHAIRMAN TYLER: Well, they shall; that's the kind of thing we will have to prepare for such a seminar. It's just that I am getting a little disturbed about how much work there is to this thing! (*Laughter.*)
MR. CORSON: Aren't we saying, really, that in each of the areas that you have defined, there are no clear, readily-agreed-upon objectives at the moment?
CHAIRMAN TYLER: All written out? No, that's true.
MR. CORSON: All written out, and of which you might say to the contractors, "This is what we want you to measure," and, lacking that, you have to say to the contractor, "We have canvassed what objectives there are to be found; we have put them down, here; we are looking to you to find devices to measure. . . ."

---

[15] Ibid., pp. 168–170.

CHAIRMAN TYLER: We are holding a seminar to help clarify and get the essence on citizenship and recording it as part of our general understanding. Then we get agreement that Mr. X takes responsibility for this part of what we have clarified, and then he begins to pursue this farther and work it out in more detail in cooperation with school people.

MR. CORSON: Might we not come up with, at the end of the seminar, with saying that, in the field of citizenship there are a dozen different objectives that are obviously held by some in that particular field. We find ways of measuring eight out of the dozen. We don't find ways of measuring the other four and, in working with the schools and measuring those eight, you may develop ways to get at the other four then, or you may not.

CHAIRMAN TYLER: That is, it's quite possible.

MRS. SMYTHE: I think we have to recognize, too, there are two sets of objectives. One is our objectives in making this measurement, in doing this survey altogether, and I think our objectives are much more easily arrived at then than the objectives of American education as a whole. I don't see that we have to establish what are the educational objectives of all America in any precise, summary form, because one of the things we wanted to do is to get a sense of the range and varieties in emphases from one part of the country to another. But our own objectives should be more clearly stated, I think, to find out what is the range of approaches, what is the range of information, what is the level of growth in various areas which are defined, already, for us in these things. I am not saying this is a definitive statement of our objectives, but it gives some idea.[16]

These lengthy extracts show clearly the discrepancy between what ECAPE was at this point willing to discuss internally and the actual portrait of the subject-matter objectives as they were finally presented to the public. Here, the differences of opinion within current curricula were explored and the question of choice among them was openly raised. As the next chapter shows, the final objectives emphasized principles which come from a single and simple point of view. The intangibles had either been lumped into "citizenship" or relegated to "understanding" and "appreciations" that were related only to the particular school subject.

As Tyler made clear in this meeting, the subject areas were to be directly related to the school's definition of them:

---

[16] Ibid., pp. 172–176.

CHAIRMAN TYLER: We are talking of the commonest classification of the schools in the curricular area—the language arts for the elementary schools, which is usually broken up in the high school into English and foreign languages, but commonly called the language arts at the elementary level; and mathematics, natural science, social studies, and you've got health and physical education. Then you get into the question as to whether you treat the various occupational objectives separately, but, generally, I would see vocational assessment of the kind of assessment we are talking about here, as of two sorts—one, the understanding of the youngsters about the world of work, what kinds of jobs are available, and something of the sort of education required for the different sorts of jobs. This is knowing their way around the world of work. Second, having some occupational skills, if they are not planning to go to college to develop them.

Then, finally, we have the fine arts area, which may or may not be separated into music and the visual arts.

I believe this represents—is this right, Paul—this represents the usual area of the public school. . . .

MR. JOHNSTON: Yes.

MRS. SMYTHE: And under "social studies," you include the catchall areas—citizenship, I presume?

CHAIRMAN TYLER: That's where it's most likely; the people teaching social studies and the supervisors are more likely to be concerned there, although there are some objectives that would be schoolwide—the concern with the habits of study and study skills, and so forth, is schoolwide as well as being contributed to by many other if not all the areas.[17]

Ultimately, as the next chapter demonstrates, the contractors came to assume a major role in the delineating the subject areas. The original ECAPE committee became an advisory group, represented mainly by Tyler and Tukey, and a permanent staff was developed to guide and mediate among the contractors. Perhaps this was inevitable, even fortunate, if the Assessment was to get off the ground. Certainly no consensus would actually have been possible among all the groups and individuals consulted by ECAPE, although Mrs. Smythe's suggestion of a pluralism of subject-matter objectives might have been viable.

The educators who believed that the intangibles were central to an evaluation of education raised significant ideas which never found their way into the Assessment. But at other meetings more conservative administrators

---

[17] Ibid., pp. 136–137.

pushed in opposite directions—toward assessing solely the most basic subjects and in the exact terms most commonly held by the schools. It is evident from the transcript that Tyler leaned toward this latter position and so influenced the Assessment. There were many reasons for this, not the least of which were the inherent difficulties in communicating to the general public if other approaches had been taken, and the substantial political clout of the established administrators and curriculum specialists. But a more fundamental reason must have been Tyler's own commitment, from the beginning, to a simple census of educational outputs which would, once it was accomplished, stimulate research into relationships among affective factors which were difficult enough even to understand, much less to measure. In terms of the Assessment's acceptability to Congress and the states as a tool for accountability, "Formal schooling is what you pay for," as John Tukey said in an interview at NAEP headquarters in Denver in August 1972.

WHO WOULD DEFINE EACH SUBJECT AREA?

The lack of clarity, evident in the ECAPE meetings, as to who would determine the detailed nature of the subject areas to be assessed was present from the first December 1963 meeting held to discuss the National Testing Project. Tyler at that time proposed a process through which dialogue between educational specialists and "intelligent laymen" might occur:

> *MR. TYLER:* I tried to speculate, when John asked me to draw up some kind of a memorandum, to see what this area might include on the question of what could be the advisory group that would attempt to approve, disapprove, suggest the specification, and so forth, and my view was that, in each area, the advisory panel would represent two kinds of people—one, the informed scholars and teachers in the area, so they'd talk about things that are ahead that they think important, but the other would be a certain number of people who would be judged, like this group, as being persons with some wisdom, some notion of what's important in adult life and would be able to ask the specialist at any point, "Why would you include this?" "What's its real relevance to living a productive and satisfying and significant life?" and, at the same time, to raise questions, "Why wouldn't you do something about the Bill of Rights?" and so forth, so there'd be a continuing dialogue between intelligent and responsible laymen and people who have specialized in the area to try to see there'd be some balance. . . .
> This may be quite unrealistic and I don't know what the Com-

missioner would have in mind as to how to get this done, but it seems to me that's one way of trying to see that what finally survives is judged important by both groups—the people working intensively with it as teachers or scholars and the people who are concerned about the product of American education and the quality of American living, and so forth.[18]

The next chapter illustrates how the nature of such dialogue, as Tyler conceived of it, and the principle of including in the Assessment only what survived such dialogue had severely limited utility if anyone's *real* interests and values were to be represented. We use the term "Cardinal Principle" to highlight the adamance with which Tyler retained his attitude that "what the schools are trying to do" *could* meaningfully be reflected through the process he proposed. Serious doubts are raised as to the ultimate wisdom of Tyler's stance on this important matter.

---

[18] *Proceedings of the National Testing Project Conference*, pp. 133–134.

4

THE SUBJECT-MATTER OBJECTIVES

Once ECAPE decided to evaluate performance in ten distinct subject areas, it began to define specific subject-matter objectives on the basis of which exercises could be written and performance measured. This chapter analyzes the process and underlying assumptions guiding NAEP's development of subject-matter objectives. Though the guidelines formulated by ECAPE and later NAEP appear to be clear and simple, these guidelines and the process that ensued from them actually contain numerous contradictory premises and procedures which can be explored through the available working papers, memos, and reports.[1] It will become clear that the subject-matter objectives as established for the Assessment's cycle reflect these unperceived and/or unresolved confusions of purpose.

This is not to say that NAEP's subject-matter objectives are any worse than such objectives are generally. Or that, in some cases, they are not at least more comprehensive than others have been. It is notoriously difficult to produce subject-matter objectives that are genuinely useful for educators who had no part in devising them. Personal involvement in that process gives one the advantage of familiarity with the concrete matters and problems which

---

[1] Major sources for this chapter are the objectives booklets themselves, a *Summary of Conference of Lay Panels Who Received Proposed Objectives for a National Assessment of Education,* ECAPE, Dec. 15–16, 1965, and "Assessing the Progress of Education: A Second Report," by Martin J. Higgins and Jack C. Merwin, *Phi Delta Kappa,* vol. 48, pp. 378–380, April 1967.

precede the generality and abstraction that characterize most lists of objectives. It is this abstractness which often makes such lists meaningless to those who might be expected to want to use them. Another somewhat ironic peculiarity of subject-matter objectives is that no matter how vague and meaningless they are, their adoption by a recognized educational body lends them an aura of authority. They exist; therefore they must be taken seriously.

The Plowden Report may have provided the first official debunking of lists of objectives since their appearance as staples in the arsenal of planning and evaluation:[2]

> . . . general statements of aims, even by those engaged in teaching, tend to be little more than benevolent aspirations which may provide a rough guide to the general climate of a school, but which may have a rather tenuous relationship to the educational practices that go on there. It was interesting that some of the head teachers who were considered by H.M. Inspectors to be most successful in practice were least able to formulate their aims clearly and convincingly. [Paragraph 497]
>
> It is difficult to reach agreement on the aims of primary education [unless] anything but the broadest terms are used; but formulations of that kind are little more than platitudes. [Paragraph 501]

The Assessment, from the beginning, was conscious of the hazards intrinsic to any stated set of objectives for the nation's classrooms. To avoid meaninglessness, it insisted that its objectives would be behavioral, that they would eschew indefinite phrases and directives, and that they would be illustrated by exercises so that an additional level of specificity would always be provided. Further, the objectives would include attitudes and "understandings" as well as the usual content which each subject area hoped to transmit to students.

Too, the Assessment was keenly aware that its very existence relied upon putting to rest fears that a centralized curriculum-setting effort might result from the subject-matter objectives. ECAPE's and NAEP's pronouncements

---

[2] Lady Bridger Plowden et al., *Children and Their Primary Schools: A Report of the Central Advisory Council for Education* (London: HMSO, 1967). More recently, Samuel Meisels has shown how the movement against explicit goals has spread through the alternative schools in this country, and he has examined the costs and benefits to those who take such a stance, in "Goal-Stating in Open Education," unpublished special qualifying paper, Harvard University Graduate School of Education, Cambridge, Mass., 1971.

consistently denied that it intended to threaten anyone or anyone's goals. To this end, it insisted that the process by which *its* objectives were to be determined would take into account the viewpoints of everyone concerned. The assumption was that because the Assessment was setting out to gather existing objectives rather than to create new ones or even new variations on old ones, it could even *incorporate* the major objectives of all concerned. Thus, the objectives were to be meaningful and acceptable to all—a condition which seems a contradiction in terms.

THE PROCESS FOR FORMULATING THE OBJECTIVES

ECAPE planned that the formulation of the objectives would include the input of lay citizens as well as of scholars and educators in each field. The involvement of lay persons was seen as a bold move, one going beyond conventional procedures involved in testing. The participation of the three groups was viewed as desirable for what seem to be both positive and defensive reasons: By making certain that the objectives were deemed important by both the producers and consumers of education, a more truly national assessment might result; by including representatives from all interested parties (students at that point apparently being considered represented by their teachers and parents),[3] an assessment could forestall assault from any quarter:

> For National Assessment, goals must be acceptable to three important groups of people. First, they must be considered important by scholars in the discipline of a given subject area. Scientists, for example, should generally agree that the science objectives are worthwhile. Second, objectives should be acceptable to most educators and be considered desirable teaching goals in most schools. Finally, and perhaps most uniquely, National Assessment objectives must be considered desirable by thoughtful lay citizens. Parents and others interested in education should agree that an objective is important for youth of the country to know and that it is of value in modern life.
> This careful attention to the identification of objectives should help to minimize the criticism frequently encountered with cur-

---

[3] Students were involved to some degree during the second round in formulating objectives in all subjects.

rent tests in which some item is attacked by the scholar as representing shoddy scholarship, or criticized by school people as something not in the curriculum, or challenged by laymen as being unimportant or technical trivia.[4]

This defensive stance and the strategic considerations motivating it must have been partly responsible for the consensus orientation of ECAPE throughout the formulation of the objectives. Rather than using the three chosen constituencies as advocates for objectives arising from the interests and expertise of each group, the process actually ensured that diversity and conflict—and perhaps searching inquiry—among and within the groups would be kept to a minimum.[5]

Several components of the process contributed to this end: the crucial role given to the contractors; the composition of members in each of the three groups; the brief time allocated for the groups to consider the objectives; and the dilution of the possible input by lay members by giving them an extremely limited role.

The prominence of the contractors' activities was evident from the outset. In most cases, the contractors formulated a list of already familiar objectives which was used as a guide for the two-day meetings of the scholars and educators in each subject area, generally held during the summer of 1965. It is difficult to know whether the contractors' working function during the meetings was that of attentive listener or mediator, gadfly or advocate. What is clear is that the agenda and sometimes the initial working papers, the minutes and reports, the ultimate decision, and probably the most lengthy deliberations were all provided by the members of each contractor's team.

---

[4] Cf. *NAEP Music Objectives* (Denver: ECS, 1970), p. 2. Almost identical statements appear in the introductions to each booklet containing the objectives for the subject-matter areas.

[5] This is not to imply that only through conflict among constituents could meaningful objectives be formulated, but to emphasize that, given the opportunity, the three groups consulted by ECAPE might have been able to present meaningful information about different areas drawn from their own experience. For example, John F. Kerr has discussed the "three main sources of data" from which objectives may be derived: first, "information about the level of development of the pupils, their needs and interests"; second, "the social conditions and problems which the children are likely to encounter"; and third, "the nature of the subject matter and types of learning which can arise from a study of the subject matter." Because ECAPE needed approval more than inquiry from its constituents, these sources of data were never seriously tapped—and the resulting objectives exhibit this lack. See Kerr, "The Problem of Curriculum Reform," in John F. Kerr (ed.), *Changing the Curriculum* (London: University of London Press, 1968), pp. 13–38.

Thus, the scholars and educators began their work from within a prepared context—one which carried the authority of actual practice. Besides, these two constituencies had been combined into a single group at the outset. Whatever forcefulness might have arisen from their different perspectives must have been blunted—although swifter agreement may have been gained. Personal involvement in and of the group, in any event, seems to have been limited. The length of time that each committee spent together as a deliberative body was as a rule only the two-day period; and subsequent input evidently was requested and received individually. From the register of the schoolpeople's affiliations, it seems debatable as to whether any actual practitioners were included at all. Instead, the "practitioners" were persons who—though they may have begun their careers actually working with children in the schools—were then representatives of representative organizations (the NEA, etc.). This is not to imply that such delegates could not contribute substantially to resolution of the problems at hand, only that their experience and insight inevitably came from a perspective that was distant from actual classrooms.

INVOLVEMENT OF LAY PEOPLE

The contractors submitted the preliminary objectives to ECAPE, which then made arrangements for the participation of lay people. The University of Minnesota was designated to take charge of seeking nominations of women and men from such organizations as the NEA, the National Congress of Parents and Teachers, and the National Chamber of Congress, and of planning conferences in four regions of the nation. Each region was then allocated a number of "lay panels," representing large cities, suburban areas, and rural areas.

Each panel, chaired by someone appointed by ECAPE, met to consider all the preliminary objectives for all subject-matter areas. Then all the chairmen gathered for two days in New York City in December 1965, to make their reports to ECAPE.

Input from lay people was designed from the start to be reactive rather than initiating. The participants had been charged with responding to lists of objectives (and subobjectives and prototype exercises) which had already been drawn up by the contractors and the other educational "experts." The members of one lay panel expressed, through their chairman, their displeasure at having been called together on too short notice and having had little time in which to examine the objectives before they met. It can be argued that input from lay people was further attenuated by the fact that the selection of panel chairmen was, as was the case with schoolpeople, top-heavy. Eight of the eleven chairmen were either members or executive officers of local or state school boards, or leaders of statewide educational associations.

Although these conditions made unlikely any substantial contribution from the grass roots or even from less-organized but interested lay people, it is obvious, from the summary of the New York conference of panel chairmen, that serious concerns and objections had been expressed at the regional meetings. The chairmen themselves seem to have been conscientious in conveying their members' opinions, although in the ensuing discussion with ECAPE, represented primarily by Ralph Tyler, who chaired the meeting, they seem to have been quite willing to come to conclusions other than those they brought with them from the lay people for whom they supposedly spoke.

There was no possibility at the conference for the many disparate views of the lay people to be brought together in any coherent statement or perspective; each chairman presented, with greetings and diplomatic thanks for the opportunity to participate, brief sequences of his or her members' criticisms and comments. Matters of small and larger import were presented together, and until discussion of specific objectives began, it is likely that the lay chairmen themselves did not know whether their panels had found points of agreement.

As the conference progressed, it was obvious that at least one vital issue had been addressed by all the lay panels. There was deep concern that the Assessment would turn out to be a mask for federal control or at least interference in educational matters, though some panel chairmen had evidently been able to allay the fears of their groups. Tyler's response to such misgivings is a classic of historical irony:

> I understand that some people see a specter of the Office of Education or somebody else behind this project, but I don't see why they talk about that in this relationship because we are starting here. You aren't from the Office of Education; we aren't from the Office of Education. We are starting with things that the schools are trying to do and figuring out how to get some information.[6]

Apart from this general apprehension, the questions raised in New York ranged over a wide spectrum—from the fit between the prototype exercises and the ages for which they were designed, to the exclusive emphasis on

---

[6] *Summary of Conference of Lay Panels*, p. 4.

Western classical culture in the literature and music objectives. When read now, some of the changes that the lay people sought seem far more advanced in educational theory and practice than the assumptions on which the objectives had been based. The interaction between the separate subject-matter fields had been emphasized by a panel member from Pennsylvania; the need for assessing five-year-olds in order to have a measure of achievement before youngsters entered school was communicated from California; and the need for a more differentiated adult sample, with thirty- to thirty-nine-year-olds as a separate category, was suggested by the Georgia panel. Several groups were insistent that the Assessment take seriously its commitment to evaluating attitudes and values and proffered various opinions as to what seemed to be omissions or unwarranted emphases—such as the lack of stress on development of esthetic and moral values, the disregard of work and study habits in the Assessment, the uncritical acceptance of the value of the work of scientists, as well as the emphasis on European civilization as the sole root of American culture. While there were some points of mutual concern, the lay people's input was by no means unified—rather there was a range of pragmatic and personal and professional attitudes deriving from varieties of experience. For example, a simultaneous call for the addition of "creative writing" and "writing mechanics" was sounded, the latter a high priority for a clear majority of the panels.

ECAPE'S RESPONSE: THE "CARDINAL PRINCIPLE"

The format of the New York conference certainly fragmented the lay chairmen's presentations and prevented any attempts they might have made to voice their opinions strongly or to lobby for their acceptance. But another, more subtle means through which their arguments were blocked seems clear: The instructions given to the participants at the start of the meeting by Tyler narrowed and considerably confused the nature of their sphere of possible influence. Tyler explained that while the lay panels could secure the *omission* of objectives which they found inappropriate, any *additions to* or *changes in* the preliminary objectives would be a more complex matter. In the words of the *Summary*:

> If the lay chairmen felt that a valuable objective had been omitted, it could be called to the attention of the test development agencies, but it would not necessarily be added to the assessment. *The school representatives must say, "These are the things we are trying to*

do." It isn't fair to assess people on what they have learned if they haven't had a chance to learn it. . . . For example, many of the chairmen expressed concern over the use of the limitation of cultural considerations to "Western Culture" in the art, music and literature sections. They raised the question whether we were confining ourselves to our own narrow little culture and implying that this is the only thing worth learning or knowing. Chairman Tyler said that he would take this idea back to the contractors, but that if the schools are not teaching music and literature of other cultures now we couldn't assess for such knowledge. *We want to assess only what the schools are attempting to accomplish.*[Emphasis added.][7]

That the objectives were to be defined in terms of "what the schools are trying to do" is a theme reiterated so often by Tyler in response to the lay people's criticisms of the objectives that it can be called the "Cardinal Principle."[8]

At first it looks like a simple principle, but as it was actually used in the determination of the objectives its meaning seems increasingly ambiguous. While it usually implied that the determining factor in the Assessment's objectives was the actual *goals* of the schools, it sometimes appears to have meant the actual *practice* of the schools. At still other times, ECAPE seems to have used the Principle to mean what it thought the goals of the schools *should be*; here the determination of certain objectives was almost wholly normative, reflecting the opinions of the early Assessment leaders or the experts from the contracting companies.

Which meaning of the Cardinal Principle was applied had great importance, of course, for the politics of the Assessment and the content of the objectives. In the working relationship between ECAPE and the lay people, however, different usages must have had the same effect: lay views would have to be weighed against the decisions of the contractors, who were advised by the experts as to the actual practice or the aspirations of the schools. The Cardinal Principle was used continuously and also inconsistently until it became a kind of mystification through which ECAPE could defend itself against criticism but by which it ultimately seems to have confused itself. Certainly it made it difficult for ECAPE to hear what the lay panels were saying or to develop logistics which might have produced a real collaboration

---

[7] *Summary of Conference of Lay Panels,* p. 1.

[8] This term, coined by the authors, is obviously in no way related to the Cardinal Principles of 1918, written by the National Education Association.

between the laymen and those who made the final decisions on the objectives.

AN ILLUSTRATION: WRITING, SOCIAL STUDIES, MUSIC, AND THE CARDINAL PRINCIPLE

Writing   ECAPE's response to the lay panels' strong determination to include writing mechanics in the objectives illustrates the way in which communication among the constituencies was muddled and the choice of objectives complicated by inconsistent application of the Cardinal Principle. According to the available documents, the decisive pronouncement against the inclusion of mechanics in the writing objectives had first been given by a member of the ETS contracting team:

> The [Writing] panel members also discussed whether grammar and vocabulary should be stressed. The panel recognized the existence of conflicting approaches to grammar and sentence structure. An ETS staff member distributed and explained a grammar test which indicated that the teaching of grammar had little or no effect on a student's written expression. In light of this information and other discussions which the panel members held, the committee agreed that the survey should not assess a knowledge of grammatical terms.[9]

It is possible of course that the Writing Panel members might well have come to the same conclusion without the intercession of the contractor—but not, and this is the central point, if they had been following the Cardinal Principle, that the Assessment should be concerned only with what the schools were actually attempting. For though omens of changes in teaching "English" and writing were present in the work of linguists and experts in the language arts, grammar was still a major thrust of the curriculum in English classrooms throughout the country.

Even while word of the linguistic theories being developed by Noam Chomsky and his colleagues at MIT and by Roger Brown and his group at Harvard was filtering down from the universities to institutions of teacher training, the linguists themselves were vehemently denying that their field was in a state advanced enough to bear application to the classroom. And while the Dartmouth Conference produced yet another theoretical blow to the classroom teaching of mechanics in English, traditional practice was not widely affected. At Dartmouth College in 1966, the same summer in which

---

[9] *NAEP Writing Objectives* (Denver: ECS, 1970), p. 5.

the Writing objectives were being developed, American and British language arts specialists criticized traditional structural analysis of English and explicit teaching of grammar as impediments to the knowledge and use of the language. But new curricula had not yet been written, much less found their way into classrooms.

The original Writing objectives reflect the orientation of the Dartmouth Conference and are clearly committed to actual rather than analyzed language use in the classroom. But then, as now, the goals and methods used in English classes stressed identifying a preposition and diagramming it in a written sentence more than using it in daily speech. These objectives exhibit the Cardinal Principle used as a normative standard of what the schools *should be attempting,* not what they were actually trying to do.

The response of the lay people could have been anticipated. Many panel members were adamant that the objectives should not downgrade the mechanics of writing; in particular, they complained about the wording of "Objective I: Write to communicate adequately in a social situation":

> It was suggested that in the amplifying statement under this objective the section, "correct spelling, grammar, mechanics, and the like are not essential to the effectiveness of social communication," indicated a tolerance of sloppiness and should be deleted. Many of the chairmen reported that their groups had felt strongly about the above statement. They realized that social writing normally doesn't stress mechanical correctness, but they didn't feel that mechanics should be downgraded.[10]

There are few educational subjects about which lay people might be expected to speak with such confidence as their own language. For this reason and also perhaps because it is difficult to accept the suggestion that the endless hours of spelling, punctuation, and usage drill in English classes may not have been important in helping one to communicate adequately in a social situation, the lay people saw the wording of the objective as a potential threat to the clarity of their language. More fundamentally, however, while experts may stress the authentic quality of interpersonal communication over what they call the "artificial" standard of "correctness for correctness sake,"[11] lay people have good reason to recognize that the social acceptance of an invitation, a thank-you note, or a formal address to a group may ultimately

---

[10] *Summary of Conference of Lay Panels,* p. 6.
[11] *NAEP Writing Objectives,* p. 10.

depend on its conformity to social conventions, rather than on what is really being said. Language arts experts may hope to change this basis for social judgment, but for the general public it is a fact of life.

Tyler's rebuttal and the lay chairmen's response are summarized as follows:

> Dr. Tyler explained that in the assessment, samples of writing for a social situation would be collected and they would be judged in terms of content, organization, clarity, legibility and mechanics. What the objective is indicating is that a personal letter is to be judged more in terms of what it says to you as a person than on the accuracy of the mechanics. However, the chairmen wanted it clear that the assessment should not be saying that the mechanics of writing is unimportant.[12]

The final form of the objective does not seem to have been much influenced by the lay people's wishes:

> . . . social situations call for the communication of thoughts, observations, and facts so organized that they will have meaning for the reader; correct spelling, grammar, mechanics, and the like are not essential to the effectiveness of most social communication. Of course, correctness is hoped for here as in any endeavor and "better" performance anticipated as the population matures, but social communication relies principally on factual accuracy, organization, and flavor.[13]

Ironically, more than five years later, NAEP was forced to compile a separate *post hoc* report on the Assessment results in "Writing Mechanics." The reason for this was continuing pressure from lay people on the ECS Advisory Council, who became involved after the Assessment in Writing had been completed and who were more successful than their earlier counterparts in persuading NAEP that the mechanics of writing deserved serious attention.

Social Studies   ECAPE took quicker action on another matter on which the lay panels sought change, the reformulation of the original Social Studies Objectives. As in the case of the Writing Objectives, the experts had ignored the Cardinal Principle and had formulated objectives of global abilities based on competence in a broad range of the social sciences rather than on the common school-meaning of the field. In most schools across the country,

---

[12] *Summary of Conferences of Lay Panels,* p. 6.
[13] *NAEP Writing Objectives,* p. 8.

knowledge of facts in history, geography, and current events dominates the field of social studies, and the lay people wanted this reality to supersede the broader aims of the original objectives. They wanted new ones which would

> assess the degree to which there is basic subject competence in such fields as history, geography, economics, political science, sociology. . . . Then, from these subject areas, objectives could be developed to assess the child's or adult's ability to draw up, stimulate, utilize, interrelate these many frames of reference.[14]

Three months after the meeting of the lay chairmen, a social studies conference was called at the Center for Advanced Study in the Behavioral Sciences in Palo Alto. Contractors applied for the redrafting of the Social Studies Objectives, partly as a result of the lay recommendation. Subsequently, ETS recontracted to produce new objectives which were sent to one member of each of the original eleven panels which had reviewed the earlier objectives the previous fall.

Perhaps the original Social Studies Objectives were unsuitable for reasons other than their distance from the actual classroom; the Objectives booklet suggests that they were changed because they were not behavioral enough. It does not seem, in any event, that the experts in this instance were any more consistent about applying the Cardinal Principle than were the lay people.

Music   In the case of the Music Objectives, both lay people and professional musicians questioned different aspects of ECAPE's formulation, and the two groups were answered by a shifting application of the Cardinal Principle. The lay panels demurred at the inclusion of music in the Assessment precisely on the grounds of whether or not it was a significant curricular goal in the schools. Tyler's response does not deal directly with their hesitancy, but stresses ECAPE's reliance on the expertise of advisory panels:

> Dr. Tyler pointed out what he felt was the philosophy of this assessment. If the [advisory] panels say that these are good things to go at, and this would be true in mathematics as well as music or art, the students won't all get to the same level. . . . If music is important enough to be included, we would report such things as a great many people have learned to sing and to get satisfaction from it. . . . We are saying that this kind of information is useful because we think music is something that is desirable to learn, although, as with mathematics, we aren't trying to say that everyone should get to a particularly high level.[15]

---

[14] *Summary of Conference of Lay Panels*, p. 7.
[15] Ibid., p. 7.

Although it is reported that the lay panel chairmen then arrived at a consensus that an assessment of music would be valuable, many of them went on to express their dismay that jazz and contemporary music had been omitted. They felt strongly that these should be included. Ultimately, as reported in the Music Objectives booklet, these latter forms of music were not included—although professional musicians who had been consulted had also requested them. The reason given was that they were not being taught in the schools!

The Cardinal Principle's vagueness and inconsistent application not only blocked the opposition of lay advisors and some professionals to various objectives, but also supported the always prevalent conception of objectives as being "objective" or "value-free." The description "what the schools are attempting to achieve" promised that an objective amalgamation of goals could and would emerge. This is, of course, impossible. But rather than squarely confront the matter of whether some choices were inevitable, and sharing problematic matters with the laymen and others interested in the Assessment, ECAPE obscured this very complicated issue. Tyler's typical statements merely implied that not *all* the goals of the schools were of equal interest, as when he suggested that the objectives should be those which scholars, teachers, and curriculum specialists believe faithfully reflect the contribution of that field and which the schools are seriously seeking to attain. What is ignored here (although hinted at by the word "seriously") is that someone or some people are going to have to make judgments about what, from the vast array of "unpopular" and "popular," "progressive" and "traditional," "diverse" and "uniform," and "stated" and "actualized" goals of education, will be considered the *real* objectives of the country's classrooms.

For the moment we can judge ECAPE's view of who should resolve these issues by considering its actions. The lay people, it seems clear, were considered unqualified to delineate the objectives and to judge them critically after they had been formulated by the experts. The experts who drew up the original Social Studies Objectives and those who decided to omit mechanics from the Writing Objectives were not held to the letter of the Cardinal Principle; professional musicians evidently were. The judgments of the ECAPE leadership and other selected professionals, especially the contractors, were ultimately those which were trusted.

It would appear, then, that the three original constituencies—scholars, educators, and lay people—never really acted as advocates for their groups' interests and concerns, and that when conflicts among their interests did arise, they were handled in ways that promoted lack of clarity and inconsistency. Over time, a large number of different persons were briefly involved, and most communication within ECAPE took place through memos and, one suspects, through secondhand reports of what others had said and might have meant. The entire process was presided over by the contractors, ECAPE staff members, and the symbolic notion that somewhere in public practice was to be found a key to what constituted appropriate objectives.

This might be called a process of pseudo-participation, one which follows the letter of the original stipulations but which ultimately involves no one's deeply held commitments. It seems likely that parents' aspirations for their children and for their society were never brought into real dialogue with teachers' goals nor with the objectives that might emanate from the cutting edge of scholarly work. This being the case, the results might be expected to be rather disparate lists of objectives which would safely conform to a generalized notion of the nation's educational (read "subject-matter") objectives—in terms of some unidentified, rather hazy, and certainly distant point of view. Vague goals or extremely specific items, none deep enough to provoke dissent or dismay from too many people, and mostly unrelated to any coherent perspective on the subject area or students' developmental growth, could have been predicted. This is indeed what the final objectives, with certain exceptions, appear to be.[16]

THE CONTEXT FOR THE DEVELOPMENT OF THE OBJECTIVES

ECAPE's original hope—that the objectives would be meaningful and ac-

---

[16] Obviously, no general statement can apply equitably to all the subject-matter objectives, and it is worth mentioning briefly some of the variations in quality which we have found among them. The quality of the content and presentation of the Literature Objectives seems very high, and the Music Objectives imaginatively address some very difficult problems. Of all the objectives, those in Social Studies and Citizenship are the most confused and would seem to require intense concentration. The Reading Objectives, according to specialists whom we consulted, are excellent: in contrast to most of the other objectives, their hierarchical arrangement is especially sound and developmentally appropriate. It should be noted, however, that since the Assessment begins in Reading, as it does throughout, with nine-year-olds, the difficulties of setting objectives for the years during which children learn to read could be and were avoided.

Special attention must be drawn to the objectives in what came to be called "Career and Occupational Development." Here the criticisms we have made of the process by which the objectives were developed are not applicable. Competing contractors with different approaches to this difficult area were involved in lengthy deliberations with professionals and lay people. The resulting objectives and their presentation are a product of *five* years of work, indicating that, had comparable time and energy been expended on other areas, the objectives might have been vastly improved.

ceptable to all three of its constituencies—could have been called naïve even in 1964; given what appear to be the realities of the process by which the objectives were formulated, and in light of contemporary developments and interests, such a notion seems woefully simplistic.

For one thing, interest in unearthing the hidden curriculum and its unstated objectives has since produced justified skepticism that explicit statements of educational purposes are meaningful indicators of what is really taking place or what was really intended to take place. Instead, as Robert Stake has pointed out, statements of objectives are often really "formal transformations of values" by which personal or institutional preferences and biases are obscured. Secondly, although most of the final objectives and subobjectives fell short of the original intent to formulate behavioral objectives, ECAPE's committment to statements of behavioral goals—very much in tune with the effort to make education a scientific endeavor—has never wavered, even though its accomplishment would be quite problematic.[17] Now, as the demand for accountability hits many classroom teachers as well as statewide administrators, behavioral objectives continue to be taken as the keystone.

Another phenomenon casts doubts upon the probability that the Assessment's objectives can succeed on their original terms: Contemporary criticism of the schools extends to the assumption and practice of homogenous educational aims and methods that have long been supported by professional educators. Pluralistic life-styles have been increasingly accepted and even celebrated in society, and pressure has been put on the nation's schools to accommodate them. A multiplicity of purposes must be reflected in complex objectives.

Another major element of the original conception of the objectives is open to question—the simple definition of the nation's education as the sum of objectives from ten separate and equally considered subject-matter areas. This definition seems never to have been seriously challenged within the policy-making meetings of ECAPE, although, as we have seen, one lay panel raised the possibility that interrelationships among the disciplines might be reflected in the objectives. It is obvious that even after the dubious decision to define educational progress in terms of a given number of distinct subject areas, it would have been possible to develop relatively complex interdiscipli-

---

[17] A much needed critique of the mystique of behavioral objectives and perhaps a reversal against this aspect of testing may be in the offing if a recent article is any indication. Included is an overview of "criterion-referenced testing," a passionate and impressively considered challenge to the entire process of directing instruction according to specified behavioral objectives. See Gene R. Hawes of Michigan State University, "Criterion-Referenced Testing," *Nation's Schools,* no. 2, pp. 35–41, February 1973.

nary objectives that reflected a more sophisticated concept of knowledge and the learning process.

There seem to be three major justifications for the ECAPE/NAEP decision to fragment the development of objectives into discrete subjects. First of all, the inception of the Assessment coincided with a renewed classicism, stimulated by an intense interest in the state of the public schools and in an attempt to improve the academic preparation of the nation's youth. Such concern was expressed in several quarters, notably by professors in prestigious universities who were dismayed at the incompetence of entering students admitted in increasing numbers from public schools, and from those like Rickover, who were fearful that America's defense capacity, shamed by the appearance of Sputnik, was being jeopardized by poor training in the sciences.

The push was on to halt the "dilution of knowledge." Top educational professionals, many of whom participated in the Assessment, joined with scholars to draw up more rigorous curricula—first in science and math, but later in social studies and English—and to lure bright college graduates into the teaching profession. The ambitious curricular projects were zealously and expensively undertaken, buoyed by Jerome Bruner's dictum that if energies were channeled toward finding the appropriate forms, any subject could be taught to anyone of any age without losing the integrity of the subject itself. In the wake of the pedagogic fervor and optimism of the late fifties and early sixties, perfecting the teaching of the subject areas in the schools was perhaps as broad an educational goal as those educators who planned the Assessment could envision.

Second, the division of the objectives into subjects emanated from the desire to formulate the Assessment as closely as possible in the conventional terminology and principles of the schools. As noted earlier, school people themselves had to be convinced that the Assessment was, on the one hand, nothing at which to take alarm and, on the other, something that might benefit them. If a major objective to be evaluated had been "to formulate hypotheses about the causes of an event"—which would have included training in science, social studies, and literature and could have involved content from any of these fields—the role of curriculum specialists advising the Assessment would have been much more complicated than under the traditional scheme. If, as one lay panel suggested, oral and written study and use of language had been seen as part of a general topic such as "Communication" or "Language Arts," reading and literature specialists might have complained that their own domains had been trespassed upon.

For instance, who would be held accountable if the Assessment were to report that 60 percent of the nation's thirteen-year-olds could not find their way from one point to another on a map of a hypothetical city? Successful execution of this task calls for a complex act of knowing, and, while most teachers would deplore such a failure and most lay people would blame the schools for it, the skill itself would probably not be listed in any conventional list of objectives for any particular subject area.

ECAPE's consideration of objectives manifestly did not begin with the needs for certain skills nor with the question of priority among various skills, abilities, and understandings. It began with the subject-matter divisions and with the contours of knowledge which each discipline had traditionally fashioned. The resulting objectives do not suggest adequately the relationships among various fields, although in some cases the objectives include abilities which are fostered and perhaps even initiated in other fields. In Science, for example, critical reading to determine what is relevant or irrelevant, what is hypothesis, fact, or opinion, would seem to have a close connection with similar activities in Reading, Literature, and Social Studies.

A third source of the ECAPE/NAEP conception of the objectives, and one which may explain the unexamined influence of the other sources on the Assessment, was a feeling among some of the project's key members that the development of objectives was merely a heuristic device to facilitate the development of exercises by the contractors. During interviews for this report it became clear that this relatively simple utilitarian view prevailed during the Assessment's formative stages, even though some interviewees on the NAEP staff now claim the delineation of objectives and publication of objectives booklets as one of the Assessment's major achievements, rather than just a means to create and validate the exercises.[18]

A related set of criticisms concerns the presentation of each subject area in the individual objectives booklet. With the exception of Literature and Music, there is scarcely any attempt to relate the list of individual objectives to a

---

[18] A competing view of the objectives has been offered recently by consultants to NAEP. They view the objectives as essentially meaningless and instead insist that the exercises should be considered as the subject matter objectives. Their rationale seems to be that the behavior or application of knowledge required by the exercises exhibits a precise and central objective of the subject. They also suggest that if reporting the results by themes is planned (rather than done *post hoc*), it be done by exercises rather than objectives. Theoretically this view would seem to have a good deal of merit, but as the next section explains, it is questionable given the inadequacies and debatable content validity of the exercises themselves.

conceptual understanding of the field—how it was perceived by those who defined the objectives, what its importance might be for those who participate in it, and what relation it bears to other aspects of human activity. Thus the objectives, no matter how commendable, seem to exist *de novo*, as if in total isolation from preferences, values, or perspectives on each subject. Within almost no area is there even a minimal attempt to point out which objectives might be considered primary and which secondary—and for which groups of the population. While it is occasionally indicated that one objective is related to others and that some may be more important at some ages than others, there is no presentation of a whole and how its parts fit together theoretically, empirically, or developmentally.

It may be objected that the objectives were designed to be simply that, and not complex statements about knowledge and cognition. Had attention been paid, however, to what Paul Hirst has called the relationship between each discipline and "the development of mind and the nature of knowledge,"[19] the objectives—even within each subject—might have been more systematically organized to present a more coherent view of each area. Within each it also would have been possible to consider the question of what is essential and abiding within the discipline and what is determined by the historical or cultural context. If such a consideration had been made, it might have been possible to respond to particular requests by the lay review panels, using broader procedures for ascertaining how the objectives could change and to what constituencies NAEP would be responsible. In Literature, for example, the request that non-Western literature be included could have been seen as an expression that the fundamental inquiry of literature takes place within particular and individual works whose salience to the individual depends upon his or her age, cultural milieu, purposes, etc. The popular appeals for inclusion of mechanics in the Writing Objectives could have been dealt with more adequately than by a belated re-analysis of the writing exercises and the publication of a special report on an objective that had originally been excluded.

Because such fundamental issues as those outlined above were given little attention, and were not taken into serious account in either the development of the objectives or in their presentation to the lay consultants, the way in which they are now offered to the public is quite superficial. Various essential

---

[19] Paul H. Hirst, "The Contribution of Philosophy to the Study of the Curriculum," in Kerr, op. cit., pp. 39–62.

educational issues have been glossed over, and in most of the subject areas the objectives themselves possess little value as guiding principles, although they may be used as content items for those who are comparing lists of objectives in an attempt to formulate their own. Little offense can be taken at them as merely yet another in a long history of lists of objectives. But little insight into substantive educational purposes or processes can be gained from them.

ALTERNATIVE APPROACHES TO OBJECTIVES AVAILABLE TO ECAPE

There was considerable existing evidence at the time to suggest that if the objectives were to have meaning, they would have to be informed by some of the serious attempts to examine the relationship of learning in the various subjects to the learning process as a whole. This would have been especially appropriate for an undertaking of national importance concerned with the general education of citizens.

One available approach could be seen in the work of Benjamin Bloom and his colleagues, whose work, extending over more than a decade, had produced *Taxonomy of Educational Objectives: The Classification of Edcuational Goals,* in 1956.[20] (The book itself was dedicated to Ralph Tyler.) The underlying analogy of the biological classification system with an "educational-logical-psychological" system can be criticized for its simplicity, as can the whole venture for what it does not explore about the interaction among its categories.[21] But for its time, Bloom's attempt to produce a hierarchy of objectives covering the spectrum of simple and complex intended changes in student behavior was an important breakthrough in thinking about objectives. The taxonomy, for one thing, was applicable to any subject matter; the acts of knowing which it described and classified are pertinent throughout the school curriculum. The taxonomy could therefore serve as a common core for workers in a variety of fields, and its early use underscored this possibility:

> The early drafts of taxonomy have already been extensively used. Some of the examiners have found it useful as an aid in helping the faculty formulate objectives more precisely and in seeing a possible range of educational objectives. . . . The parallelism of

---

[20] Bloom, *Taxonomy of Educational Objectives* (New York: McKay, 1956).
[21] See Hirst, op. cit.

objectives in different subject-matter fields is highlighted by this procedure, thus suggesting possible points of integration.[22]

Throughout the *Taxonomy* is an impressive concern that it be useful to practitioners at every level. Here teachers accustomed to uttering global, vague objectives, such as that their students should "really understand" or "grasp the core or essence" of a thing, were encouraged to inquire what they really meant.[23]

ECAPE might also have taken heed of the memo from John Flanagan of Project TALENT, to which we referred on page 21. It was dated April 14, 1964, and titled "Evaluating the Effectiveness of Elementary and Secondary Education: The Need for Objectives in Terms of Behavior."[24] This memo was provocative but pessimistic; Flanagan's description of objectives was imbued with a profound awareness of the relationship of learning to the needs of the individual, but he was doubtful that existing instruments could adequately evaluate the attainment of such objectives. What might have been of particular interest to the Assessment's goals was his insistence that behavioral outcomes could be designated for the "progress which each student has made along the unique pathway leading to his or her self-realization." Such an approach was, he argued, consistent with the general aims of education, usually agreed upon as "developing the individual's maximum potentials and producing free and responsible citizens."

Flanagan added an opinion about his work which ECAPE might have at least considered:

> In accordance with most recent thinking in regard to public education these statements refer to individuals and not to fields of knowledge or disciplines.

The growth of the individual thus takes precedence over the specific content which may further it. Flanagan went on to say that AIR (American Institute for Research) had developed procedures for describing the individual's needs in terms of behavioral objectives, although satisfactory means for assessing the outcomes of responsible citizenship or individual fulfillment through vocational efforts had yet to be devised:

---

[22] Bloom, op. cit., p. 22.
[23] Ibid., p. 21.
[24] Carnegie files.

> . . . in spite of the emphasis by scientists on such goals as appreci-
> ation of science, understanding the scientific method, the need for
> rational decisions, and the fostering of ingenuity and imagination,
> these outcomes are represented either not at all or in very inade-
> quate fashion by present instruments. The outcomes that are easy
> to measure such as knowledge and application of prescribed for-
> mulas account for most of the questions.

Perhaps it would have been impossible for the Assessment to make substantial use of either Bloom's taxonomy or Flanagan's perspective. The commitment to separate subject areas came early and was sensible because it would
be readily accepted by professional educators. And viewing the objectives
from the individual learner's point of view must have seemed somewhat distant from the purposes of a national assessment, in which large numbers of
people were to be reached and for which one of the early hopes was comparison among states or even local school districts.

Within the limitations of subject-matter objectives, however, an attempt to
make distinctions among objectives—which was undertaken in some subjects
but not in others—might have produced a more meaningful presentation of
each field; serious attention to Bloom's work could have been useful in delineating the cognitive processes at work on each level and might have guided
the designers of the exercises as well. Once the Assessment was, for political
reasons, designed to make comparisons among states impossible, the objectives might also have gained depth from Flanagan's work. Modal types of
individuals from many situations and with many life purposes could have
been posited, educational objectives for them could have been described, and
appropriate means designed to assess their progress over time. The numbers
of respondents would have been smaller in such an assessment, and NAEP's
substantial resources could have been channeled into developing instruments
that Project TALENT, according to Flanagan, lacked the funds to develop.

THE MEANING AND IMPORTANCE OF OBJECTIVES
TO THE ASSESSMENT

The apparent lack of interest in considering different models for the objectives or even in making serious inquiry into the nature of objectives themselves and their possible uses, reinforces the evidence that, at least in the early
days of the Assessment, objectives were not seen as worthy of much serious
thought. While ECAPE saw objectives as necessary to isolate and define *before*

the Assessment could begin, this precedence was one of practical procedure, not of priority.

Yet, as noted briefly above, in later years the objectives have assumed major importance. All the booklets describing them to the public contain a statement almost identical to the following one, which is taken from the Introduction to the Music Objectives:

> After objectives for Music and the other assessment subjects were initially developed, they were compared to other statements of objectives in these areas which had appeared in the literature during the past twenty-five years. . . . It was clear that National Assessment had not produced "new" objectives in any subject area. Rather these objectives were restatements and summarizations of objectives which had appeared over the last quarter of a century. This was a desired and expected outcome in that one criterion of National Assessment objectives was that they be central to the teaching efforts of educators. . . .
>
> The job of developing objectives has not ended, however. For as the goals of the educational system evolve and change, so must the objectives used by National Assessment likewise change. This means that there must be continual re-evaluation of the objectives in each National Assessment subject area. . . .
>
> By providing this continuing process of re-evaluation, the National Assessment program hopes that it can attain its primary goal of providing information on the correspondence between what our educational system is attempting to achieve and what, in fact, it is achieving.[25]

The contradictions in this excerpt are significant for what they reveal about the ambiguities in the objectives. First, satisfaction is expressed that the objectives within each subject area are virtually identical to those already prevailing in the literature of the past twenty-five years. That satisfaction rather than chagrin is articulated at this outcome to a lengthy and expensive process may indicate NAEP's wish to assure educators that the Assessment did not threaten current practice. The assumption here is that continuity in subject-matter objectives occurs because what is "central to the teaching efforts of educators" does not change, has not changed.

Second, this recognition and celebration of the traditionalism of the objectives is significant because it is inaccurate and misleading—largely through omissions which were partly intentional and partly the result of insufficient

---

[25] *NAEP Music Objectives,* p. 8.

understanding of the latent functions of the delineation of subject-matter objectives. Clearly in some areas the Assessment *is* creating "new" objectives in a variety of subtle and not-so-subtle ways. At a general level the emphasis on national educational objectives itself is a significant force in the new definition, or renewed definition, of educational objectives at the state and local level. Old objectives may remain unchanged, but if they have been virtually moribund their revival constitutes creation of new objectives. More specifically, and more discreetly, the Assessment developed new objectives in the way in which it chose to define the field of Career and Occupational Development, and in the very creation of the new subject area of Citizenship, as well as in its handling of some of the traditional subject areas. In Writing there was the clear attempt on the part of the contractors and Assessment staff to deemphasize the importance of grammar and other aspects of writing mechanics. Surely, whether one favors such a deemphasis or not, it constitutes a new definition of the objectives of teaching or learning Writing.

The statement included in each of the objectives booklets which is quoted above explicitly contains a further and important contradiction. Immediately following the comment that the objectives are not new and have not changed over the past quarter-century is the assertion that NAEP assumes the subject-matter objectives are likely to change in the near future. Part of its claim then becomes that it will document such changes (not initiate them), reconstitute the Assessment's objectives contained in accordance with these changes, and, we may assume, revise the exercises to measure the achievement of the new objectives.

If NAEP has come to consider part of its task a continuing census on the *"goals of the educational system"* and continues to define those goals as synonymous with subject-matter objectives, it will be taking on a difficult job. How new educational *purposes* within the country, such as expanded decision making for students or stronger self-concept for minority and female children, can be translated into separate subject-matter areas is a challenging problem.

It is difficult also to imagine how the process that produced the original objectives—which supposedly had not changed from those of the previous quarter-century—could be sensitive enough to register changes in objectives over each period of the Assessment, or even over a decade of assessments. This question seems to be still very much alive in NAEP. Those members of the Exercise Development Team in Denver who are working up the Assessment's second phase speak of the major changes in present educational objectives which their work is reflecting. Yet those responsible for the more encompassing aspects of the Assessment, including Dorothy Guilford of the Office of

Education's Center for Educational Statistics, are rather certain that, when they are translated into stated objectives, what appear to be changes will turn out to be largely restatements of the existing NAEP objectives. What those who focus on the near terrain take for major crevices and outcroppings may turn out to be, when viewed with extended perspective, mere shadows on a generally continuous surface.

It might be argued that much of this analysis is critical of the objectives from a position outside that which ECAPE was working from, and that political acceptance of the Assessment necessitated a bland and simplified set of objectives and a process which would produce them. Since this was to be a national list of objectives, the argument might continue, only a list derived from a defensive stance—to preclude attack from regions and organizations—would suffice. Besides, in 1965, it was bold to involve so many constituencies, even if the actual level of involvement was low. To begin to consider the wide variety of approaches to schooling and even the major discrepancies across the country might have made impossible any resolution at all.

Even if we accept these excellent arguments, we are left with crucial questions: What meaning can there be in a national assessment which is so enmeshed in compromise and superficiality from its very beginning? Are there ways of ensuring that, once a benign and nonthreatening assessment is brought into being and is accepted, it can be transformed into a more profound assessment? What would a more meaningful set of objectives include and what would be its purpose? Further consideration of these questions and issues must await the remaining sections of this book, which are concerned with the National Assessment's management, politics, and utility.

5

THE ASSESSMENT'S
EXERCISES

Once NAEP had developed subject-matter objectives, its next task was to create the exercises to be used in evaluating achievement of the objectives. NAEP established a number of challenging criteria the exercises had to meet, but as we shall see, there were challenges that NAEP did not anticipate or acknowledge and these led to a variety of problems.

Certain of NAEP's criteria were given special emphasis. First, each exercise was to have *content validity*; that is, each individual exercise was to measure, directly and clearly, achievement of one (or more) of the behavioral objectives. Second, equal numbers of "easy," "average," and "difficult" exercises were to be written. Some exercises were to be so easy that 90 percent of the respondents would answer them correctly (the so-called 90 percent exercises), while others were to be so difficult that only 10 percent would answer correctly. In this way, the range of abilities, skills, and understandings of the population would be quite fully described. Finally, the exercises were not to be restricted to the traditional multiple-choice format, but were to take whatever forms (e.g., interview, essay, or task performance) would be most appropriate for the behavioral objectives involved.[1]

To prepare the exercises, NAEP contracted with the agencies that had

---

[1] For a complete list of the exercise development criteria, see Carmen J. Finley and Frances S. Berdie, *The National Assessment Approach to Exercise Development* (Denver: NAEP, 1970), p. 15.

written the subject-matter objectives, but the exercise development criteria proved difficult to meet. In part, the problem was due to the contractors' inexperience with the kinds of exercises NAEP sought; the standardized tests with which the contractors were then familiar did not emphasize content validity of items, nor did they make use of 90 percent exercises. Also, in part, difficulty arose because of NAEP's poor management and planning of the exercise development process. Most important, the exercise criteria themselves contained several unresolved predicaments concerning the relationship of exercises to objectives, and these continue to make the writing of Assessment exercises a formidable task.

THE EXERCISE DEVELOPMENT PROCESS

There is little evidence that either the Assessment leadership or the contractors were aware of the magnitude of the exercise development effort required. The Assessment's initial plan required that all exercises submitted by the contractors be reviewed twice, first by lay people to ascertain that no exercise was potentially offensive to any large group of people, and second by experts to verify that each exercise did indeed evaluate the educational objective for which it was intended and that it had no identifiable flaws.[2] The entire process was expected to take a year and a half. Before work was complete, however, at least three other major lay and professional reviews were undertaken, as well as a myriad of in-school and out-of-school feasibility studies and pretests. More than three years was required.

The first review provided for in the orginal NAEP plan was the review by lay people. Of the 21,000 exercises developed by the contractors by spring 1967, about 1,200 were judged by the Assessment staff to be sufficiently controversial to require lay study. These were discussed at conferences attended by representatives from organizations including the American Association of University Women, AFL-CIO, NAACP, National Conference of Christians and Jews, PTAs, school board organizations, and the U.S. Chamber of Commerce. About 300 exercises were dropped as a result of the review, primarily in Literature, Reading, and Social Studies. Some 200 Citizenship exercises were revised.[3]

---

[2] Much of the historical information on the process of exercise development is based upon Finley and Berdie, op. cit.

[3] For a detailed account of the exercises dropped or revised, see Finley and

The other review included in the original plan was a mail review by subject-matter specialists. About 70 percent of the 21,000 exercises developed were submitted to reviewers, the remainder having been eliminated by the staff or the lay panels. Three to five reviewers for each subject area were selected from nominees proposed by major professional associations in education, and each exercise was studied by one reviewer.[4] While the review provided a wealth of commentary, the contractors who had written the exercises were perplexed in interpreting much of what was said or reconciling conflicting views. Reviewers often asked how particular exercises fit into the broad picture: Each reviewer had been sent only the objectives relating to the specific exercises he was to review.

One problem about which the reviewers agreed, however, was that considerably less than 90 percent of the population would respond correctly to the "easy" exercises. As a result, several studies were commissioned to determine how easy the "easy" exercises in fact were. About fifty "easy" exercises were administered to respondents from high and low socioeconomic backgrounds for each of the ten subject areas. As expected, the responses showed that few "easy" exercises could be answered by the hoped-for 90 percent: There were clear difficulties in communication, vocabulary, and format. As a result of the study, contractors were asked to write new, easier exercises.

Following the mail review several conferences were held and participants continued to come across substantial problems. Some reviewers complained that the exercises merely "scratched the surface"; others found them textbookish, pedantic, unimaginative, and sometimes imprecise or just plain incorrect. Most consultants agreed the vocabulary was too difficult and the exercises reflected an exclusively middle-class bias.

Additional conferences were arranged between November 1967 and June 1968 to evaluate the contractors' revisions following the summer reviews. This time it was felt that significant progress had been made, and it was agreed that five subject-matter areas—Writing, Citizenship, Literature, Science, and

---

Berdie, op. cit., p. 40.
[4] Nominations for participants were requested from the International Reading Association, National Council of Teachers of English, National Council of Teachers of Mathematics, National Association of Industrial Teacher Educators, National Science Teachers Association, American Industrial Arts Association, American Vocational Association, National Art Education Association, National Council for the Social Studies, American Historical Association, Music Educators National Conference, and National Association of Schools of Music.

Social Studies—were suitable for final pretests and lay review. The Science, Writing, and Citizenship areas were selected for the first round of the Assessment.

At this point there remained the matter of reducing the exercises in each area to a number which could be administered in the time available—160 aggregated minutes per subject area. Once the professionals and lay people were done with all their reviews, there remained about 181 minutes in Citizenship, 348 in Science, and 224 in Writing. The contractors then rank-ordered the exercises on the basis of quality, reportability, and balance across objectives and difficulty levels, and the Assessment staff determined each area's final set of exercises.

Overall, there seems to have been a minimum of effective planning and control by the Assessment staff. There is no evidence of systematic scheduling of contractor activities, time allocation ("pert diagramming"), or clear decision points. Special studies appear to have been undertaken in a strictly *ad hoc* fashion, without considerations of careful design so that maximum information might be obtained at minimum cost. Nor is there any evidence of a precise formulation of the desired goals of the exercise development program; i.e., in judging the quality of the exercises, *"How good is good enough?"*

NAEP has made some effort to remedy certain of these ills. For example, disappointment with the exercises has led the Assessment staff to rely less heavily on outside contractors and to establish increased internal exercise expertise. In addition, the staff has concluded that the system of checkpoints along the exercise-writing path was insufficient. Because reviewers often evaluated exercises only when they had reached their "final" form, many had to be rejected, representing a considerable investment in time and money. For this reason, NAEP established a five-phase exercise development process for future rounds: (1) development and review of objectives and prototype exercises, (2) preparation of exercises, (3) review and revision of exercises, (4) field testing and revision of exercises, and (5) final review and selection.

The major alterations incorporated in the new five-phase program occur in phases 1 and 2. During the review and revision of objectives (phase 1), a group of subject-matter specialists prepares a small number of complete prototype exercises designed to explicate the nature of the objectives and serve as models for later exercises. When the objectives and prototypes are complete, phase 2, the actual writing of exercises, begins and involves two stages. One-half the desired number of exercises are completed first, to be evaluated by the Exercise Development Advisory Committee or Assessment staff. Only when any problems uncovered at this juncture have been solved are the remainder of the required exercises written. The review and revision, pretest, and final review (phases 3, 4, and 5) are similar in method to that utilized for the first round, embracing both lay and subject-matter reviewers. The entire process consumes about three years.

While these steps may be wise, they are also only a beginning. Technical problems, including large questions about the relationship of many of the exercises to the subject-matter objectives, indicate that adequate exercise development requires an effort characterized by a degree of comprehensive planning and imagination so far not evidenced. The primary weakness of the exercise development process can perhaps best be analyzed as a failure to establish an effective research and development organization. Manifestations of this failure have been enumerated above: insufficient understanding of the magnitude of the task, minimal overall scheduling, and inefficient utilization of contractors and other resources.

In part, the trouble may have arisen because of the novelty of the project, but on the other hand, such novelty might have been expected to inspire unusually high management ingenuity.

TECHNICAL ASPECTS OF THE NAEP EXERCISES

Many of the exercises used in the Assessment's first round do not meet the standards that NAEP itself set for them, disregarding for the moment any more stringent criteria that might have been employed. In particular, item analysis indicates that along several important dimensions, the exercises have an extremely poor fit with the subject-matter objectives and subobjectives which they are supposed to measure. The critical aspects of this lack of fit are analyzed below. All released exercises in Science, Citizenship, Reading, and Literature were reviewed, and those cited below are intended to illustrate the range of problems and prospects.[5]

Distribution of Exercises by Objectives and Subobjectives

The NAEP behavioral objectives written for each subject-matter area are cast as *objectives* and *subobjectives*. In each subject area, the objectives organize the subject in terms of a few large divisions, and the subobjectives particu-

---

[5] Not all exercises used in each Assessment round are "released" to the public. About 50 percent are retained for use in future rounds, in order to preclude "teaching to the test," which the Assessment staff fears may complicate attempts to measure change in achievement over time. NAEP publications claim that the released exercises are representative of the entire exercise pool, in terms of format and difficulty. For further discussion of NAEP's exercise release policy, see Chapter 8.

larize these divisions in more or less detail. Sometimes the objectives organize the subject on the basis of content; for example, in Writing, one objective concerns business communication, and another scholastic writing. Sometimes the division of a subject area is based on the kinds of knowledge or ability involved. For instance, in Science, there are four objectives: the first covers knowledge of facts and principles; the second, skills and abilities; the third, understanding of the methodology of science; and the last, appreciation of the role of science and scientists in society.

The number of subobjectives related to each objective varies considerably from one objective to the next. For example, objective I in Science (Knowledge of facts and principles) contains twenty-nine, one involving electricity and magnetism, another involving evolution; objective I in Literature (Read literature of excellence) has only two. Objective I in Literature and its related subobjectives are shown in detail in Figure 1.

FIGURE 1
LITERATURE OBJECTIVES

I. Read Literature of Excellence.

A. *Be acquainted with a wide variety of literary works:* by many authors, in all genres, from diverse cultures, from diverse periods.

Generally speaking, this goal demands of an individual a broad reading background and the ability to use that background in dealing with works new to him.

Age 9 Recognize children's "classics" (*Mother Goose, Winnie-the-Pooh, Child's Garden of Verses, Mary Poppins,* Dr. Seuss).

Age 13 (in addition to Age 9)

Recognize certain authors and works (Aesop or La Fontaine, Andersen or the Brothers Grimm, *The Jungle Book, Tom Sawyer, Charlotte's Web,* Benet's *Book of Americans,* Robert Frost, Alfred Noyes, Carl Sandburg, Walter de la Mare).

Age 17 (in addition to Age 13)

Recognize typical passages of Shakespeare, major nineteenth-century novelists (English and American), Pope, Swift, Whitman, Frost, E. E. Cummings, Keats, and others.

Adult Given a similar division on the basis of years of formal education, the definition of goals is approximately the same as that for Age 17, if one grants the balance of attrition from memory and addition from experience.

B. *Understand the basic metaphors and themes through which man has expressed his values and tensions in Western culture.*

Not unlike IA, this goal calls for an individual's knowledge of the major texts and literary or cultural figures and themes of Western culture. This knowledge constitutes a cultural shorthand, by which one may recognize similarities between the past and present, by which one may recognize certain universals, be they prototypes like Oedipus, symbols like the blind seer, or themes like the struggle of Job to understand the nature of divinity. The end of this goal, again like the end of goal IA, is the ability to use this knowledge when confronting a new situation, either in literature or in life.

Age   9 Know some of the common Biblical figures. (This goal is assigned to this age group, although it is hard to predict when, where, or if this knowledge is acquired.)
Know about the Arthurian legends, a few of the Greek myths, American folk figures (Paul Bunyan, Pocahantas).
Be able to recognize the use of these figures in a modern context (a work of literature, a sentence, a slogan, or a trade name). *NB:* This goal is applicable at all age levels.

Age 13 (in addition to Age 9)
Know most of the common Biblical figures.
Know most of the Greek pantheon and such legends as those of Jason and Odysseus.
Know the Arthurian legends, Robin Hood, several American figures (Tom Sawyer, Ichabod Crane, Rip Van Winkle).

Age 17 (in addition to Age 13)
Know certain of the major characters of European, English, and American literature (Hamlet, Captain Ahab, Don Quixote, Gargantua).
Know the themes of certain Greek works (*The Odyssey*).
Know certain post-Christian themes (Faust, Arcadia, Utopia and ideals).
Know certain American themes (*Huckleberry Finn, Moby Dick*).

Adult As for Age 17, but with somewhat more sophistication, and, at the upper levels, more knowledge. The college-educated adult might be better able to understand Job, Oedipus, or Antigone, or any of the archetypal stories, simply because he is older (see the introduction to II).

According to NAEP's exercise development criteria, each exercise should measure attainment of one (or more) objectives or subobjectives. One fact a reviewer of the exercises must face, however, is that the exercises treat some objectives and subobjectives more exhaustively than others. Certain subobjectives are left essentially untested.

Table 1 indicates the number of exercises employed and, in parentheses, publicly released, for Science. For objectives I and II, there are about ten exercises per subobjective, while for objectives III and IV, there are about six. Within age groups, there are two or three exercises per subobjective for objectives I and II, while only one or two for objectives III and IV. Finally, within age groups, there is about one *released* exercise per subobjective for objectives I and II, and about one-half a *released* exercise per subobjective for objectives III and IV.

The number of exercises released for objectives III and IV is much too small to permit of forming conclusions concerning achievement of these objectives. In fact, the numbers indicate that within age groups, certain subobjectives under III and IV were measured by only a single exercise, or perhaps by none at all.[6] This is certainly an inadequate base from which to make inferences.

Perhaps objectives III and IV, which concern attitudes, were considered less important than I and II, which concern facts, principles, and processes; or perhaps III and IV are more difficult to measure. Nevertheless, once a commitment was made to include these objectives, it seems necessary that each subobjective should be tested by several exercises.

Table 2 gives parallel information for Citizenship. The coverage of Citizenship exercises is more nearly balanced, although objective D (Know the structure and function of our government) apparently is given more weight than objective C (Help maintain law and order) or objective H (Personal responsibility).

In both Science and Citizenship, the strict recall objectives (Know the facts and principles of science, or Know the structure and function of our government) receive a large proportion of the exercises.

The coverage of Writing appears reasonably well-balanced, but because objectives I, II, and III do not contain subobjectives, it is impossible to perform the calculations carried out for Science and Citizenship. (See Table 3.)

---

[6] Unfortunately, NAEP publications fail to list the Science exercises by subobjective; thus, coverage of the Science subobjectives must be inferred indirectly, by counting exercises.

A balanced distribution of exercises need not imply equal coverage of all

Table 1
Science: Number of Exercises Employed and Released

Age	Facts I		Process Skills II		Understanding III		Appreciation IV	
9	98	(41)	28	(13)	11	(5)	10	(2)
13	74	(28)	27	(12)	8	(4)	10	(3)
17	88	(38)	19	(9)	5	(3)	5	(3)
Adult	85	(36)	19	(11)	5	(2)	5	(2)
Total	345	(143)	93	(45)	29	(14)	30	(10)
Number of subobjectives	29		10		6		5	

Source: Data obtained from NAEP, Report 1, 1969–1970, Science: National Results (Denver: ECS, 1972), pp. 8–11.

Table 2
Citizenship: Number of Exercises Employed and Released

Age	Welfare/ Dignity A		Rights/ Freedoms B		Law/ Order C		Government structure D		Participation E	
9	4	(2)	3	(2)	2	(1)	11	(4)	2	(2)
13	14	(7)	8	(5)	2	(2)	23	(10)	6	(3)
17	7	(4)	4	(2)	3	(2)	21	(9)	11	(7)
Adult	10	(5)	5	(2)	5	(3)	23	(10)	13	(8)
Total	35	(18)	20	(11)	12	(8)	78	(33)	32	(20)
Number of subobjectives	7		3		6		6		6	

Age	International relations F		Rationality G		Personal responsibility H		Families I	
9	5	(3)	8	(3)	4	(2)	3	(2)
13	6	(3)	10	(5)	2	(1)	3	(2)
17	3	(2)	9	(6)	2	(1)		
Adult	4	(2)	12	(8)	2	(1)	3	(2)
Total	18	(10)	39	(22)	10	(5)	9	(6)
Number of subobjectives	2		6		4		3	

Source: Data obtained from NAEP, Report 6, 1969–1970, Citizenship: Group Results for Sex, Region, and Size of Community (Denver: ECS, 1972), app. C and D.

Table 3
Writing: Number of Exercises Employed and Released

Age	Social I		Business II		Scholastic III		Appreciation IV	
9	11	(4)	2	(2)	7	(4)	3	(2)
13	7	(4)	5	(3)	4	(2)	10	(5)
17	4	(3)	4	(2)	4	(2)	7	(3)
Adult	4	(3)	5	(3)			7	(4)
Total	26	(14)	16	(10)	15	(8)	27	(14)

Source: Data obtained from NAEP, Report 3, 1969–1970, Writing: National Results (Denver: ECS, 1972), pp. 11, 23, 35, 44.

A balanced distribution of exercises need not imply equal coverage of all objectives and subobjectives. Perhaps, for example, some subobjectives are deemed more important than others, although NAEP gives no systematic rankings. Whatever the relative importance of the subobjectives, however, certainly more than one exercise should be used to test each of them (for each age group), simply to provide some judgment of validity. In fact, more than one exercise *at each of the three difficulty levels* should be used to test each subobjective.

Finally, there is little reason to think that the number of exercises devoted to an objective should be a function solely of the objective's importance. Instead, objectives that are most *difficult to measure* probably require the largest pool of exercises, to achieve validity. In short, formal criteria should be established for balancing exercises across objectives and subobjectives.

Exercises Which Measure More than One Objective or Subobjective

According to NAEP criteria, each exercise should provide information about the level of achievement of some objective or subobjective. Some exercises, however, appear to relate to several objectives at once. Thus, while a correct response to such an exercise may indicate achievement of all objectives to which the exercise relates, *it is uncertain what an incorrect response indicates.* For example, consider the Citizenship exercise, Exercise 1.[7]

---

[7] The numbers that appear within parentheses below the exercise numbers in this book are taken from the Assessment's testing packages. The Assessment's numbers indicate age (13), package (12), exercise (11).

Exercise 1
(13:12-11)

Objectives: Support rights and freedoms of all individuals (recognize that everyone has a right to have a fair trial if accused of a wrong act). Recognize the main functions of governmental bodies (recognize that courts resolve disputes).

Age 13: Interview Suppose the police arrest someone they think steals things. The person arrested may or may not be guilty of stealing things. What decides if a person is guilty and has to go to prison for stealing?

(If answer has to do with "evidence" or "confession" or the like, probe for further understanding; for example, "Is there anything else that must happen before a person can be sent to prison?")
Acceptable Responses: Jury; trial; judge; court.
Unacceptable Responses: No response; legally oriented response not mentioning any of the above acceptable responses; factors such as fingerprints or eyewitness which could be used as evidence at a trial.
Results state that a jury, trial, judge or court decides whether or not a person is guilty.

Age 13

81%

Are we to conclude that the 19 percent who failed to respond correctly *do not* support individual rights and freedoms? Or *do not* recognize the main functions of government bodies? Or both?

Exercise 2
(13:13-21a5)

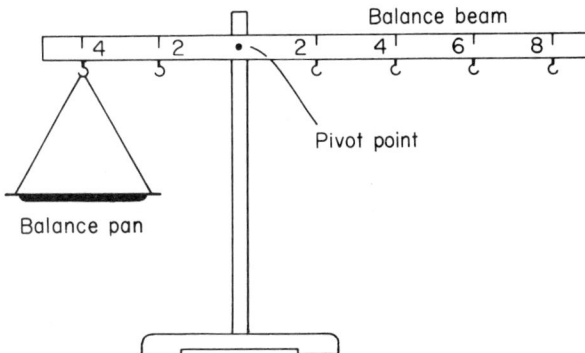

The apparatus before you is the same as that shown in the picture. This balance is balanced when the balance beam is level as shown above. The number by each mark on the beam tells the number of inches that mark is from the pivot point.

(The apparatus also included 10-gram fishweights, a centimeter ruler, and a block of wood 10 x 3 x 2 centimeters. Respondents were given 20 minutes to answer several related questions (e.g., see Exercise 234). The following question was preceded by others which required them to make measurements which would assist them in answering it.)

5. What is the density of the wood block? It is _____ grams per cubic centimeter. (An answer between .38 and .64 was scored correct.)

Age 13

4 %	Correct
70	Incorrect
25	No Response
99 %	

An extreme case occurs in the Science exercise, Exercise 2. As Richard J. Merrill has pointed out,[8] the exercise relates to several specific subobjectives: ability to propose or select validating procedures—both logical and empirical; ability to obtain requisite data; ability to interpret data; ability to reason quantitatively and symbolically; and facts and principles relating to density. Which of these subobjectives has the 96 percent who did not respond correctly failed to achieve? Respondents were asked to complete several exercises related to the example at hand, and these may provide some additional information—but they were not released.

To clarify the relationship of the exercises to the objectives, some effort might be devoted to arranging and analyzing the exercises in hierarchical form (see Figure 2). Exercises at the bottom of such a hierarchy or tree would measure single subobjectives, and those at the top would measure a composite of those at the bottom. Development of hierarchies might call attention to the difficulty involved in determining with any precision the subobjectives a respondent must master in order to perform correctly on a particular exercise.[9]

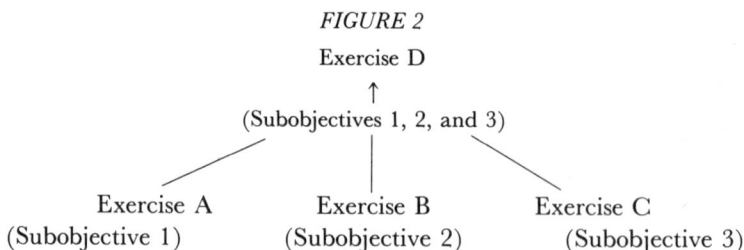

FIGURE 2

Exercise D

↑

(Subobjectives 1, 2, and 3)

Exercise A	Exercise B	Exercise C
(Subobjective 1)	(Subobjective 2)	(Subobjective 3)

[8] "National Assessment of Science Education—A Beginning," in *Report 1— Science, Observations and Commentary of a Panel of Reviewers* (Denver: ECS, 1970).

[9] For example, in the hierarchy in Figure 2, it might turn out that not all respondents who perform correctly on exercises A, B, and C also perform correctly on exercise D, indicating that some subobjectives are involved in D other than subobjectives 1–3. On the other hand, some respondents might perform correctly on exercise D without properly answering A–C, indicating that mastery of subobjectives 1–3 is not required for exercise D. Analysis of this sort might improve both exercises and objectives.

Exercises Which Fail to Measure Particular Objectives
or Subobjectives

Some exercises fail to indicate much about achievement of their related subobjectives. For example, consider Exercise 3, a Science exercise. Presumably this exercise is related to the subobjective (IIG)—Ability to reason quantitatively and symbolically—or perhaps (IIE)—Ability to interpret data. The relationship between performance on the exercise and achievement of either of these subobjectives, however, is tenuous at best. Does selection of the correct response indicate an ability to reason quantitatively, to interpret evidence, or, more likely, simply to read and comprehend straightforward English?

Exercise 3
(9: 3–2)

Big leaves usually give off more water than little leaves. Which of the following leaves gives off the most water?

Age 9

89% ☐

2 ☐

4 ☐

3   ☐

3   ☐   I don't know.

0   No response
‾‾‾‾
101%

Similarly, analysis of the Reading exercises indicates that although the objectives and subobjectives are relatively refined, the exercises themselves are not of adequate quality to test for the objectives. Some Reading exercises employ written passages inappropriate for the objectives to be assessed. For example, fact-finding questions, which would imply the use of literal and factual material, are sometimes affixed to "flight of fantasy" passages, which might be better used for assessing more literary skills. Exercise 4, a paragraph taken out of context from *How Many Miles to Babylon?,* is used as a basis for questions involving the skill, "remembering significant parts of what is read—remembering pertinent details." Nothing within the excerpt itself indicates which information will turn out to be significant and pertinent. Nor is there any sign that this selection might be taken from a mystery, which might alert the reader to seemingly inconsequential cues. Because there is no inkling that any nugget of information in the paragraph is either more or less germane than any other, the selection is not ideally suited for winnowing out and remembering important information. Although the questions are relatively easy, the skill assessment is confounded by the nature of the exercise.

Exercise 4
(13:8–12, A:2–15, 7:5–10)

Read the story carefully so that you can answer the questions on the next page without looking back at the story.

It was morning, and James Douglas awoke frightened. Perhaps it was because the light had not been turned on, and the morning city light itself was gray and cold, hardly different from early evening. Maybe it was because of the three old women, one bending over the sink, one standing against the wall opposite his bed, one sitting at the table, her head bent over an empty dish. Maybe it was because he had been thinking about how to run away from school when he went to bed the night before. Maybe it was because it was a cold November Monday in Brooklyn. He closed his eyes and pretended to sleep.

Answer the following questions without referring to the story.

A.   In what city does the story take place?

_____

B.   In what month does the story take place?

_____

C.   On what day does the story take place?

_____

Other Acceptable Responses

A.   1.   New York
      2.   New York City

Exercise 5 is another example of the choice of a poor paragraph with which to demonstrate a skill, in this instance, finding the main point or topic sentence of a passage. The main idea is not embedded in any one particular sentence, nor is the first sentence the topic sentence. The paragraph is incomplete when taken out of context; presumably the sentences covering the definition of "beat" are a way station to the discussion of the paragraph's opening subject, the beat generation. The beat generation is thus the overall *implied* topic.

Exercise 5
(13:1–9, 17:8–11)

_____

Read the paragraph and answer the questions which follow it.

Any attempt to label an entire generation is unrewarding, and yet the generation which went through the last war, or at least could get a drink easily once it was over, seems to possess a uniform, general quality which demands an adjective. It was John Kerouac, the author of a fine, neglected novel "The Town and the City," who finally came up with it. It was several years ago, when the face was harder to recognize, but he had a sharp, sympathetic eye, and one day he said, "You know, this is really a *beat* generation." The origins of the word "beat" are obscure, but the meaning is only too clear to most Americans. More than mere weariness, it implies the feeling of having been used, of being raw. It involves a sort of nakedness of mind, and, ultimately, of soul; a feeling of being reduced to the bedrock of consciousness. In short, it means being undramatically pushed up against the wall of oneself. A man is best whenever he goes for broke and wagers the sum of his resources on a single number; and the young generation has done that continually from early youth.

A. What is the MAIN point of the paragraph?

    ☐ The beat generation
    ☐ The labeling of a past generation
    ☐ The definition of the word "beat"

    ☐ I don't know.

B. Where would you MOST likely find this paragraph?

    ☐ In the encyclopedia

    ☐ In a collection of essays
    ☐ On a sports page
    ☐ In the *Dictionary of American Slang*

    ☐ I don't know.

C. What does the writer suggest when he mentions a "fine, neglected novel"?

    ☐ Kerouac had the right idea about the war.
    ☐ Kerouac had a clear understanding of the new post-war generation.
    ☐ Kerouac had not received the recognition of "The Town and the City" that was deserved.

    ☐ I don't know.

D. According to the paragraph, the origins of the word "beat" are

    ☐ obscure.
    ☐ clear to Americans.
    ☐ attributed to Kerouac.
    ☐ attributed to jazz musicians.

    ☐ I don't know.

The objective of Exercise 6 is to "interpret the sentence structures and intonation patterns which signal both meanings and attitudes." The Reading Objectives specify that this subobjective requires the student to have some comprehension of context. Inquiring, "Which of the following asks a question?" calls for not an interpretation of meaning implied in context but a knowledge of grammar applied in isolation.

Exercise 6
(13:12–8, 17:5–1)

Which of the following asks a question?

    ☐ Already the has answer given been
    ☐ Been the answer already given has
    ☐ Has the answer already been given
    ☐ Has the given already answer been
    ☐ The answer has been given already

    ☐ I don't know.

Exercise 7 is meant to demonstrate ability to "verify the facts through experience." One might expect a relatively direct passage to accompany this higher-level objective. Instead, there follows a flimsy and labored excerpt about Amos the Ant. Performance on such an item tells very little about a person's ability to verify fact through experience.

Exercise 7
(9:7–14)

Read the story and answer the question which follows it.

One day Amos the Ant took his lunch to the park. He sat down under a tree and started to eat. Then some children came over. Amos gave them each a sandwich. It was a fine day for a picnic.

How do you know this story is make-believe?

- ☐ Ants don't eat.
- ☐ Ants aren't in parks.
- ☐ Ants eat lunch at home.
- ☐ Ants don't give people food.
- ☐ Children are afraid of ants.

NAEP publications repeatedly note that the Reading exercises were developed to be "meaningful" and "relevant" and were selected for "importance and quality," [10] but there is considerable disparity between such descriptions of the exercises and the exercises themselves. Beyond the problems already cited, there is the additional fact that some of the material is, in Charles Silberman's term, "mindless." Consider, for example, the Silky the Spider episodes (Exercises 8 and 9), Amos the Ant (Exercise 10), Big Eyes the Fish (Exercise 11), or Johnny (Exercise 12). All of these selections are vapid in content and erratically and poorly written. Amos the Ant is unworthy of the

Exercise 8
(9:4–9)

Read the story and answer the question which follows it.

Of all the things to eat in the world, Silky the Spider liked bean soup the best. He could eat a whole riverful of bean soup. The trouble was that bean soup was hard to find, especially for a spider, so Silky used to knock on door after door asking whoever opened the door if he had any bean soup for sale. One day, a woman named Mrs. Bean opened her door. When Silky found out her name, he gulped her right down. Boy, did he have a pain in his stomach after that!

How did Silky feel about bean soup?

- ☐ Silky hated bean soup.
- ☐ Silky couldn't stand bean soup.
- ☐ Silky never thought about bean soup.
- ☐ Silky thought bean soup was delicious.
- ☐ I don't know.

---

[10] See *General Information Yearbook (02-GIY)* (Denver: ECS, 1972).

Exercise 9
(9:5–13)

Read the story and answer the question which follows it.

The thing that Silky the Spider hated most was rain. Whenever it rained, his mother would take a big bar of soap and scrub him all over. Then the rain would wash all the dirt and soap away. That didn't make Silky happy because he really liked dirt.

Which one of these sentences tells BEST how Silky felt about rain?

- ☐ Silky liked the rain.
- ☐ Silky thought rain was fun.
- ☐ Silky was happy when it rained.
- ☐ Silky didn't like the rain at all.

- ☐ I don't know.

Exercise 10
(9:3–1)

Read the story and answer the question which follows it.

One day Amos the Ant took his lunch to the park. He sat under a tree and started to eat. Then some children came over. Amos gave them some food. It was a fine day for a picnic.

What did Amos do FIRST in the story?

- ☐ He had a picnic.
- ☐ He ate his lunch.
- ☐ He climbed a tree.
- ☐ He went to the park.
- ☐ He found some children.

- ☐ I don't know.

Exercise 11
(9:6–9)

Read the story about a fish and answer the question which follows it.

Once there was a fish named Big Eyes who was tired of swimming. He wanted to get out of the water and walk like other animals do, so one day without telling anyone he just jumped out of the water, put on his shoes, and took a long walk around the park.

What do you think the person who wrote this story was trying to do?

- ☐ Tell you what fish are like
- ☐ Tell you that fish wear shoes
- ☐ Tell you a funny story about a fish
- ☐ Tell you that fish don't like to swim

- ☐ I don't know.

Exercise 12
(13:7–12)

Read the passage and answer the question which follows it.

Johnny told Billy that he could make it rain any time he wanted to by stepping on a spider. Billy said he couldn't. Johnny stepped on a spider. That night it rained. The next day Johnny told Billy, "That proves I can make it rain any time I want to."

Was Johnny right?

☐ Yes

☐ No

☐ Can't tell from the passage

☐ I don't know.

associated objective, Follow development of an author's idea, since nothing approaching an idea is developed. The reading skills and understandings of American young people, even at the nine-year-old level, should not be assessed by responses to inferior material of this sort.

The Knowing versus Doing Distinction

Knowledge of fundamental facts and principles can be acquired in a number of ways, but the way in which this is done may affect the way knowledge is used in practice. For instance, if a respondent has merely memorized a fact or principle being tested, he may not be able to use the principle in appropriate empirical circumstances. Consider the Science example, Exercise 13, which falls under objective I, Knowledge of facts and principles. Can we conclude that the 61 percent who answered correctly would be able to apply the complete circuit principle being tested in a real-life situation (e.g., to repair a faulty flashlight or electric train), where the battery, wire, and light are not as clearly set forth as in the example? Probably not. Although a student may respond correctly to the exercise, he may never in fact be able or motivated to employ the knowledge in question.

It may demand a more fanciful set of exercises to assess the extent to which factual knowledge is used in practice. In the case at hand, for example, the respondent might be presented with a number of items which can be used to establish electric circuits (lights, buzzers, switches, etc.). He could then be asked to build something with the items. The child's sophistication in fundamental principles of electricity might thus be determined by the complexity of his product and the facility with which he works. (Of course, some students might decide to construct a sculpture rather than a circuit!)

Exercise 13
(9:6–15)

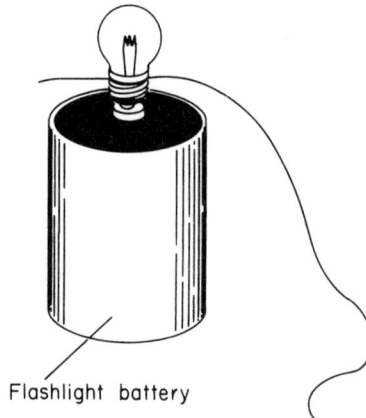

Flashlight battery

Jane wrapped the end of a piece of wire around the base of a flashlight bulb. When she touched the bottom of the bulb to the center of the top of a new battery, the bulb did not light. What should Jane do next to *light* the bulb?

Age 9

13%	Touch the end of the wire to the bulb.
4	Put the end of the wire in a drop of water.
11	Touch the bulb to the bottom of the battery.
61	Touch the end of the wire to the bottom of the battery.
10	I don't know.
1	No response
100%	

Examples such as Exercise 13 are widespread. The measurement of doing as distinct from knowing appears to be a problem NAEP has not yet been able to solve. A systematic research effort is needed to develop test instruments which assay performance, although such effort might best be carried out by some group other than NAEP. The results of such an effort would have applications for the Assessment, but also for the testing field generally.

Process versus Factual Knowledge

While some objectives concern factual knowledge, others concern the skills and abilities needed to engage in the process of a subject-matter area. The assessment of process in Science is often quite inventive. For example, Exercise 14 provides an excellent vehicle for the respondent to demonstrate whether he can think about problems in a scientific way.

Exercise 14
(9:8–9)

Someone said that if you mix salt and sugar with water and let the mixture stand you get salt-water taffy—a kind of candy. Which of the following would be the best way for you to test this idea?

Age 9

3%	Take a vote among your friends.
13	Buy some salt-water taffy and see if it has salt in it.
7	Find out if salt and sugar have the same chemicals in them.
6	Grind up some salt-water taffy to see if you get salt, sugar, and water.
66	Try to mix salt, sugar, and water, let them stand, and see what happens.
5	I don't know.
0	No response
100%	

Exercise 15
(9:2–10)

Why do very few people get smallpox in the United States today?

Age 9

12%	The weather conditions have changed.
50	Most people get smallpox vaccinations.
6	People move more often than they used to.
4	People drink more milk today than ever before.
17	All the germs that cause smallpox have been killed.
11	I don't know.
0	No response
100%	

Some exercises unfortunately fall into the trap of really measuring fact, while purporting to measure process. For example, in Exercise 15, the proper response requires knowledge of facts—since weather, milk, or eradication of germs, although unlikely, are possible causes for reduction of smallpox. The alternative hypotheses must be tested by evidence not at hand in the exercise.

Measurement of Attitudes

The measurement of attitudes, like other psychological measurement, usually involves multiple test items, which bear complex interrelations. Attitude measures are commonly obtained by summing the results on several test items, and lie-scales and measures of internal consistency often are built in.

The NAEP decision to create exercises each of which can stand alone independent of the others forced a departure from these conventional attitude-measurement techniques.

Unfortunately, the individual attitude exercises developed in this way are often trivial. For example, to what extent does Exercise 16 really measure the desired objective, Have attitudes about and appreciations of scientists, science, and the consequences of science? First, it is difficult to interpret the response choices (often, sometimes, never) because no basis for comparison is provided. The exercise would be more useful were it part of a set of similar items concerning several types of television specials—political documentaries, dramatic productions, concerts, and so on. Furthermore, should not a careful-thinking respondent be selective in choosing TV science programs? Would a seventeen-year-old with positive attitudes toward science choose a scientific program over a sports program scheduled simultaneously? Also, might not a respondent prefer doing science to watching it on television? Problems of interpretation render this exercise of little value.

Exercise 16
(17:11–10a)

(a) If you learn about a special television program dealing with a scientific topic, do you watch it?

Age 17

17%	Often
64	Sometimes
19	Never
0	I don't know.
1	No response
101%	

The Citizenship exercise, Exercise 17, provides some insight into another area of difficulty. A respondent to this exercise must be influenced strongly by what he believes is the desired or expected response. But there is no way to assess the depth of conviction or the behavioral consequences of belief. An objective of such importance (Treat all persons with respect; do not condemn others on the basis of irrelevant personal or social characteristics) merits a more complex evaluation, perhaps by means of an open-ended interview.

A few attitude exercises begin to assess the degree to which respondents are able to make complex and subtle judgments and distinctions, for example, Exercise 18. However, most attitude exercises suffer from poor construction,

Exercise 17
(13:11–18, 17:4–10, A:5–22)

A4* - Objectives: Treat all individuals with respect; do not condemn others on the basis of irrelevant personal or social characteristics. (Do not avoid associating with others because of such differences. Reliance on stereotypes in reacting to members of minorities shows little respect for them as individuals.)

Ages 13 and 17:   Tape-accompanied paper-and-pencil

Adult: Paper-and-pencil in individual interview
People feel differently toward people of other races. How willing would you be to have a person of a different race doing these things?

		% willing to		
			Age	
[For each situation below, the choices were: willing to, prefer not to]		13	17	Adult
A.	Be your dentist or doctor?	80%	70%	74%
B.	Live next door to you?	82	71	67
C.	Represent you in some elected office?	80	77	82
D.	Sit at a table next to yours in a crowded restaurant?	82	83	88
E.	Stay in the same hotel or motel as you?	88	85	89
Willing to associate with a person of a different race in 3 or more of the above situations		90	89	87
. . . 4 or more . . .		77	79	77
. . . all 5 . . .		57	57	57

*Not administered to the in-school sample in one large Western state, one Southeastern county and one Southwestern city at the request of state or local authorities.

Exercise 18
(9:11–21, 13:12–7)

A2* - Objectives: Are loyal to friends. Treat all individuals with respect; do not condemn others on the basis of irrelevant personal or social characteristics. (Do not avoid associating with other children because of such differences. Respond to each individual on the basis of his own merits and actions.)

Ages 9 and 13:   Interview
A.   Suppose the father of one of your friends was put in jail for stealing. Would you want your friend to come to your house to play after you knew that the father was in jail? (Yes, No) (At Age 13, "to a party" was used rather than "to play.")

B.   (If "No" to A) Why not? (Part B was not scored; it was asked to insure that children understood Part A and to give them a chance to explain their position.)

C.   (If "Yes" to A) Why?
Acceptable reasons to C**: My friend didn't do anything wrong; friend couldn't help it; the child didn't steal anything; he (she) is my friend; if I trusted the friend before, there is

no reason not to now; don't take it out on the friend; you can't just let a good friend go; to cheer the friend up; she would be lonesome without her father: I would like to make the child happier; it doesn't matter to me.

Unacceptable reasons to C**: No response, I don't know, or a few responses inconsistent with a "Yes" to A: Child might steal like the father; friend would be too worried or too embarrassed to come; I wouldn't want the other child around; it might get me in trouble; I'd want him to stay home with his mother.

Results

	Age	
	9	13
Indicated willingness to associate with friend whose father was in jail (Yes to A)	56%	79%
Indicated willingness to associate and gave an acceptable reason for doing so (acceptable reason to C as well as Yes to A)	48	76

*Not administered at Age 9 in one Southwestern city at the request of local authorities.
**Descriptions of acceptable and unacceptable responses for all exercises are summaries of the responses actually made, but are not verbatim, of course, since each type describes a variety of wordings from a large number of respondents.

insufficient relation to the objectives, and an undue likelihood that the respondent will be influenced by his perception of the desired response. NAEP might have experimented with alternate formats, such as the semantic differential and the Q-sort.

Innovative Exercises

While most NAEP exercises are traditional multiple-choice, some are quite unusual. For example, in a number of Science exercises the respondents were given items of equipment (a balance and weights, a block of wood and a ruler, a pendulum and a clock, etc.) and asked to complete specified tasks. Although in certain cases (notably Exercise 2, the density exercise discussed earlier) the experiments to be performed overlap a number of objectives at once, in general these exercises begin to tap the ability of respondents to behave in a scientific way. The Science exercises in which students perform experiments are among NAEP's greatest achievements in testing.

One of the most interesting and unconventional exercises is a Citizenship example, Exercise 19. The exercise provides some information on the extent to which participants in small-group decision-making situations take clear positions, defend their points of view, and reach compromise.

Exercise 19
(13:10–1, 17:12–1)

E14 (Group Task). Objectives: Apply democratic procedures on a practical level when working in a group. Try to inform themselves on socially important matters and to understand alternative viewpoints. Weigh alternatives and consequences carefully, then make decisions and carry them out without undue delay. Have good ideas for solutions. Support free communication and communicate honestly with others (willingly express their own views on civic and social matters, however controversial the issue; encourage the hearing of dissenting viewpoints). Defend rights and liberties of all kinds of people uniformly (defend the right of a person to express his opinions).

Ages 13 and 17:   Observed group interaction

Exercise Description   The purpose of this exercise was to provide a standard situation in which to measure effective cooperation in a group task. A group of eight students was asked to choose from a list of twelve issues (see lists below) the five most important issues between teenagers and adults, to rank them in order of importance, and to write a recommendation for at least the two most important problems, and for all five problems if they had time. They had thirty minutes to complete the task. The only rule was that a majority of the group must agree on anything they wrote.

Two observers recorded individual acts of group members as they discussed the issues, each observer recording different types of behavior. At no time did the observers participate in the discussion. Observers were specially trained in recognizing the individual actions they were responsible for recording.

The task seemed appropriate and interesting to all groups and some groups tackled it with enthusiasm. The types of behavior measured included cooperation, organization, contribution of substance and defending a viewpoint. The complete set of separate behavioral categories is listed in the results section on the next page.

List of Issues

Age 13	Age 17
Time Limits (for being home, in bed, etc.)	Censorship
	Curfew
Home Duties	Voting Age
School Assignments	Drinking
Adult Books and Movies	Smoking
Sports and Other Activities	Working Rules and Laws
Dating and Parties	Marriage
Parents' Approval of Friends	Auto Insurance
Money (where from and how spent)	Dress and Appearance
Dress and Appearance	Military Service
Smoking	School Attendance
Swearing	Civil Liability
Being Talked to Like an Adult	Criminal Liability

Results (Positive Actions)

	% Who Did This at Least Once Age	
	13	17
Took a clear position	62%	67%
Gave a reason for a point of view	67	79
Sought information related to the game from other team members or from the administrator	54	55
Steered the task by organizing the group or by suggesting a change in procedure	51	39
Defended the right of another group member to be heard or to hold a different opinion	4	1
Defended own viewpoint contrary to a previous consensus*	6	24

In addition to the positive actions, one negative action was recorded. The percentage of students who *never* acted in such a manner throughout a session is reported here.

Avoidance of Negative Actions

	% Who Never Did This Age	
	13	17
Never committed act which was totally unrelated to task or which demeaned the task	93%	99%

Group Effectiveness

	% of Groups Performing Action Age	
	13	17
Selected five most important issues	94%	95%
Selected five issues and wrote recommendations for at least two of them (completed minimum task)	93	92
Selected five issues and wrote recommendations for all of them (completed full task)	58	23

(Although it was not necessary for effective group interaction to establish any formal procedures, some of the groups did so by selecting a chairman. At age thirteen, 23 percent, and at age seventeen, 30 percent selected a chairman.)

*To be credited for this behavior, it was necessary for a student to argue against a position previously taken by at least two other members of the group. He had to "stand alone" in this act, at least initially. At times one who defended a contrary view was able to convince the group to accept that view. Of those who introduced a contrary view, 22 percent at age thirteen and 17 percent at age seventeen were able to convince the group. At other times, some of those defending a contrary view explicitly yielded, either being convinced of the majority view themselves or yielding so that the group could continue the task. Of those who initially defended a contrary view, 18 percent at age thirteen and 26 percent at age seventeen yielded in this way.

Dr. Tobe Johnson has offered some telling criticisms of this and similar NAEP exercises:[11]

> [These exercises] are rather pallid simulations of the kind of effective cooperation essential to getting complex and controversial things done cooperatively in this society—and which will be, increasingly, the real test of effective citizenship, and even the survival of this country as a nation state. [One such exercise] measures cooperation only at the cognitive level—that is, orientation toward a simple task where goals and values are not in conflict. The same is largely true of exercise (13:10-1, 17:12-1) [Exercise 19], which might have occurred among heterogeneous groups as contrasted with more homogeneous ones.

It is certainly essential that exercises involving decision making in situations of conflicting goals and values be developed in the future, but the Assessment has made a good beginning in creating a number of nonstandard exercises in group process. The fact that, as Dr. Johnson correctly notes, some of the group exercises are presently "pallid simulations" does not cancel out the reality that they do innovatively measure some important abilities, albeit not all or even the most important.

THE NAEP EXERCISES AND CRITERION-REFERENCED MEASUREMENT

Criterion Referencing: Some Theoretical Considerations

NAEP's attempt to create exercises that bear a close relationship to subject-matter objectives is not only an important distinguishing feature of the Assessment but is also one of the most difficult challenges it has faced. In the last decade, a growing literature has appeared on the problem of relating tests to instructional objectives, and a new form of testing—often called "criterion-referenced measurement"—has emerged. This relatively new phenom-

---

[11] "Critical Response to the National Assessment," *Report 2—Citizenship* (Denver: ECS, 1970), p. 21.

enon has generated considerable excitement and an original set of questions about testing. Any judgment of the success of the exercises developed by NAEP must be informed by a critical understanding of criterion referencing.[12]

The current excitement surrounding criterion-referenced measurement among educational measurement specialists was initiated by Robert Glaser in a paper published in 1963.[13] There, Glaser contrasts criterion-referenced measurement (CRM) and the traditional norm-referenced measurement (NRM).

At the most elementary level, the difference between CRM and NRM lies in the standard used as a reference in judging respondent performance. CRM depends on an absolute standard of performance as measured against mastery of specific knowledge and skills, while NRM depends on a relative standard, as measured against the performance of other students. Glaser writes:

> Underlying the concept of achievement measurement is the notion of a continuum of knowledge acquisition ranging from no proficiency at all to perfect performance. An individual's achievement level falls at some point on this continuum. . . . The degree to which his achievement resembles desired performance at any specified level is assessed by criterion-referenced measures of achievement or proficiency. . . . The term "criterion," when used in this way, does not necessarily refer to final end-of-course behavior. Criterion levels can be established at any point in instruction where it is necessary to obtain information as to the adequacy of an individual's performance. The point is that the specific behaviors implied at each level of proficiency can be identified and used to describe the specific tasks a student must be capable of performing before he achieves one of these knowledge levels. It is in this sense that measures of proficiency can be criterion-referenced.
> . . .
> On the other hand, achievement measures also convey information about the capability of other students. In instances where a student's *relative* standing along the continuum of attainment is

---

[12] NAEP publications often use the term *criterion-referenced* to describe the Assessment exercises, but recently NAEP has decided that "objectives-referenced" is more appropriate. Whatever the word used, the issues raised by the debate on criterion referencing are central to the Assessment's attempt to relate exercises to objectives.

[13] Robert Glaser, "Instructional Technology and the Measurement of Learning Outcomes: Some Questions," reprinted in W. James Popham, *Criterion-Referenced Measurement* (Englewood Cliffs, N.J.: Educational Technology Publications, 1971), pp. 5–16.

the primary purpose of measurement, reference need not be made to criterion behavior. Educational achievement examinations, for example, are administered frequently for the purpose of ordering students in a class or school, rather than for assessing their attainment of specified curriculum objectives. When such norm-referenced measures are used, a particular student's achievement is evaluated in terms of a comparison between his performance and the performance of other members of the group.[14]

A second distinction between CRM and NRM concerns the characteristic ways the scores on the two types of tests divide groups of respondents. A criterion-referenced test should be designed to divide students into just two groups—those who have mastered the material, and those who have not. A norm-referenced test, on the other hand, should be designed to rank students and therefore should be constructed to maximize the variability in scores, even among students all of whom have mastered the material involved. (It is interesting to note that in the great number of heroic attempts to find educational production functions, i.e., functions relating schooling inputs to outputs, the output measures used have invariably been norm-referenced. Perhaps it is partly because such tests are explicitly written to maximize variance within rather than among treatment groups that no systematic results have been found.)

How can we tell if a measurement instrument is well constructed? Traditional educational measurement emphasizes two standards developed for norm-referenced tests: reliability and validity. Reliability is essentially a measure of repeatability. A reliable test should produce the same results each time it is administered, as long as the respondents remain the same in all relevant respects.

Validity is an indicator of whether or not a test measures the behavior it sets out to measure. Theorists talk of predictive, content, and construct validity. For example, the validity of the Scholastic Aptitude Test (SAT) might be judged on the basis of the success with which SAT scores can be used to predict college performance (predictive validity). The validity of a third-grade spelling exam might be judged on the basis of whether or not the words on the exam are a representative sample of the desired vocabulary of third-graders (content validity). Finally, the validity of a measure of anxiety might be judged on the basis of the degree to which it correlates with other measures of anxiety (construct validity).

---

[14] Ibid., pp. 8–9.

When viewed from the vantage points of reliability and validity, criterion referencing begins to lose some of the "charisma" it enjoys at first consideration. Several contradictions become evident, and these have not yet been resolved by measurement theorists. For example, the usual statistical estimate of reliability cannot always be applied to CRM tests (due to small within-group variances), and when the estimate can be computed, it often is difficult to interpret.[15] What is required for CRM is an index of reliability that indicates the power of a test to discriminate reliably between pre- and post-treatment groups, rather than the usual index designed for norm-referenced tests, which indicates the power of a test to discriminate reliably among individuals.[16] Such an index has not yet been developed, nor is it clear what it would be like.

A related problem concerns the consistency of test items. Theorists have provided a number of tools which can be used in NRM to analyze the extent to which an individual item in a test contributes to the overall power of the test. One of these is the discrimination index, which is a measure of the percentage of those performing highly on the overall test correctly answering the item under consideration, less the percentage of those performing poorly on the overall test who correctly answer the item. An item should be retained on a test only if it is "positively discriminating" (that is, if performance on the item and on the test-as-a-whole are positively related).

The discrimination index, however, may not be an appropriate way to judge the value of items in a CRM test. R. C. Cox and J. S. Vargas have defined a "pretest-posttest difference index" which is "the percentage of those passing the item under consideration following treatment less the percentage passing before treatment."[17] Interestingly, in a study of two arithmetic tests, the correlations between the Cox-Vargas index and the discrimination index were only 0.37 for one test and 0.40 for the other. Apparently, items which

---

[15] See for example, T. R. Husek and K. Sirotnik, "Item Sampling in Educational Research: An Empirical Investigation," paper read to American Educational Research Association, Chicago, February 1968.

[16] Test reliability is generally estimated as the PM correlation coefficient of the items on a test (so-called internal consistency) or as the correlation coefficient of test scores obtained by subjects taking the same or similar tests twice (or by subjects taking a single test which is divided into split halves for scoring and estimation purposes).

[17] R. C. Cox and J. S. Vargas, "A Comparison of Item Selection Techniques for Norm-Referenced and Criterion-Referenced Tests," paper read to the National Council on Measurement in Education, Chicago, February 1966, cited in Popham, op. cit.

receive high marks on one index receive low marks on another. Thus, depending on the purpose of the test (discrimination between individuals or discrimination between treatments), different item-analysis techniques may be in order.

Validity is a more difficult issue than reliability. Most proponents of CRM argue that content validity (rather than predictive or construct validity) is most important for criterion-referenced measures: test items should be representative of the actual proficiencies being assessed. To date, criterion-referenced measurement has been used most successfully in basic skills training, such as programmed arithmetic instruction, where content validity is relatively easy to define. For example, the criterion "all students should be able to add columns of ten, three-digit numbers with 80 percent accuracy" is easily measured by constructing a test choosing essentially random samples of such long-addition problems. CRM has also been used to evaluate basic reading skills (see especially Rodney Skager's work at UCLA).[18]

In discussing performance criteria, Alfred Garvin of the University of Cincinnati has proposed a radical thesis:

> Our primary concern is with measuring the attainment of instructional objectives. The relevance of meaningful criteria to these instructional objectives dictates both the possibility of, and the necessity for, CRM. The relevance of criteria to instructional objectives is inherent in the content (and the level) of the instructional unit involved. Thus, for any given unit of instruction, we are not free to choose between CRM and NRM.[19]

Garvin asserts that performance criteria can be meaningfully established only if some extra-classroom proficiency is required. He then applies this principle to reach several important conclusions:

1. Unless at least one of the instructional objectives of a unit envisions a task that must subsequently be performed at a specified level of competence in at least some situations, CRM is irrelevant because there *is no* criterion.

2. If public safety, economic responsibility, or other ethical considerations demand that certain tasks be performed only by those

---

18 "Objective-Based Evaluation: Macro-Evaluation," *Evaluation Comment*, vol. 2, Center for the Study of Evaluation of Instructional Programs, Los Angeles, June 1970.

19 "The Applicability of Criterion-Referenced Measurement by Content Area and Level," in Popham, op. cit., p. 56.

"qualified" for them by formal instruction, then CRM of the outcomes of such instruction is clearly indicated. The criterion here is the licensing standards of the profession involved. . . . However, entry to such professional trains is typically based on NRM since training capacity imposes a "quota."

3. In any instructional sequence where the content is inherently cumulative and the rigor progressively greater, CRM should be used to control entry to successive units. However, if there are several different sequences, differing widely in rigor, NRM is more useful in making appropriate placements.

4. There are certain content areas to which criteria *do* apply but not everyone need meet them. There are the "required subjects"; everyone must try to learn them—if only as a matter of public policy—but it is almost preordained that some of them will not.[20]

If any conclusion is supported by the research on criterion referencing, it is that there are as yet no strictly logical or statistical procedures for assessing the validity or even the sense of a criterion-referenced measure. Trying to decide whether a test is in fact truly a measure of some criterion behavior is about like trying to decide whether a machine exhibits artificial intelligence—a completely rigorous decision procedure is not possible. In the field of information science, the notion of a Turing Test has been proposed: a machine is said to pass the Turing Test of intelligence if an observer cannot tell whether he is communicating with a person or with the machine.

Similarly, a Turing Test of criterion-referenced measurement might be established: A test is valid if an observer can, after looking at a respondent's test results, make a correct judgment about the respondent's capabilities with respect to a criterion. This certainly seems to be a weak tool for test analysis, but Glaser, who started it all, has reached a similar conclusion:

The distinction between norm-referenced and criterion-referenced tests can often be determined by examining the specificity of the information that can be obtained by the test in relation to the domain of relevant tasks. Logical transition from the test to the domain and back again from the domain should be readily accomplished for criterion-referenced tests, so that there is little difficulty in identifying with some degree of confidence the class of tasks that can be performed. This means that the task domain measured by criterion-referenced tests must be defined in terms of observable behavior and that the test is a representative sample of the performance domain from which competence is inferred.[21]

---

[20] Ibid., pp. 62–63.

[21] Robert Glaser, "A Criterion-Referenced Test," in Popham, op. cit., p. 44.

Criterion Referencing and the NAEP Exercises

The issues raised in the debate on criterion-referenced measurement provide some standards by which NAEP's attempt to relate exercises to objectives can be judged. We will consider the NAEP exercises in two ways: first, through analysis of the exercises as they actually were constructed in the Assessments to date, and second, through analysis of the NAEP philosophy of criterion referencing.

Although the examination above indicated that CRM remains a cloudy concept, certain explicit features of the CRM topology are recognizable: CRM involves absolute standards of performance and its goal is to discriminate between groups with inadequate mastery ("pre-treatment groups") and groups with criterion-level mastery ("post-treatment groups"). More precisely, CRM is intended to maximize variability of response between treatment groups, and minimize variability within groups.

A study of nine sets of NAEP subject-matter objectives reveals that only two come close to stating performance *criteria:*

> *Music.* While each ability level of the four age groups would be presented tasks relative to each major objective, it is not expected that this would be true for the subobjectives. In reading music or in knowledge about it, for example, certain subgoals would be appropriate for only the top 10 percent and then would not necessarily be accomplished by all persons in that group.

> *Science.* The delineations are, in general, written in terms of what approximately half of the people at a given age level might be expected to know or be able to do.[22]

Neither of these, of course, is very far on the path toward explicit standards of performance. Music sets only a vague 10 percent standard for some subgoals, while the science standard is somewhat more specific. A more important problem, however, is that the criteria are worded not in terms of the fraction of the exercises a student must be able to perform correctly in order to achieve each major objective, but rather in terms of the fraction of the students that should achieve each subgoal or major goal. The fact that only two of seven subject-matter areas even attempt to set standards, and that the standards set are stated in an inverted form reminiscent of norm-referenced testing, is highly disturbing.

The Assessment has not provided specific statements of the behaviors of which a student

---

[22] NAEP objectives booklets.

must be capable in order to meet each objective or subobjective. Although the exercises are loosely related to the objectives, there is no way of knowing the level of performance on the exercises that would indicate achievement of the objectives. Thus, it is impossible to determine, for example, the number of seventeen-year-olds who have mastered (at the appropriate level) the facts and principles of science (Science objective I). To make this determination would require resolving difficult problems of reliability and validity as well as setting performance criteria.

It may well be, as Alfred Garvin has suggested, that performance criteria in some subject-matter areas *cannot* be established, since no specific extra-classroom performance is required in these areas. If this is the case, it is foolish to speak of criterion referencing such subject-area tests.

The Assessment has more closely approached CRM with respect to variability than with respect to standards. The released exercises include many 10 percent and 90 percent examples in addition to the usual 50 percent—thus it is expected that within treatment groups, variability should be low. Since the exercises have not yet been used to measure treatments as such, however, there is not empirical evidence concerning treatment variability (discrimination).

In summary, the Assessment appears to have developed a modified testing model, somewhere between the norm-referenced and criterion-referenced approaches, relying on the development of 10 percent, 50 percent, and 90 percent exercises. But even this small step toward criterion-referenced measurement is reduced in its significance by inadequacies involved in NAEP attempts to predict the number of exercises answerable by particular percentages of the population. Analysis of the reading exercises indicates the problems NAEP was unable to deal with in defining difficulty levels.

Working Definition of "Difficulty"

One of the prime requisites for the development of exercises at various levels of difficulty, and fundamental to a claim of comparability among exercises, is a concise working definition of "difficulty." As used in the Assessment, it is not defined in the NAEP literature, and an examination of the exercises leads to the conclusion that the term is loosely construed and erratically applied.

Classification of Exercises   NAEP has not provided a scale or criterion reference against which the difficulty of material might be judged. In Reading, for example, the level of difficulty of an exercise is probably a function of conceptual complexity, density, vocabulary, and length, interacting with the reader's experience and ability. Little systematic weighting of these factors is apparent in the exercises, however, and ranking seems to have been governed solely by committee consensus, with no common guidelines.

This consensus method of ranking exercises for difficulty did not yield accurate predictions; many exercises do not reflect the anticipated difficulty levels. Perhaps had there been some definition and agreement on the factors constituting difficulty, consensus of experts would have been more meaningful. Consider, for example, Exercise 20, which is rated medium for nine- and thirteen-year-olds. The objective here is to demonstrate ability to use function words as an aid to getting the meaning. Since the picture shows only one object (the sign) anywhere about the door, the respondent need not even know the meaning of "sign" or "hanging" and is left with the task of recognizing and deciding among "by," "on," "over," or "near" to describe the location of the sign. Since "on" is an easily recognized and commonly understood word, it is not clear what, if any, criteria were used to rate this exercise as medium instead of easy.

Exercise 20
(9:3–2, 13:3–15)

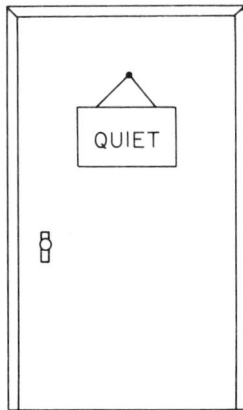

Look at the picture and fill in the oval beside the sentence which tells BEST what the drawing shows.

☐ A sign is hanging by the door.
☐ A sign is hanging on the door.
☐ A sign is hanging over the door.
☐ A sign is hanging near the door.

☐ I don't know.

Comparability   It is not always possible to use examples of passages rated easy, medium, or hard, to rank other exercises. Exercise 21, for example, is easier than Exercise 22 on any measure such as complexity of thought, vocabulary, or length, yet both passages are ranked as easy. In fact, the national response for nine-year-olds was 83.4 percent correct for Exercise 21 and 26.9 percent for Exercise 22. Although the respective objectives involved—Follow the development of an author's idea and determine the main idea—are more or less equivalent in complexity, application of the skill to Exercise 22 is more difficult due to the density of information. It is not apparent on what grounds the passages were estimated to be of comparable difficulty.

Exercise 21
(9:6–5)

Read the story and answer the question which follows it.

The wind pushed the boat farther and farther out to sea. It started to rain and the fog grew thick. The boy and his father were lost at sea.

What happened FIRST in the story?

☐   It became foggy.
☐   It started to rain.
☐   The boat turned over.
☐   The boat went out to sea.

☐   I don't know.

Exercise 22
(9:7–6, 13:2–14, 17:6–11, A:6–7)

Read the passage and answer the questions on the next page.

One spring Farmer Brown had an unusually good field of wheat. Whenever he saw any birds in this field, he got his gun and shot as many of them as he could. In the middle of the summer he found that his wheat was being ruined by insects. With no birds to feed on them, the insects had multiplied very fast. What Farmer Brown did not understand was this: A bird is not simply an animal that eats food the farmer may want for himself. Instead, it is one of many links in the complex surroundings, or *environment*, in which we live.

How much grain a farmer can raise on an acre of ground depends on many factors. All of these factors can be divided into two big groups. Such things as the richness of the soil, the amount of rainfall, the amount of sunlight, and the temperature belong together in one of these groups. This group may be called *non-living factors*. The second group may be called *living factors*. The living factors in any plant's environment are animals and other plants. Wheat, for example, may be damaged by wheat rust, a tiny plant that feeds on wheat; or it may be eaten by plant-eating animals such as birds or grasshoppers.   . . .

It is easy to see that the relations of plants and animals to their environment are very complex, and that any change in the environment is likely to bring about a whole series of changes.

A. What is the MAIN idea of this passage?

    ☐ Farmers should not shoot any birds.

    ☐ Insects eat up all the farmer's crops.

    ☐ No crops can be grown without sunlight.

    ☐ Birds eat up most of the farmer's grain.

    ☐ All living things are affected by living things.

    ☐ I don't know.

B. The passage also points out the importance of which fact?

    ☐ A bird is simply an animal that eats up grain.

    ☐ Wheat rust is similar to the rust on your own bicycle.

    ☐ Only living factors determine how much corn can be raised.

    ☐ How much wheat is grown depends only on how much is planted.

    ☐ Any change in the environment is likely to cause other changes.

    ☐ I don't know.

Across Age Difficulty Ranking

Overlap exercises were designed to be given to more than one age group, in order to allow a comparison of abilities by age, and a few exercises were administered to all four groups. These overlap exercises raise special problems for the assignment of difficulty levels. Often, overlap exercises are classified as uniformly easy, medium, or hard across several age groups, in contradiction to NAEP's claim that the exercises take into account increasing sophistication with age in the use of skills. While a particular overlap item might remain easy, medium, or hard at all age levels, most would seem to be of varying difficulty to nine-year-olds, thirteen-year-olds, and seventeen-year-olds alike. For questions of the relationship between difficulty and age, NAEP should give some attention to developmental theories of cognitive growth and related testing efforts.

Artificial Elements of Difficulty   There is considerable inconsistency in the manner in which exercises are made difficult. Some Reading exercises, for example, quite legitimately derive their difficulty from factors such as the material's conceptual complexity, the length of sentences or paragraphs, the amount of information embedded in passages, or the use of sophisticated or specialized vocabulary. Sometimes, however, exercises are made difficult by the inclusion of distractors—items which are irrelevant to the passage or objective being assessed and serve only to distract the subject from his assigned task. If the purpose of presenting a particular passage is to evaluate a specified objective, why work at cross-purpose by attempting to obscure the

Exercise 23
(9:7–16)

Read the passage and answer the question which follows it.

   Colorado has many mountains. Colorado has more than 1,000 peaks two miles high. Gold was discovered in Colorado in 1859. A total of 54 of the 69 highest mountains in the United States are in Colorado.

Which words tell what this passage is MAINLY about?

☐ Fish in Colorado

☐ Hunting in Colorado

☐ Mining in Colorado

☐ Mountains in Colorado

☐ I don't know.

---

correct answer or the information necessary to reach a correct conclusion? For example, the objective of Exercise 23 is Finding the main point of a paragraph. The paragraph presented in the exercise is primarily about mountains in Colorado, but a *non sequitur* distractor sentence has been inserted in the middle, creating a poorly written paragraph. There is no reason to select a hodgepodge passage to assess this objective, when there are well-written paragraphs, containing distinct main and subordinate ideas. If an objective requires difficult or challenging material, the related exercises should be constructed through the selection of innately complex material rather than through adulteration of simple passages. Alternatively, the exercise at hand could have been improved by including answer choices relevant to the paragraph but still distinguishing between matching and getting the main idea. For example, the choices might have read: (*a*) peaks two miles high, (*b*) 54 of the 69, (*c*) mountains in the United States, and (*d*) mountains in Colorado.

The Assessment's View of Criterion Referencing

   In spite of these many difficulties, it is clear that the Assessment staff considered the creation of exercises at three difficulty levels a major step in the direction of criterion referencing. This can be confirmed by considering the criterion-referencing philosophy elaborated by the NAEP Research Director, Frank Womer, in a research proposal to the Carnegie Corporation entitled "Exercise Development of Criterion-Referenced Materials":

   Criterion-referenced exercises (items, questions) are designed specifically to sample knowledge, skills, and understanding directly.

Their purpose is to describe what students know rather than to rank-order students from low achievement to high achievement. If one wants to describe achievements that almost all students have mastered (base-line information), one must develop exercises that relate directly to an accepted objective of instruction (criterion-referenced) and also are very easy.[23]

It seems clear that Womer is more interested in finding a common core with which nearly every student is familiar than in measuring whether students have achieved specific performance standards. In fact, in the last sentence of the quotation above, the entire distinction between objectives and behaviors indicating criterion-level achievement of the objectives seems lost.

In a later paragraph, Womer reasserts NAEP's commitment to criterion referencing:

In its first attempt to secure materials for the project, National Assessment selected four agencies . . . to develop behavioral objectives for its ten subject areas and then to develop criterion-referenced exercises to assess the objectives.[24]

In contrast to Womer's claim, however, the Assessment objectives actually developed are seldom behavioral, and, in any event, there are no performance criteria related to the objectives.

Womer's proposal deals with none of the very interesting and important issues regarding criterion referencing: reliability measurement, alternate conceptions of validity, item analysis, differences between subject-matter areas with respect to the possibility of defining performance criteria at all, and others.

In short, it seems that although NAEP asserts its intention is to measure the achievement of objectives, its actual intention is something different. NAEP's desire seems to be to develop a set of exercises which sample the tasks students learn to accomplish in school—or some people think students ought to learn in school. This provides a sort of sampler of the kinds of things students can do.

Thus, while the exercises are in some general sense *objectives-related,* they are not in any meaningful sense *criterion-referenced.* The individual exercises say very little about the percentages of the population meeting NAEP's educational objectives and subobjectives, let alone more complicated combinations

---

[23] April 1971, Carnegie files.
[24] Ibid.

of objectives such as might be involved in a judgment of functional literacy. Even in the basic skills subject areas, it is impossible to move from the response percentages on individual exercises to an assessment of the achievement of subobjectives and objectives—vital questions of coverage, validity, reliability, consistency, and difficulty remain to be resolved. Unless these problems are faced with energy and imagination, the Assessment's exercises will continue to provide only odd and disconnected bits of evidence, having limited application to research or policy.

6

NAEP'S MEASUREMENT
OF BACKGROUND VARIABLES

Several studies have been made attempting to relate various background variables to educational achievement in recent years, but it is clear that the knowledge and techniques available for such analyses are still in their infancy. Despite increasing precision and sophistication, the capacity to identify explanatory variables has remained virtually the same throughout the last several years. Similarly, there has been little progress made, either through analysis or experimentation, in distinguishing and employing variables that are more or less manipulable.

Thus, the basic conclusions of the Coleman Report (1966), that school has less influence on educational achievement than was generally expected, and that family background has more, remain as the most important findings. Surprisingly few new insights have been attained in this particular regard, despite several major studies and reanalyses, including Project TALENT (1967); T. Husen's IEA Study of Mathematics Achievement in Twelve Countries (1967); the Plowden National Survey in England (1967 and 1971); the Coleman reanalysis, *On Equality of Educational Opportunity* (1971); and the Jencks reanalysis of earlier studies, *Inequality: A Reassessment of the Effect of Family and Schooling in America* (1972). Finally, there are the findings of the IEA Study of Literature Achievement in Nine Countries (1972–1973). This last study was specifically designed to measure an increased number of school variables in order to counter criticisms of the earlier studies, but its main results are essentially similar to those of the earlier work: no strong, positive, and consistent relationships could be found between existing combinations of school inputs and educational achievement. Findings regarding the importance of socioeconomic variables were essentially those of preceding studies.

Thus, progress has been painfully slow for those who are attempting to develop a causal model of educational achievement. For those who would attempt to draw policy implications from such research the frustrations have been all the greater.[1]

This context is of great importance in understanding the past and future of the National Assessment of Educational Progress. Little thorough analysis has been made of why the Assessment is measuring certain background variables and what can and cannot be expected from such measurements. Certainly, there has been no systematic effort to consider whether the Assessment should attempt to measure a greatly expanded number of background variables in future years. The only independent consideration given to these issues has come from Martin Katzman and Ronald Rosen,[2] and they merely provide a facile inference that politics watered down the research design; they ignore the prior questions of which research design was actually proposed or, more importantly, *what could be expected to come from the measurement of additional, or more refined, variables.*

An accurate evaluation of the politics of this aspect of the National Assessment requires a respect for historical context and for the original intentions and statements of the Assessment's leaders. It must be remembered that the first major policy discussions and meetings regarding the Assessment occurred in late 1963 and early 1964, before any of the large survey studies analyzing the sources of educational achievement had been undertaken. Furthermore, it is clear from recent interviews and from reading the internal memoranda and transcripts of meetings of that period that the two major social scientists leading the project, Ralph Tyler and John Tukey, had very limited, and indeed, quite realistic expectations and aspirations concerning the measurement of explanatory variables. In essence, they expected to avoid such efforts almost entirely.

This point was the source of considerable debate among the social scientists

---

[1] For an analysis of the limitations of existing survey research in this area, see Gerald Grant, an essay review of *On Equality of Educational Opportunity,* in the *Harvard Educational Review,* vol. 42, no. 1, pp. 109–125, February 1972.

[2] "The Science and Politics of National Educational Assessment," *The Record,* vol. 71, pp. 571–586, especially pp. 579–580, May 1970.

attending the first major policy conference December 18–19, 1963. But Tyler and Tukey were virtually decided on the matter from the outset—the Assessment would measure general levels of knowledge, skills, and understandings without regard to whether those levels were the result of schooling or other specific factors. They maintained this modest view throughout and retained basic control over the decision since they were more intimately related to the Assessment than any of the other distinguished social scientists present. Excerpts from the transcript of that first policy meeting illuminate this issue, as well as the general intent that Tyler and Tukey had for the Assessment:

> *MR. ORVILLE G. BRIM, JR.* [Russell Sage Foundation]: But, Dr. Tukey, regardless of what the original mandate of the Office of Education was, I will not sit here all day tomorrow just to be involved in appraising the outcomes of the gross educational process of the United States which lumps together television and the school system without the assessment process being able to give some differentiation of the impact of each. So, I draw the action implication—otherwise, why the hell do it?
> *MR. TUKEY:* But the action implication can be drawn without assessing where the results come from.
> *MR. BRIM:* I deny it, completely.
> *MR. TUKEY:* I will give you an example I'd like to see you deny.
> *MR. KEPPEL:* God, it's nice to be back in the club—I haven't felt better in years. Bless you! Go ahead, will you? [*Laughter*]
> *MR. TUKEY:* If, as we all know would not be the case, the result of this assessment was that everybody knew everything they ought to and were behaving in all the ways they ought to, et cetera, et cetera, we would have no great feeling that we needed to improve the school system. If we find deficits, we have a feeling something ought to be done about them. We have a feeling the school system is where the public hand is on the throttle, and we should do something in the school system to correct it.
>
> Now, I don't see that where the present information comes from matters at all, in terms of action.
> *MR. BRIM:* It sounds like more of a shotgun instead of a rifle approach. If you are able to pinpoint the sources, variabilities between counties or states with some reference as to whether it's television or the school system, you sharpen your focus of activity.
> *MR. TYLER:* You sharpen it—but look at the problem. Take reading, which is in the minds of many people. There is plenty of evidence to indicate the level of reading depends a great deal upon the language used in the home. Will you pull that out and say you will consider only the reading the school contributes?
> *CHAIRMAN GARDNER:* You can never disentangle it.

MR. BRIM: What you are suggesting, then, is—in fact, if I can resort to a kind of disciplinary observation as a sociologist, I would think of dividing up the sources in terms of the different institutions of society in this sense. What you are suggesting, Ralph, is a different cut, almost in terms of the functional reading, mathematics, and so forth, and that the efforts resulting from the survey should be oriented toward subject matter, like we don't care who does the deficit in mathematics; let's pour it on.

My target is not subject matter, but institutions. I think this is good to get out in the clear.

MR. TYLER: Take a field you aren't so intimate with—the field of public health. It is important to know, for example, that there is a great deal of malnutrition in a community, or there isn't, and the question as to whether some of the kids are fed at home and others eat in dormitories and so forth is interesting if you can find it, but, I think, if you try to load on your initial appraisal of where this community is in terms of valid learnings, and also the question of finding out where they got it, it adds so much to the problem of analysis that it defeats the whole enterprise.

I'd like to know, for example, where Negro children and rural children are with reference to the kinds of knowledge they have, certain basic skills they need, and so forth. Just to find that out, which we now don't know, would be useful in terms of further action.

But I agree with you, if you can go on and make further analyses to find out, in many cases it would be very difficult to find out whether it was a deficit in the home or in the school, and so forth, but at least you'd know where they are.

MR. TUKEY: I wouldn't be against more detailed knowledge, but it sounds to me it costs somewhere between ten and a hundred times as much to get it than it costs to get the basic information, so I will stick up for getting the basic information, first.[3]

MR. TYLER: If we think of the analogy in the employment field, our first question is, do we have six percent unemployed, and the next question might be beginning to test off in what areas are they losing their jobs most rapidly, and so forth; what is their educational level. But I think, if you start out by the notion of what can you attribute to the school system, you are licked because most of the things we value highly are such a combination of what the homes do, the schools do, what the community contributes, too, that it's very difficult logically to say it's this much.

---

[3] *Proceedings of the National Testing Project Conference, December 18–19, 1963,* Carnegie files, pp. 19–22.

Take the Scarsdale schools, for example; how much of that is done in the home, the school, how much by the excellent other kinds of community enterprise they have? Do we have to know that to answer the question, "Is Scarsdale relatively undereducated?" And I can think of times when you want to test out, but I think that we shouldn't want to start out by that level of analysis.

MR. DYER: I don't see the point of starting out with the other level of analysis.

MR. TYLER: The Congress and people in general are concerned with such questions. Do we have a large level of people having a relatively low level of education, and where are they and what are the inadequacies they have? After all, for the moment, our first question, like the question of do we have typhoid, is to find out what the state of the nation is, where are our uneducated and are they among the Negroes or white/rural, or European. . . .

MR. BRIM: There is a little difference in your analogy, there, because in the instance of typhoid, we know the cause and what to do about it. I don't think that's fair in this case; we are taking the census without knowing the cause, trying to accomplish two things—both the incidence and an analysis of the cause at the same time.

I think you are right, now; you can certainly do the census without any trouble but, with a little additional data, you can also proceed from your census data to an epidemiological analysis.

MR. TYLER: I just don't want the impossibility of something to cause us to finally say that it's too big a job.

MR. BRIM: I see what you mean.

MR. TUKEY: The facts put forward, here, I don't think are right. People were collecting typhoid statistics before they knew the cause.

MR. BRIM: But it didn't do them a damned bit of good until they knew the answer to typhoid.

MR. TUKEY: I wouldn't agree with that, either. People began to find out only after they had some indication of what the facts were.

MR. BRIM: After you get your prevalent statistics, you begin to make epidemiological analyses; it wasn't until they realized the rates were different and began to develop hypotheses—we've already got the hypotheses. Let's build them into the census and realize, ahead of time, there are differences attributable to the family—right—to the community and to the school systems, and let's apportion out these and build into our plans the possibility of an analysis of these epidemiological causes.

In this sense, now, Ralph's point about let's not get hung up on this if it comes to an issue of do we have to have this or nothing at all, I certainly go along with the point of view, let's start with the census rate, because that would generate the motive power to look into the causes.

But we are social scientists sitting here and know better than to start with census rates.

MR. DYER: I don't see how a census means anything unless you begin to work with classifications, and as soon as you work with classifications, you begin to get data that are meaningful in terms of the worlds Brim is talking about.

MR. TYLER: You aren't arguing with me on the value of additional data—and I repeat what I said to Bert, that additional data that you can build into it, that will not make the thing so complex that it fails in the early stage. I am all for that, but I realize that you are on touchy questions when you get into trying to find out about the family, the notion of many of the Congress that this is—that this is privacy; that is nobody's business, and so forth.

And I come back to the original one. Let's be sure we get a defensible level of education for different age groups that we are talking about and as much else as we can feed into it that might have legitimate use in analysis. This is my view of it—but not to demand that unless you can pick out how much of that was due to the school and how much to the home, that you wouldn't have anything to do with it because I don't think, even with the most sophisticated data at present we can tell, in Scarsdale, how much of that was due to the home and to the school.

MR. TUKEY: I will take it one statement further—that is to say, I don't think this question is answerable. I mean, the argument is, what was due to nature and what was due to nurture. The biological level has been now thrown out the window on the ground a lot of it is interaction. The same thing is to be expected here.

MR. BRIM: Dr. Tukey, with all due respect, I think that's clouding the issue—I really do.

MR. FIRMAN: Among communities that are like Scarsdale, though, we found real differences in the way in which they scored a standardized achievement test, holding Scarsdale constant insofar as we now know how to hold Scarsdale constant.

MR. CRONBACH: He is giving us trouble by bringing in the word "cause." The appropriate question at every point, whether national, state, or Scarsdale, is what might we reasonably hope to accomplish, and the expectancy figure doesn't get you into all this sort of thing, and what we have to do is to think of some reasonable control variables to go into an expectancy table so the data get meaningful at the local level.

I see the point, Ralph, of saying something in the educational field comparable to today's unemployment rate is seven percent, but you have to move down a couple of steps to where are the pockets of unemployment, and it seems to me, it's only a question of conditional probability, and it seems to me, when you start talking about it as a pure science problem, it really distorts.

MR. FLYNT: . . . I wanted to add one more thing, Mr. Chairman. It seems to me, the lay mind, . . . operate[s] on a rough series of assumed correlations, and I have been impressed that we have been going in two directions here. We have been discussing the theoretical and desirable. We need to discuss the pragmatically practical; whether you want it to be or not, the findings of such a survey will be regarded as having these approximate correlations.

We have, in the last forty years, I should say, brought the lay mind to believe there is a strong correlation between high salaries of teachers and high level of preparation of teachers, good school buildings, good laboratory equipment and the product. The product is just, there is some assumed correlation, and my experience in legislation going back a long time is that sometimes a rough-and-ready, crude chunk of data, some of which I might quote but won't take the time to do so, which have been practically used with executive sessions of committees—that these crude chunks of data which assume, let us say, the state, to mention one—a survey of the qualifications of math teachers in the State of California was a turning point in one of our major pieces of legislation.

If we are going to penetrate further into this in depth, I think we have to devise instruments which are more acute than anything we have now. And, as Commissioner Keppel pointed out last evening, where the lay minds represented by Congressmen have been unable to accept these rough approximations, such as in the case of school buildings at the elementary and secondary level, we have had no forward movement.

Now, they have assumed some kind of correlation between superior facilities and high education and have enacted some legislation. But the rubric is narrow, may I say—math, science, modern foreign language, and engineering.

And, another one, Mr. Chairman, it seems to me, in your effort to keep austerity in the proposal, let's not forget that there is an assumed correlation between size and composition of libraries and performance, and this one is a very high correlation factor in the lay mind, and these things, whatever is put in the hands of the Commissioner of Education, is obviously going to be used in this way, whether he wants it or not; it will be teased out of this.

CHAIRMAN GARDNER: Are you suggesting we should measure facilities?

MR. FLYNT: If there is to be an assumption that we are not real sure that there is a coefficient of a correlation of one-to-one between superior facilities and outgoing product, I think we ought to be honest enough and, as public officials, our integrity is challenged, here, if it isn't so, and we ought to be prepared to say so.

I put it in reverse; if it's so, then it will be very clear to the Congressmen appropriating money that the federal government, after all, is a problem-solving agency in the field of education. . . .

The ultimate use of this data is going to be an attempt to measure the product against the provision, and if there is an assumption that superior facilities produce superior products, then I am sure that ready acceptance will be found for this.

Up to now, that hasn't been any too clear to the lay mind; they have seen good teachers in poor buildings produce good students.

MR. TUKEY: It seems to me, this is an argument which says, evaluation at the higher levels is eventually going to be an essential. . . .

MR. FLYNT: Yes, that's right.

MR. TUKEY: . . . because it seems to me, the lay mind doesn't believe, I think, these things are crucial for the core subjects. I would feel that you had to come higher up the scale before you had assumed that correlation.

MR. FLYNT: Oddly enough, the lay mind assumes it to be quite crucial for football—an absolute willingness to buy seventeen thousand steel seats for a stadium for a high school football team, a band room, a small choir room, and very expensive storage spaces for instruments. . . . There is some correlation between some kind of equipment. We have just taught the schools that there is a correlation between effectiveness of science teaching and laboratories—in fact, the Office of Education spent some millions of dollars on improving the science laboratories in secondary schools, which has the effect of getting the teachers in and holding the teachers, without regard to salary and anything else, simply by improving the working conditions.

All of these things are apparent in what Dr. Tukey is saying—it seems to me inevitably you are driven to this high-level evaluation of this thing, whether you want to or not.

MR. ROSSI: It seems to me, we ought to play the game straight; it doesn't come out the right way, we are stuck with it.

MR. FLYNT: That's right, it is. This is, essentially, what I'd say. I have struggled with this for twenty to twenty-five to thirty years, and I am not at all sure that some of these assumed correlations which are tentative and haven't been accepted would, if thrust through, prove out; we have seen my own field of history. You go to the English public school, to Eton or Harrow, the equipment and instructional facilities are antiquated in the extreme—the buildings constructed in the fifteenth century, and not very comfortable by any means. We were frozen to death in one of them, and it seems to me, Dr. Rossi, that we are—these are the leading, around this table, are the exponents of the greatest wisdom that could be accumulated in one room, and we are challenged, here at the highest level, to consider what the meaning of all this is.

If it's true that better prepared teachers produce better pupils regardless of socioeconomic status, we'd better know it; if it isn't true, we'd better start some sort of school organization at the local level.

MR. THORNDIKE: The last comment suggests maybe, whenever we go into a school and test the pupils, we might have a parallel set of tests to be given to the teachers.

MR. FIRMAN: In the ten schools I mentioned last night, we found some to be universally good and others to be universally ineffective in teaching basic skills. In the good schools, fifty-five percent of the staff had masters' degrees and in the poor schools twenty-four percent had masters', and I think that's significant.

MR. TUKEY: But, is it significant about the teachers or about the policies of the board of education?[4]

These discussions, aside from suggesting the inadequacies of making policy judgments through verbal discussion, also provide evidence on several other crucial matters. Francis Keppel, then Commissioner of the Office of Education, had earlier asked for the Assessment to provide hard data with which to approach Congress, particularly regarding relative inequalities in educational achievement and also concerning the absolute levels of achievement in various subject areas. Tyler and Tukey were suggesting—on technical, practical, and political grounds (in that order of salience)—that the Assessment should concentrate on measuring the educational equivalents of the incidence of malnutrition, typhoid, unemployment, etc. Further, Tyler and Tukey agreed all along with Cronbach's analogy that one also needs to know "*where the pockets of unemployment are.*" Thus, they would attempt to collect some background data about the students so that comparisons could be made of levels of knowledge, skills, and understandings among a variety of distinct groups, in each of the subject areas, and at each of the age levels. And, finally, it was clear they did not expect the Assessment to determine *why* the pockets were where they were, or how they might be eliminated.

The issue raised by Mr. Flynt of the U.S. Office of Education in the final excerpt quoted is a subtle and critical one which never was resolved. What he was suggesting elliptically was that merely determining the inequity of edu-

---

[4] *Proceedings of the National Testing Project Conference,* pp. 139–145.

cational achievement among a variety of subgroups might lead to a greater recognition of problem areas in the field but that it would also lead to an undiscriminating invocation of the many assumed correlations which then dominated the determination of educational policies. In other words, it might mean that more money would be poured into teacher education, building, or other educational inputs which in fact could have inconsistent effects on educational achievement but which were then popularly assumed to produce inevitable gains. Thus, he was suggesting that it would be necessary to test the assumed correlations and find out which of them held and which did not. At the time (prior to Coleman), it might have been reasonable to assume that some relationships between educational inputs and educational achievement would hold, and that the more manipulable of these could be employed to produce greater achievement and greater equality in American education. Flynt's concern was particularly perceptive and timely, but in fact if the Assessment had tried to gather input data to resolve this issue, by the time it issued its first reports in 1970 it merely would have added one more voice to those that have since demythologized the assumed correlations. It would not have been able, with techniques available either then or now, to identify any variations which could produce strong, positive, and consistent variables with which to guide systematic educational policy making.

The Tyler-Tukey position, doubting the utility of attempts at causal analysis, prevailed virtually unchanged from the first meeting in 1963 until very recently. There is one exceptional moment worth noting, however. Stephen Withey, the first staff director for ECAPE, compiled a foresighted memo during 1964:[5]

INPUT FACTORS

There seems to be no systematic treatment of the educational system input factors that influence educational progress. A publication such as *Evaluating Criteria,* 1960 edition, of National Study of Secondary School Evaluation (Washington, D.C.) hints at some of these items in its comprehensive enumeration of criteria for evaluating high schools. But many are missing because much of the input is somewhat independent of the educational offering itself. Input factors run all the way from psychological factors to sociological conditions. The bearing of these areas on education is still a question with changing, developing, and innovative answers.

---

[5] "Input Factors," ECAPE memorandum, Denver, Carnegie files.

The listing of input factors raises questions as to which variables would be most valuable in an assessment such as that proposed. Thinking of the items in terms of research methodology also raises questions on the multiplicity of sources of information, the relative cost of securing items, informational comparability, and the degree to which these factors reflect each other. A further question asks: which items are most meaningful when only a few pupils will be sampled from the area described?—and so forth.

The following list, culled cursorily from individual studies, is suggestive of the multiplicity of items:

Pupils

1. Sex of student
2. Age and grade
3. Years since starting school
4. Pupil potential as expressed on standardized tests
5. Educational readiness or measures of preschool preparation
6. Pupil motivation, interests, values and aspirations
7. Pupil self-image
8. Expenditures per pupil for instructional purposes
9. Size of class in which pupil is a member
10. Special status of pupil

Family

1. Intactness of family
2. Size of family
3. Parents' expectations
4. Family behavior on intellectual and academic interests
5. Parent participation in school affairs
6. At-homeness of parents—working mothers, etc.
7. Degree of reinforcement of school values in the home
8. Parents' attitude toward school
9. Educational attainment of parents
10. Socioeconomic position of parents

Community

1. Size and population
2. Type of community—main economic supports
3. Geographic location
4. Total assessed property
5. Climate of support for school financing
6. Average level of educational attainment
7. Stable versus transient membership
8. Community services
9. Ancillary community educational resources

10. Rate of community growth

Teachers

1. Teacher turnover or average length of tenure
2. Teacher preparation
3. Teacher salaries—some measure of the distribution or the position of the pupils' teacher in the salary distribution
4. Teacher identification with the community
5. Teacher-pupil ratio
6. Teacher benefits
7. Teacher expectations for her pupil(s)
8. Length of teaching experience
9. Certification of teachers
10. Teacher qualifications above the minimum
11. In-service teacher training
12. Teacher-pupil relationships

School System

1. Class size
2. Size of school system and rate of growth
3. Special services—e.g., guidance, health, library, etc.
4. Instructional supplies and equipment
5. "Desirability" of school plant
6. Professional preparation of school administrators
7. School evaluation procedures
8. School retention rates
9. Ethnic and racial composition of the school
10. School climate
11. Breadth, scope, and organization of school offerings
12. School policy (promotional procedures, etc.)
13. Public or private school system
14. Formal and informal school relationships
15. Quality of administrative leadership
16. Preschool services
17. Compensatory school services
18. In-service program
19. Articulation and coordination of curriculum
20. Expenditures per pupil
21. Capital outlay
22. Budget
23. State and federal aid versus local financing
24. Proportion of budget spent on salaries
25. Assessed valuation of school district
26. Percent of funds obtained by local taxation
27. Staff morale

28. Distribution of responsibility within the school
29. Degree of resemblance between the learning situation and the life situation of the student
30. Specialized education offerings
31. Entrance, progress, and graduation policies and practices
32. Objectives of the school
33. Appraisal of student progress
34. Relationship of school to other agencies providing education
35. Relationship of educational programs to current kowledge of the nature and needs of youth in the community
36. Relationship between teachers and pupils
37. Relationship between administrators and teachers
38. Attitudes of staff toward students
39. Age-grade distribution within the school
40. Proportional educational and occupational intentions of students

Whatever the desideratum of this memorandum, the effect could only have been to support the Tyler-Tukey position that such an analysis was too much to attempt. Indeed, none of the survey research projects since that time have been able to develop adequate measures for many of the inputs which were listed; most notably, attempts to measure the various affective factors mentioned (Pupils, 5, 6, and 7; Family, 1, 3, 4, 5, 6, 7, and 8; Teachers, 7 and 12; School System, 7, 10, 28, 29, 32, 33, 34, 35, 36, 37, and 38) have been totally lacking or almost totally inadequate.

DESCRIPTIVE DATA VERSUS EXPLANATORY
OR PREDICTIVE DATA

Thus, NAEP eventually took a relatively descriptive stance toward background data: The units for reporting would be those that would allow for the gross identification of pockets of more or less educational achievement and progress. This distinction is critical: Most of the background factors to be recorded were intended merely to describe the various subgroups; they were not to be used either to explain or predict levels of achievement, with the possible exception of the SES measures. (Surely it is easy, as we indicate later, for descriptive data to be used and/or abused in drawing predictive or explanatory conclusions.)

Thus, while politics did exercise some influence on which particular background factors would be described, Katzman and Rosen and other critics of the Assessment's design are wrong in their conclusion that politics was the key factor preventing the Assessment from becoming a rigorous input-output system of national educational accountability. As noted earlier in this chapter, the startling but essentially negative "schooling" findings of the Coleman Report and subsequent studies suggest that Tyler and Tukey were astute and judicious in their recognition of the limitations of social science as a means of providing a comprehensive and sensitive causal model of educational achievement.

THE SELECTION OF DESCRIPTIVE CATEGORIES

With this descriptive intent in mind, ECAPE and NAEP decided to record information by sex for four age groups, four regions of the country, four types of communities, and two levels of SES. Later, after various political considerations, a decision was made to record race as well, in two broad categories—black and nonblack. These categories provided the Assessment's first round with a potential of 512 descriptive subgroupings (2 sex × 4 age × 2 race × 4 regions × 4 community types × 2 SES levels).

The NAEP description of its first reporting categories is as follows:[6]

> Various reporting categories have been and are being developed. The basic categories are the four different age groups—9, 13, 17, 25–35. In a few instances the same exercises will be used across three or even across all four age groups. In many instances the same exercise will be used at two different ages. Thus it will be possible to see some comparative data across two or more age levels. The choice of age groups to assess was made in order to sample near the end of primary education, near the end of elementary education, near the end of secondary education, and after most adults have completed all of their formal education.
>
> A second set of reporting categories is by geographic region. Four regions were used in the sampling; the same four will be used for reporting purposes—Northeast, Southeast, Central, and West. The Northeast includes all the middle-Atlantic and New England states. The Southeast contains most border states between the North and the Southwestern and West Coast states, plus Hawaii, Alaska, and West Texas. The Central area contains the other states. These divisions correspond closely to geographic

---

[6] *What Is National Assessment?* (Denver: ECS, 1970), pp. 39–41.

divisions used for many other statistical reports. Whether or not geographic differences appear remains to be seen.

A third set of reporting categories is based upon type of community, basically size. These categories are:

Large cities (above 200,000 population)

Urban fringes (cities adjacent to the large cities)

Middle-size cities (25,000 to 200,000)

Small town–rural areas (below 25,000)

In addition to these basic reporting categories, additional information about community size and type was collected. Thus, it may be possible to report finer breakdowns by separating out central cities areas or truly rural areas, if the data warrant.

A fourth reporting category will be sex. Numerous studies have demonstrated that boys and girls produce different results in various subject areas. Such differences certainly will appear in National Assessment results.

A fifth reporting category is labeled SES. Originally it meant socioeconomic status. It now is read as socioeducational status. Neither term may truly represent the intent of this breakdown. The intent was to be able to report results separately for assessees from disadvantaged homes. The great concern of contemporary society with the education of the disadvantaged requires an all-out effort to provide information about the knowledges and skills of that group as they exist today.

Defining SES or describing the intent of the classification is simple. Finding a good index or indices of SES is extraordinarily complex. The literature of educational measurement yields numerous attempts at measuring SES, each one of which has some major flaw. Ideally one might want to classify assessees according to parental income. In practice such information cannot be collected as it verges upon invasion of privacy. Obvious substitutes are educational levels of parents and/or occupational levels of parents. Such information can be secured relatively easily for 17-year-olds by direct questioning. But 9-year-olds are not apt to have the information. One can consider the use of existing school records (complete in some schools; incomplete in others) or one can consider trying to get the information directly from parents (a tedious and only partially successful scheme). Or one can ask a series of simple questions that 9-year-olds and 13-year-olds can answer, such as whether a home contains an encyclopedia or a daily newspaper or books, etc., and infer family educational level from such indices. National Assessment is trying all of these approaches in the hope that one or more of them will provide a meaningful breakdown into two or more meaningful SES levels.[7]

The final reporting category is race. This category was added to the reporting scheme less than two years ago at the urging of persons concerned with obtaining maximum information about minority groups. It is a controversial category that offends some people if included and offends others if omitted. The policy committee for National Assessment felt that the need for this type of information outweighed the dangers inherent in collecting it.

An additional practical reason for including race as a reporting category is the fact that it offers an additional category to be used in connection with low SES reports. Many persons assume, incorrectly, that most low SES individuals are members of a minority group. Statistics, however, say that more members of the white majority in this country are low SES than are members of minority groups in the country as a whole. The use of race as a separate reporting category will enable one to look at SES and race both independently and together.

Unfortunately, the small size of the National Assessment sample means that meaningful statistics will be available only for black, white, and other or for simply black and other. The designation of race is being made by the exercise administrators. No individual assessee is asked to indicate his race. While this is not a perfect categorization, no other scheme is perfect either. It is a categorization that is close to common usage.

By the Assessment's second round, the Reading and Literature exercises, NAEP had attempted to produce somewhat more refined descriptive categories. The measures of age, sex, and regions remained the same, but the measure of race was expanded to include "Black, White, and Other"; the four sizes of communities were substantially altered to include seven "Sizes and Types of Community," which provide a combined measure of size and "community-occupational" status (STOCS); and the two levels of parental education were expanded to four. The *General Information Yearbook, 02-GIY*, describes the STOCS changes.[8] Although these refinements are sophisticated, they in no way alter the basic intent or value of the categories, which remain largely descriptive, and should not be taken to be explanatory or predictive. The question of which descriptive reporting categories are likely to prove most useful is important. For instance, what are the implications for educational change of findings associated with sex, race, or parental level of education?

---

[7] The first cycle tail sheet collected information on whether the respondent's family had a telephone, an encyclopedia, an automobile, a daily newspaper delivered, subscriptions to any magazine, and more than thirty books in the home. The telephone and automobile questions were eliminated in later cycles.

[8] Denver: ECS, 1972, app. D.

Returning to the earlier analogy—that of measuring pockets of unemployment—the seven STOC measures seem potentially useful in the development of federal and state aid policies. Given more refined objectives and exercises, if consistent differences show up among these different sizes and types of communities, then it is conceivable that particular categorical aid programs might be useful in these different places, although the Assessment could provide little guidance as to what those programs should consist of. Data comparing specific communities and specific states might have produced more direct information and impetus to change. After all, many policies are implemented by local districts or state legislatures and state departments of education, and directly relevant data might have helped them develop these policies. However, the states and local districts can collect some comparative data of their own, and some of NAEP's existing reporting categories (such as sex, race, and STOCS) may be helpful in a general way in the determination of state and local policies.

The ECAPE-NAEP decision not to sample and report the results by specific states and communities is quite complex and it too has generally been misinterpreted, like the decision to undertake descriptive rather than explanatory analysis. For example, as noted earlier, Katzman and Rosen have argued that politics prevented NAEP from collecting state-by-state data, which is true, but they have failed to inquire whether such collection was seen as a crucial objective or as relatively debatable.

Several facts are worth noting here. The transcripts, memoranda, and interviews suggest that Tyler and Tukey had no rigid expectation at the outset that they would gather comparative data by particular states and communities. Their primary interest was in establishing a national census of educational progress. They indicated a desire to report subpopulation data for the sake of comparisons and identification of pockets of special need, and Keppel at one point stated that he hoped the Assessment would promote healthy competition among communities and states (while avoiding invidious comparisons). In one instance, the January 27–28, 1964, conference, providing states with comparative data was listed as a major tentative aim. But in fact, many at that meeting assumed the states and communities would actually crave such intelligence about themselves, and in terms of the current accountability movement this assumption was partly true. But even given an overly optimistic sense of state and local demand for such information, Tyler and Tukey in no way indicated that states and communities were high-priority reporting categories. Their flexibility or ambivalence on this matter is reflected in the fact that they considered numerous alternative reporting categories, including brief consideration of congressional districts and telephone area-code zones. The ultimate decision not to draw comparative samples from each of the states and from specific local communities also derived partly from the substantially greater costs for a truly national sample which also included meaningful samples from the fifty states and various specific communities.

The history of the Assessment's political development certainly testifies to substantial opposition to drawing state and local comparisons, led by school people who saw themselves as fighting national control and invidious comparisons. But no matter how intense and vocal this opposition was, and regardless of whether NAEP's early leaders bargained with these schoolpeople and gave in, the record also shows that Keppel and Tyler and Tukey, rightly or wrongly, did not see state and local reporting categories as prerequisite, and that, partly as a result of this bargaining, they succeeded in implementing the national census population, which was their top priority.

Furthermore, those who opposed reporting by states and communities, and critics who bemoan the fact that the Assessment cannot report by these categories, neglect two distinct possibilities. First, the existence of the National Assessment and the dissemination of its results have spurred and coincided with the accountability movement and lent encouragement to demands for state-by-state data. Second, and more subtle, both the opponents and advocates of state and local comparisons have failed to consider the possibility that in the long run the present generalized system of reporting might produce more leeway for federal influence than a state-by-state or district-by-district comparison. The results of the Assessment, if they are ever to have real policy implications, might very well stimulate federal programs that are regional in their focus, or policies that might be better implemented because they are not intended to go directly through particular state departments of education or local school districts.

The above facts should not be construed as suggesting that the politics of the National Assessment was in any way nominal. Political considerations were quite important at virtually every stage of the Assessment's design and implementation. As we have seen earlier, politics was central in the delineation of subject-matter areas, the determination of objectives within the subject areas, the omission of particular exercises, and so on. However, distinctions must be made continually between the political limits of such an assessment, the conceptual limits of such an assessment, and the original intent and expectations—political and conceptual—of its creators.

NAEP'S FUTURE MEASUREMENT OF INPUTS

NAEP's early decision to put its emphasis on a descriptive rather than explanatory evaluation of educational achievement has been undergoing review. John P. Gilbert, of the Harvard Computing Center, and Frederick Mosteller of Harvard, now chairman of the Analysis and Advisory Committee, have proposed that the massive NAEP national sample and administrative operation be turned to the complex measurement of input factors affecting educational achievement. While the idea may have been tentative, it was taken quite seriously at NAEP and has been followed up in subsequent meetings and studies. Their memorandum follows:

> Because of the Civil Rights Movement and other reasons, improving the educational achievement of disadvantaged segments of the society has become a major national priority. Progress on this problem has been seriously hampered by lack of information as to how to improve achievement in individual schools let alone on such a large scale. The Coleman Report was initiated to document the existence of inequalities; however, the data it provided were carefully analyzed both by Coleman and others for clues to what factors could be manipulated to institute improvements in achievement. Although the Coleman Report and Coleman's data stimulated fresh thinking on these problems, as in Mosteller and Moynihan, more data on factors affecting achievement are desperately needed. Ideally, these data would come from large-scale experiments or randomized trials. In the absence of large-scale randomized trials a large observational study could be a major contribution to the possible improvement of educational achievement. It would also serve as a preliminary step for any later randomized trials. Such an observational study would correlate achievement measures with a variety of possible determinants. These determining factors could not be limited to only those that might be modified but would also have to include as many important factors as possible since the nonmodifiable factors will undoubtedly mediate the action of those factors that could be changed. The aim of the study would be to identify the variables affecting achievement and insofar as possible to quantify their effects and interactions. The planning and implementation of such a study will require major effort if it is to make a contribution.
>
> It is clear that NAEP stands in a unique position with regard to this problem because it already has an active sampling mechanism and has perfected and tested tools for assessing educational achievement in a variety of areas. Thus from a technical point of

view, the existence of NAEP puts the "impossible dream" well into the realm of possibility.

Two opposing observations need to be made. First this activity is clearly outside of NAEP's original charge and would possibly endanger NAEP's capability to carry out its primary task of providing periodic unbiased assessments of the nation's achievement in education. On the other hand, the widespread demand for information for building social legislation to provide equality of educational opportunity has already moved NAEP and the Analysis Advisory Committee in particular to try to quantify the "effects" of such factors as parents' education, region, and race. The data currently collected that characterize groups of respondents present serious problems of interpretation because of their limited scope and may be quite misleading particularly in the hands of others.

Because the existing data will be used in spite of serious drawbacks, one responsible position may be for NAEP to collect data as carefully and with as much thought as it is now collecting on achievement itself.

To provide data of this sort coordinated with the present data on achievement will require an effort of about the same magnitude as was required to develop NAEP's present system. However, the methods used and the experience gained by NAEP in devising the assessment scheme will of course be of great aid in developing the new variables and methods required.

The following is a brief description of some of the issues that might be involved in this enlarged study.

1. We would get background information, probably on a subsample of the total NAEP sample, and we would probably follow the present rule of not asking all questions of all the children.
2. We would wish to determine some additional things about the child, such as IQ, attitude, hearing, sight, and general health.
3. We might wish to obtain some special school-child variables, such as the teacher's assessment of the child, the length of time the child has been in that school system, attendance record, level of discipline, whether the child was bused.
4. We would need to follow the child home to determine the makeup and life-style of the home, income, attitude of home to school, expectations for the child, availability of age to learning, help with homework, etc. How does the child relate to parents and the establishment.

There is no shortage of experts to provide NAEP with opinions as to which variables would be most valuable to measure and what the best procedure might be in order to go about measuring them. Some possible mechanisms for tapping this expert opinion are:

1. Have conferences of interest groups.
2. Contract to special firms such as SRI or ADL.
3. Obtain the services of a School of Education.
4. Assemble an in-house group at NAEP.
5. Set up an ad hoc group of consultants to work on this problem.

NAEP must have a well defined charge to give to any such group; however, its success in defining measures of assessment would be one of NAEP's strongest assets for this task.

In summary, we find ourselves, at a time when society is eager to work on the problem of improving educational achievement, in possession of a valuable tool for contributing to this goal. If we continue to collect descriptive variables of the child and his position in society in an ad hoc manner, the results will still be used possibly by ourselves as well as others to try to solve problems for which they are not appropriate. If we can correlate our data on achievement with fairly complete data on probable determinants of that achievement we may be in a unique position to shed light on the educational process.[9]

Despite the fact that this memorandum comes from two of the nation's leading statisticians, or perhaps because it does, it is very striking in its similarity to the amorphous and unsystematic planning memos which preceded and generally characterized the development of the Assessment itself.

There are four points here which seem intuitively and empirically defensible. First, more data on factors affecting educational (hopefully, more broadly defined) achievement are desperately needed. Second, in the long run randomized trials might be very helpful in isolating important factors. Third, NAEP's sample population or some subsample thereof might be useful when the time for such randomized trials comes.[10] Fourth, as we noted above and as we discuss in Chapter 7, the existing NAEP reporting categories have created "serious problems of interpretation because of their limited scope and may be quite misleading particularly in the hands of others."

But there are no logical or empirical grounds for suggesting either that NAEP would be the appropriate sponsoring agency for the effort that Gilbert

---

[9] June 22, 1972, Carnegie files.

[10] Eventually as the definition of educational achievement is consistently broadened to include more than merely scores on achievement tests, some of NAEP's exercises measuring actual skills and understandings might be useful, although as of now these measures are quite unrefined. Superior measures seem likely to emerge from other smaller-scale efforts to produce valid and reliable measures of skills and understandings that might reveal interesting relationships with the determinants of educational growth.

and Mosteller propose or that the next appropriate step in the field of analyzing the determinants of educational achievement should be a large observational study. Indeed, there is a great deal of evidence to the contrary.

In the first place, as previous sections of this study have indicated, even given its relatively limited intent and mandate, NAEP has had a wide variety of serious problems, in terms of both management planning and quality control. It is surprising that Gilbert and Mosteller suggest that NAEP has "perfected and tested tools for assessing educational achievement."

Second, even if NAEP were to correct its many inadequacies and then demonstrate that it has some real utility that warrants its cost to the federal government, such a demonstration would not prove, in any way, that it has the technical and political capacity to oversee or undertake the sort of path-breaking research analysis that is necessary. NAEP was started in 1963 to provide hard data for USOE, Congress, and a variety of educational interest groups. Various people wanted stronger proof of diverse conditions in education. But, in fact, standards for proof have increased so considerably in the past several years that NAEP's hard data is actually quite soft; as considered in more detail in Chapter 7, it does not hold up under the kinds of public scrutiny that it was originally intended to withstand. Stated differently, as standards of measurement and evidence have become more sophisticated, NAEP has been unable to keep up. And there is much to suggest that it will be difficult for NAEP to catch up to current standards, not to mention keeping up with standards as they continue to rise in the future. To ask this same organization to move ahead in the extremely difficult area of causal analysis, given its administrative, technical, and political limitations, seems clearly to be asking too much.

Third, and perhaps most importantly, there is no evidence that *the* next logical step in the field of causal analysis is a large observational study—or even that *one* next logical step is a large observational study. The memo's conclusion that "thus, from a technical point of view, the existence of NAEP puts the 'impossible dream' well into the realm of possibility" is preposterous, both when contrasted with Tyler's and Tukey's humility on this subject, and, more significantly, when placed against the findings and conclusions of the most sophisticated attempts at causal analysis completed to date.

Impending omniscience is clearly much less a reality than a vocational hazard for statisticians. As indicated above, surprisingly little progress has been made as a result of several large observational studies and numerous reanalyses following the publication of the Coleman Report. Despite substantial and increasing investment and rigor the subsequent studies in the United

States and abroad have failed to move rapidly ahead toward isolating manipulable factors that positively, significantly, and consistently affect educational achievement.

The memo, before its statement about fulfilling the "impossible dream," does recognize that progress in this field may be extremely difficult. The stated aim would be "to identify the variables affecting achievement and *insofar as possible* to quantify their effects and interactions" (emphasis added). On the other hand, this seems to ignore the existing studies identifying such variables and the limited uses (and in some cases, limited analyses) of these studies. IEA has data on educational achievement in twenty-two countries which include measurement of a total of some eight hundred (as yet underanalyzed) background variables. And yet its tentative conclusions regarding the relative importance of family background factors and the relative unimportance of school factors are much the same as those which have been repeated again and again over the past several years. The memo by and large does *not* suggest that it will be feasible to move beyond these studies toward a more sophisticated understanding of the interactions and effects of identified variables. Why would one move ahead with another large observational study before the presence of some rigorous evidence—at least conceptual, if not empirical—that the study would advance the field?

The memo itself provides one rationalization for moving ahead with such a study: It correctly suggests that NAEP's present reporting categories are subject to serious misinterpretation and abuse. But it then goes on to argue that if only NAEP could collect a great deal *more* background data, this problem would be remedied. First, this position ignores the distinction between reporting the results in terms of descriptive categories and analyzing them in explanatory or predictive terms. Gilbert and Mosteller, despite their connections with the project, appear to be misinterpreting the earlier NAEP intent when they suggest that NAEP and the Analysis Advisory Committee have been trying to quantify the effects of a few crude factors such as parents' education, region, and race. It is insulting for them to claim this. In all its publications, NAEP has been attempting, though often unsuccessfully, to avoid any such casual analysis; it is unfair to misinterpret NAEP's intent and to allege now that if only it could do more of what it is not doing it would be done better.

Furthermore, Gilbert and Mosteller's suggestion that complicating the analysis by measuring more variables would mitigate against misinterpretation and abuse has no basis in reality. All the most sophisticated studies done to date have filtered down to the media, policymakers, and the public at large in terms of a few gross generalizations about the nominal effects of school resources and the significant effects of family background. Indeed, the more sophisticated the analysis preceding the conclusions, the more likely it seems the conclusions will be misinterpreted and abused with increasing zeal. There is no doubt that NAEP's attempt to be purely descriptive is thwarted by various interpreters once the results are in the public domain. To some extent this seems an inevitable problem, but insofar as it is not, the realistic alternative policies available to NAEP include (1) rigorous refusal to suggest causal factors and (2) specific, thoughtful attempts to interpret results, repeatedly emphasizing their descriptive nature, and what should not and in fact cannot be inferred from them.

One final set of remarks regarding the June 22 proposal: First, the description of some of the factors that might be involved in the study seems quite unimaginative and redundant from the start. Second, *school factors,* either because of politics or pessimism concerning the future, have been omitted from the list of priorities. While this would have to be corrected in future efforts before they could be considered complete, even then it would be shortsighted to undertake another extensive survey of the effects of school factors without first redefining school outcomes and inputs. It is known from past studies that the present variation between the schools measured is too slight to produce strong, consistent, positive relationships between school factors and educational achievement.

The memo casually suggests that this new analysis would make use of NAEP's matrix sampling system, which is described in the next chapter. Naturally, one of the only reasons to ask NAEP to make such an effort would be to make use of its sampling mechanism, but at the same time this notion introduces subtle but severe complications. The goal would be to build a comprehensive theory of the determination of individual educational achievement, but instead of studying individuals in depth and over time, the method would aggregate highly fragmented data on individuals representative of population subgroups.

This approach seems unnecessarily convoluted from the start. The use of this sampling system for these purposes would create new and unexamined inference problems more complex than those which Coleman and all the subsequent reports have faced and failed to overcome. Measuring the determinants of growth by following an individual or a group of individuals, in depth, from Time One to Time Two, so far has proved impossible. Aggregating data about individuals studied in less depth has been even less feasible. As James Coleman noted in 1964:

It is painfully evident to anyone who attempts to study a social system that our quantitative research techniques are in their infancy. For, by sensitive observation and description (as exemplified, say, by William Foote Whyte's *Street Corner Society*) we can trace the functioning of a social system. Yet, when we attempt to carry out quantitative research in such a system, we find ourselves stymied. We switch from a sensitive examination of events, in which intimate sequence in time suggests causal relations between events, to a crude measurement of 'characteristics' and a comparative cross-sectional analysis that relates one characteristic to another. That is, when we shift from qualitative reporting to quantitative analysis, we change our very mode of inference.[11]

In the years since the above statement was written, little progress has been achieved in improving quantitative techniques enough so that this change in the mode of inference can be fully understood and accounted for. And now in the June 22 NAEP memo comes the suggestion that the next step might be an aggregation of various partial quantifiable characteristics of many individuals, none of whom would be studied in any depth. Such a change in direction involves still another change in the mode of inference, moving away from the important problems suggested by Coleman before they have been resolved and without proposing to resolve them by other means. Quite apart from the more obvious practical difficulties of asking NAEP to oversee such a project, there is a substantial burden involved in demonstrating that a matrix sample has any superior virtues to recommend it for attempted causal analysis at this time. It is much more likely that the next major breakthroughs toward a causal analysis of educational achievement will come from in-depth studies of various individuals, and from exacting experiments based on imaginative efforts to introduce new inputs, or old inputs, in substantially different proportions.

---

[11] "The Adolescent Society," in Phillip E. Hammond (ed.), *Sociologists at Work* (New York: Basic Books, 1964), p. 192.

7

THE SAMPLING DESIGN
AND EXERCISE PACKAGES

The Assessment's matrix sampling system is one outcome of the NAEP intention to measure the knowledge, skills, and understandings of groups rather than individuals. While the matrix design was carefully fashioned to yield precise estimates of group responses on the exercises, as we shall see, it imposes some serious limitations on the usefulness of the Assessment results.

SAMPLING

The NAEP probability sample was designed to represent subgroups of the population, classified by sex, age, region, size and type of community, socioeconomic status, and race. NAEP sought a sampling system that would permit subsequent manipulation of the data in order to obtain estimates for subpopulations not defined in the original design, and, in addition, NAEP wanted a sample that would facilitate smooth field operations, provide simple estimation procedures, and achieve these aims at the lowest possible cost.

Consideration of these objectives led to the selection of a stratified multistage design.[1] In the first stage of a multistage design, the population to be

---

[1] For a more detailed account of the NAEP sample design, see *NAEP Report 1, 1969–1970, Science: National Results and Illustrations of Group Comparisons* (Denver: ECS, 1970), app. C.

132

sampled is divided into cells, and a sample of cells is drawn. In the next stage, samples are drawn from the populations of each of the cells selected in the first stage.

For the Assessment, the first stage involved construction of an *area sampling frame,* in which every square foot of land area in the United States was assigned to a listing unit—a small geographic area with a recognizable boundary (such as a county) and containing at least 16,000 persons. Each listing unit, depending on its population, contains one or more *Primary Sampling Units* (PSU's), which are units of roughly uniform population. Listing units were stratified by region, size of community, and a combination of income and geographic location within the region.

NAEP determined that about 2,000 responses per exercise for individually administered exercises and about 2,500 responses per exercise for group-administered exercises would provide a sample large enough to detect small differences in attainment over time at the national and regional levels. The staff decided, on the basis of variance and cost considerations, to administer each exercise package to nine to twelve respondents in each PSU. This led to the decision to select 208 PSU's in all, fifty-two in each region. For each of the four regions, then, the first-stage sample was constructed by drawing PSU's from size of community strata on a proportional to population basis.

The second stage involved sampling the population within each selected PSU and determining weighting factors. This amounted, in effect, to designing several separate surveys, one for each exercise package for each age level. About 150 respondents were chosen for each age level in each PSU.[2] For seventeen-year-olds and adults, low-SES respondents were deliberately over-sampled in order to provide a large enough sample in this category to make reasonable estimates.

PACKAGING THE EXERCISES

Exercises from two or three subject-matter areas are placed together in packages, one of which is completed by each in-school respondent.[3] Most

---

[2] In each Assessment year, there are about ten to fourteen exercise packages, each requiring nine to twelve respondents in each PSU.

[3] Because it is difficult to locate and test large numbers of out-of-school seventeen-year-olds and adults, each such respondent was offered the opportunity to complete up to four packages, receiving $10 for completing two, $15 for completing three, and $20 for completing four.

packages contain between ten and fifteen exercises and require thirty-five to forty-five minutes to complete. Each individually administered package is given to nine students in each PSU, and each group-administered package is given to twelve students in each PSU.

The exercises and instructions, in addition to being available in written form, are read to the respondents by a tape-recorded voice in all subject-matter areas except reading, for all ages except adults. The packages are administered by NAEP staff or by local staff who have been specially trained by NAEP.

THE INTERPLAY OF SAMPLING, PACKAGING, AND UTILITY

The remarks below concerning various limitations of the data collected by the Assessment are not intended to be a criticism of the sampling system or packaging criteria per se. *The sample design and packaging did not create the limitations we discern: Rather, limitations in the original conception of how the Assessment might be useful created a sample design and packaging system that has very distinctly limited uses.* The limited testing period—fifty minutes or less—is partly a function of the same limitations in the original conception; but it is also a major source of those limitations.

From the very outset (1963), NAEP's leaders maintained that they wanted to move away from the norm-referenced testing of individuals toward the measurement of national and subgroup levels of achievement.[4] The matrix sampling system provides several major benefits: First, it allows the Assessment to measure performance on large numbers of exercises in each subject area without requiring long testing periods and without being limited to quickly answered memorization items. Second, this collection of data on many exercises, given the sample design, permits the analysis and dissemination of results for the national population, as well as comparisons of the performances of various subgroups within subject areas. Third, the structure

---

[4] Given this orientation, NAEP was not interested in testing the same individuals over time and does not do so. Instead, in each cycle it will test different children who have background characteristics similar to those tested earlier.

and the size of the sample make it possible to detect relatively small differences in group performance over time. Fourth, the packaging system produces certain economies as well as ease and relative uniformity in administration. And, finally, according to NAEP claims, with which we disagree, the short testing period of thirty-five to forty-five minutes is per se a positive benefit of this system.

While the sampling design and packaging system are reasonably well designed to provide aggregated data comparing performance over time within, between, and among various groups, the Assessment's data would have been much richer with educational implications if it had simultaneously gathered more information on the performance of individuals. Disregarding for the moment the major limitations resulting from the selection of distinct subject areas, the selection of objectives, and the development of the exercises, more complete information on the performance of individuals, within and across subject areas, might have produced hard data that could be used in the advancement of learning theory or in the delineation of specific research questions and perhaps even curricula.

The packaging system of ten or fifteen exercises per package constrains the analysis of individual performance in the following ways: The first major criterion for the packages was that each must contain material from more than one subject area. In the first cycle this meant that each package had questions in Science, Writing, and Citizenship; in the second cycle each package had questions in Reading and Literature. Thus, there was extremely small leeway for asking an individual even as few as seven or eight questions within any one field; at the same time there was small leeway for having an individual complete an array of exercises that would be meaningful across fields.

This constraint was exacerbated by the second major packaging criterion: Each package had to contain exercises written at the three levels of difficulty. For example, a given student might have six reading exercises at three different levels of difficulty. Even if the exercises had been of such high quality that they could precisely indicate the attainment or nonattainment of specific subobjectives or objectives, this packaging system would have virtually precluded the gathering of useful material for research on the development of reading skills. A student operating at only the easiest level might have completed two exercises acceptably and not the other four. Thus, it would be possible to know what the student could not do, but it would be impossible to analyze what the specific characteristics of the student's reading capacities and problems were. Similarly, it would be impossible to critically analyze the performance of a student who could operate at two or three difficulty levels on some exercises, preventing the generation of hypotheses about the relationships between different difficulty levels. This objection is not intended to negate the group-analysis utility of including the difficulty levels within each package. Rather, it is intended to point out that it would have been quite useful to also know how often, and in what instances, students operate at different levels of difficulty, either within a particular subject or across subject areas.

Beyond what educators would like to know about performance within and across subject areas, and within and across difficulty levels, the packaging and sampling system also prevents the creation of a critical mass of individual data in another way. A major goal of the Assessment is not only to measure knowledge of subject area *contents* but also to measure *skills, understandings,* and *attitudes.* Again, the Assessment can do this by subgroups of the population. These comparisons are interesting, but because of the inadequate measurement of the skills, understandings, and attitudes, the resulting generalization characterizing the reporting of subgroup performance produced little that can directly aid researchers, much less educational policymakers. In addition, however, information about differential *individual* performance on contents, skills, understandings, and attitudes *within* a subject area would be quite useful. Information about individual performance in each of these four categories *across* subject areas would be still more interesting. And all this information about individuals, when measured *across difficulty levels,* would be even more productive for rigorous educational research.

This last-mentioned constraint, that individuals are being superficially tested, or not tested at all, for their differential performance on contents, skills, understandings, and attitudes, also feeds back into the first two limitations discussed and further exacerbates their cursory qualities. Even as an individual is tested on a strictly circumscribed number of questions within a subject area, at varying difficulty levels, the nature of the exercises is also subject to change, sometimes measuring contents, sometimes skills, sometimes understandings, and sometimes attitudes, thus further reducing the possibility of any adequately informed and complex statement about how individuals perform within and across subject areas and within and across difficulty levels, as well as across the four categories of contents, skills, understandings, and attitudes.

It must be emphasized again that NAEP did not try to measure these complex areas and fail. What we have considered is a combination of NAEP's limited conception of what kinds of information would be useful and the relatively subtle interplay among the sample design, the packaging system, and the data that emerges from the Assessment. These factors indicate the very limited extent to which present Assessment results can be used by the educational community. And here we are not even talking about answering research questions or informing policy decisions; we are merely talking about the generation of research hypotheses, a function which the present group results serve only in an extremely narrow and indirect way.

One further subtle but important restriction inherent in the problems described above in this chapter also places serious constraints on the complex understanding of the performance of *groups*. While the gross comparative performance of groups can be reported within subject areas, across subject areas, and across difficulty levels, there is no way really to assess how performance capabilities are distributed within groups or whether they are differentially distributed across groups. For example, within the grouping of low-SES, white, rural, thirteen-year-old males, it is impossible to say with authority whether many individuals can answer only the easiest questions in all subject areas, whether some can do some types of difficult questions in some areas but not the same types or other types of difficult questions in other areas, or whether the capacity to complete difficult exercises across subject areas is clustered within a small population of the individuals who make up the group. Stated differently, in trying to understand the inner qualities of a group, do some students that make up particular groups perform poorly or well in all subject areas? Or are there substantial variations in performance across subject areas, across difficulty levels, and across the categories of contents, skills, understandings, and attitudes? Are the students who do well in science in a particular group the same students who would do well in art and citizenship? And so on. For some of these questions there is a nominal amount of information from which only weak inferences can be made, and for others there is no information whatsoever.

Beyond our wanting to understand these issues within groups, such differences in capability may be distributed differently in various groups and knowledge of these differences would be quite useful. This inadequacy is one of the problems involved in changing the mode of inference as mentioned at the end of Chapter 6. Collecting such fragmented data from individuals not only strongly restricts what can be said about individuals, but also ultimately restricts what usefully can be said about groups.

Finally, in examining the relationship of the packaging system and the results, there is the question of the length of the testing period. Given NAEP's limited intentions in terms of group testing and its limited concern about the costs of omitting data on individuals, it is not surprising that NAEP decided to test within no more than a single fifty-minute classroom period. For one thing there was a practical and, therefore, political gain from this decision since there would be minimal interruption of school routines. Surely there might be reasons why NAEP might not have wanted to go to a two-day testing period similar to that employed in Project TALENT. (During the first meetings in 1963 and 1964, John Flanagan of Project TALENT strongly suggested to the Assessment's backers that the Assessment would be much more useful if it measured individual educational progress, in depth, over time, as well as measuring group performance. But there was no deliberated response to his suggestion.) A more realistic and complex concept of what knowledge is and how educational research might proceed would have produced an optimal testing time that provided hard data for individuals as well as groups.

NAEP tends to obscure these serious issues by making a link between the conventional testing and ranking of children and its decision to have short testing periods. Again and again NAEP promises not to gather enough material to rank students against each other. Its publications repeatedly observe that the Assessment is measuring performance on exercises, not measuring and scoring the performance of individuals.

> Package number 1 for use with age seventeen assessees in assessment year 01 contained eleven exercises. Of these eleven there were seven multiple-choice Science exercises, three free-response Citizenship exercises, and one essay Writing exercise. If one attempted to add scores from seven Science exercises, plus three Citizenship exercises, plus one Writing exercise, the total score would have no meaning. But the purpose of National Assessment is to report separately for each exercise, not to report a score for an individual assessee. Therefore, the project was free to package the exercises in any convenient fashion that added up to about forty or forty-five or fifty minutes of assessment time for each assessee.[5]

Surely, the attempt to move away from norm-referenced testing did not require such an extreme fragmentation of the data collected from individuals. Even if students had been tested for several hours, there was no possibility that they would be ranked against each other since there were so few students involved at any given age level within any given school. In reality, NAEP's

---

[5] *General Information Yearbook*, 02-GIY (Denver: ECS, 1972), p. 34.

objective of avoiding the norm referencing of students has no inherent bearing on the length of time during which individuals might be assessed.

8

REPORTING THE
ASSESSMENT RESULTS

The potential uses and abuses of the National Assessment results depend critically on how they are reported. Naturally, this dependency can be considered only after analyzing the complex issues discussed in the preceding chapters. The *quality* of the results available to be reported is affected by the strengths and limitations in the selection of subject areas, the delineation of subject area objectives and subobjectives, the development of exercises, the measurement of descriptive background characteristics, and the use of a matrix sampling system, packages, and short testing periods. These decisions, plus several other types of factors, including the technical limits of social science, the politics of federal-state-local relations, economic constraints, time restrictions, the intentions of the Assessment's original leaders, poor management planning, and mediocre service by many of the major contracting groups, have led to very serious weaknesses in the results that the Assessment has obtained to date. Beyond these weaknesses, several developments in the larger society have further limited the utility of the results. (These developments are considered later in this chapter.)

But given the results that it has, regardless of their limitations, NAEP is obliged to make decisions as to how they might best be reported. The primary audiences for the NAEP reports, according to NAEP's own definition of purpose, include politicians, the lay public, scholars, and educators. The intent is to convey results in ways that are "understandable, meaningful, and useful." [1] To accomplish these ends, NAEP's efforts produced several detailed reports containing exercises and results in the five subject areas tested during the first two years of operation,[2] a variety of summary reports published in NAEP magazines and newsletters, several articles written by NAEP staff members or consultants to appear in non-NAEP publications, and releases distributed by the NAEP public relations office to professional associations and newspapers throughout the country.

Analysis of virtually all the NAEP publications and a sampling of mass media articles on the Assessment indicate that none of the report formats, with the potential exception of the several detailed reports, can be used as a basis for major research or policy guidelines in improving education. Clearly, the more popular reporting formats are intended in part to draw people's interest to the basic, more detailed reports, since the popular reports, though thoughtfully edited, in and of themselves are unquestionably of little substance. Beyond stimulating interest in the longer reports, they can be justified only as having some very generalized symbolic value, in that they might convince the public and concerned politicians of NAEP's purpose and the fact that education is in some way evaluating itself and becoming accountable.

But herein lies a major irony. The Assessment results were meant to *inform* the lay public and relevant politicians about the status of educational achievement in the society, but some also expected the results to assist in determination of specific policies, voting of school budgets, etc. Again and again, despite Tyler's and Tukey's more humble view of what the Assessment

---

[1] *General Information Yearbook*, 02-GIY (Denver: ECS; 1972), p. 60.

[2] Assessment Reports:

No. 1	Science: National Results	July 1970
No. 2a	Citizenship: National Results—Partial	July 1970
No. 2	Citizenship: National Results	November 1970
No. 3	Writing: National Results	November 1970
No. 4	Science: Group Results A	April 1970
No. 5	Writing: Group Results A	April 1971
No. 6	Citizenship: Group Results A	July 1971
No. 7	Science: Group Results D	December 1971
No. 8	Writing: National Results—Writing Mechanics	
02–R–20	Reading: Selected Exercises	May 1972
02–GIY	Reading and Literature (*General Information Yearbook*)	May 1972

would produce, ECAPE and then NAEP publications promised that policy guidance would be a major function. Yet the several substantive, detailed reports are quite unhelpful reading for either the lay public or politicians. If they are to be useful to anyone it will be to curriculum developers and perhaps certain other education specialists. The public and inquisitive politicians are once again left with an implicit caveat that "only the experts can really understand." On the other hand, reading the popularized reports on the exercise results, which provide neither an overall sense of the levels of functional literacy nor specific data that can lead to educational changes, is much like flipping through a pile of unrelated curiosities—a form of Ripley's "Believe-It-or-Not," in which all the surprises have been edited out.

One more reservation must be expressed about the more popularized reports of the Assessment findings. Again, ironically, it seems that if they have any major potential whatever, it is likely to be their potential for misinterpretation. The more generalized the level of statements about the results, the more likely their meaning is to be misconstrued or even purposefully misrepresented. This issue was considered briefly in Chapter 6; later in this chapter it will become clear that concern on this count is grounded in actual events and is shared by some leaders at NAEP. The general superfluity of the more popular reports means that NAEP's utility must rely heavily on the more detailed reports that NAEP has published. Yet to date there is little evidence that these reports contain findings that are both new and sufficiently detailed to be of specific use to researchers, curriculum specialists, or teachers' professional groups working in specific subject-matter areas. Moreover, the detailed reports have not supplied enough data to provide the overall conception of a census of levels of educational achievement, much less a gross indicator of the society's level of educational achievement. Finally, there has been considerably less interest in the reports than was initially expected, as evidenced by numerous in-house memoranda attempting to figure out how to cultivate such interest. In order to increase the potential utility of the results, NAEP changed its reporting format between the first and second years of the Assessment and described the change as follows:

> The results for the year 01 assessment (Science, Citizenship, and Writing) have been reported in what might be called a "phase" format. Each phase volume treated a different aspect of the results for all the exercises within a given subject area. For example, within the subject area Science, the phase I report gave the national results for all the Science exercises; the phase IIA report represented results for regions of the country, the sexes, and sizes

of community; and the phase IIB report presented results for color, levels of parental education, and sizes-and-types of community. A major disadvantage of this format is that it is difficult for our readers to follow the results for specific exercises through the various phases.

Because we feel that National Assessment results should be easily understood and both meaningful and useful to educators and other concerned persons, we have adopted an alternative reporting format with the following qualities: (1) the data are presented in a larger number of relatively small volumes so that the reader will not be overwhelmed by the sheer size of a report; (2) each volume contains exercises which cluster together in a way that is meaningful to educators and scholars in the relevant subject area; and (3) along with each exercise the reports give all data—national and group—relevant to that exercise.

We believe that the clusters of exercises most meaningful to educators and scholars are what we call *themes*. A theme is a set of exercises which share a common idea but which may require diverse behavioral responses. For each subject area in the year 02 assessment, there is a summary volume which provides all information specifically relevant to the subject area (including the themes and objectives for the area) and the general trends that appear in the data. A separate volume is devoted to each theme in which the data for the specific exercises within the theme are given along with a summary of the data for the theme.[3]

While it is apparent that the inadequacies of the phase format of reporting have been significant, it is not altogether clear how substantial the gains will be with the thematic reporting format. At least in the first attempt to do it, the development of the themes around which exercises are clustered is necessarily *post hoc*, presenting problems of validity and disproportionate measurement. Staff members at NAEP are presently debating the disadvantages and advantages of this approach. In addition to problems of format, NAEP has had to deal with two other major policy questions concerning the reporting of results, both of which have created serious blocks to their use. The first question involves the percentage of the Assessment exercises and data that NAEP releases in its detailed reports and more popular documents. The second pertains to the society's shifting knowledge, standards, and interests and the difficulties of NAEP's attempt to describe the results without attributing causality to background factors that correlate with particular levels of performance. Obviously, NAEP has more control over the first area than the second.

---

[3] *General Information Yearbook,* 02-GIY, pp. i–ii.

DECIDING WHICH RESULTS TO DISCLOSE

NAEP has expended a great deal of energy in deliberating, designing, and implementing an exercise release system, but there is strong evidence that much of this energy has been spent unnecessarily because the basic premises of a partial release system were not fully analyzed by those responsible. The policy for the Assessment's first round was that one-third to one-half of the exercises and their related results would be released in the detailed NAEP reports. Given the fact that the first-round results—in Science, Citizenship, and Writing—were received with a mixture of disinterest and criticism because they did not provide enough information within any particular subject area or in terms of particular objectives and subobjectives, NAEP altered its policies in the second round so that "at least 50 percent but less than 100 percent" of the round-two exercises in Reading and Literature would be released.

The procedures for selecting the exercises to be reported are quite complex. Their basic aspects are described as follows:

> The primary purpose for developing a selection procedure was to insure that, although exercises would be selected randomly, they would nonetheless be representative of the total pool of exercises available. With such a procedure we can be reasonably certain that a report provides coverage across objectives and across all population group differences to the extent that such coverage exists in the entire pool of exercises assessed.
>
> It is critical in a report that includes only a portion of the exercises assessed that we have exercises which represent the entire spectrum of data. For example, there should be exercises for which males do much better than females, exercises which show no difference between males and females, and exercises for which the females do much better than the males. Our selection procedure enables us to achieve this kind of representative coverage for each group, i.e., males, females, NE, SE, etc.
>
> After a computer randomly selects exercises for reporting, we fill whatever gaps remain by looking for exercises which will provide us with an example of the type of data which is not in the set of exercises to be released. For example, if none of the exercises that were selected for release represent a large female advantage, one or more exercises are selected specifically because they show a large female advantage. This systematic selection proved necessary for the year 02 Reading report but not for Literature.
>
> Using systematic selection of 10 to 15 percent of the exercises, we are able to identify a set of exercises which are truly represen-

tative of the subject area being reported. In year 02, the selected exercises amounted to about 50% of all exercises.[4] Since the exercises *not* selected for release during the first assessment cycle are withheld to be released during the second assessment cycle, those exercises designated for immediate release and those withheld for later release should be equivalent in two ways. First, both sets of exercises must be equivalent in their coverage of objectives, themes, exercise formats and/or any other relevant characteristics. Second, both sets of exercises must be statistically equivalent; i.e., they must have similar representation across the entire spectrum of percentages of success. This latter requirement prevents currently reporting, for example, that girls can read charts better than boys (on the basis of the released exercises) and then reporting five years hence that boys can read charts better than girls (on the basis of the unreleased or withheld exercises). The same consideration applies to all reporting categories.

In order to insure the necessary equivalence National Assessment selects exercises for release in two steps. First, we group the exercises by their nonstatistical characteristics (objective, theme, format, etc.). Then within each of these groupings, we attempt to achieve statistical equivalence by developing an index which reflects group differences and can be used to form sets of similar exercises.[5]

These partial release plans have several important shortcomings, however, including restricted report coverage, exercise obsolescence, planning rigidities, and, despite the efforts mentioned in the quotation above, nonequivalence of the exercise pools between and within cycles. We do not discuss these shortcomings here, partly because NAEP has already expressed some inhouse awareness of them, and partly because there is a more fundamental issue which decreases their importance.

The original decision to design some form of partial release plan was based on security concerns. Various educational interest groups feared that teachers throughout the nation would teach to the test and that this would lead to the creation of a national curriculum. To some extent NAEP set up the partial release plan as a response to these fears. But more important to the decision was NAEP's own alarm that full exercise release would invalidate the Assessment—if the nation's students knew the answers to the exercises because they had been taught the exercises, the Assessment's usefulness as a census of

---

[4] *General Information Yearbook,* 02-GIY, pp. 43–44.

[5] *General Information Yearbook,* 02-GIY, p. 85.

knowledge would be undermined. Among other problems, over time the schools within the NAEP sample might do better and become unrepresentative of the nation.

Under the NAEP system, however, it is absurd for any particular teacher to "teach to the test." Given the sample design and the packaging system, only a small number of students within any given school is tested at any of the three in-school age levels. A teacher has no idea of which of his or her students will be tested and, therefore, would have to prepare them all. Furthermore, teachers would have to prepare all these students to answer several hundred exercises in the subject areas to be assessed, since they will not know beforehand which exercises will be in the specific packages to be administered. And, finally, the results of student responses would not be known anyway to either the local teacher, the child's parents, or the local school administration, and would not be reported nationally by identifying the local district.

There has been much continuing debate at NAEP about alternative exercise release policy, which would ease if not eliminate several of the existing problems, including inadequate report coverage, exercise obsolescence, and planning rigidities. The problem of nonequivalence between cycles must still be dealt with, but it seems certain that a combination of selection from past exercises and the use of new exercises could provide a sensible balance between the demands of comparability and flexibility. One aspect of the 100 percent release option requiring further study is whether 100 percent of the *assessed* exercises should be released or whether 100 percent of the *entire pool* of exercises, including unused exercises without results, should be released. In most subject areas the pool of exercises available is larger than the actual number used in the Assessment, although more selective judgments about which exercises are really valid measures might reduce this surplus sharply.

In any case, whether or not the entire pool or just the assessed exercises are released, the 100 percent disclosure would be of substantial help to states that are establishing assessment systems and wish to use Assessment exercises for economic reasons and in some cases for comparability. At present the pool of NAEP exercises that states can select from is relatively small, especially when the imperfections of many of the exercises are taken into account. Also, some states are now independently paying the NAEP contractors to develop exercises for them; in some instances it appears that they are paying for exercises that are essentially no more than recast versions of many of the unreleased NAEP exercises. Insofar as this practice might become quite widespread as more states develop their accountability systems, the states could avail themselves of substantial economies if the NAEP pool were fully disclosed. Of course, there would be additional costs involved in NAEP's updating the pools, handling the related clearinghouse functions, and disseminating the exercises, but these might be considerably less than for each of the fifty states to establish its own exercise pool independently.

Another issue deserves attention here. While the apprehension that teachers will teach to the test appears to be completely unfounded, the possibility remains that teachers might teach *from* the test. This, of course, is true whether 50 percent or 75 percent of all the exercises are released. And it is likely to be even more the case if states decide to use the same exercises to a large extent. Within each of the subject areas, the objectives, subobjectives, and exercises might to some degree become curricula for some local systems, some states—perhaps even nationally, although it is difficult to say whether overall this would produce major changes from what is now being taught in America's schools. While some critics might say that such a development would be deleterious because it might *lead* the schools into new areas, either unwillingly or unwittingly, other critics would argue the contrary position, that because of its least common denominator quality, the Assessment would become a drag on educational change by too strongly affirming the importance of what is now being done in the schools.

It is these issues that make the earlier discussion of the Assessment's subject-matter objectives so important. Should the Assessment be testing performance on the actual practices of the schools, on the stated goals of the schools, or on the normative goals as defined by the Assessment leaders and educational experts? If they are to evaluate either the schools' actual practices or stated goals, which schools should be considered representative? If, as suggested in Chapter 4, the consensus model of defining objectives is relatively vacuous, is it possible for NAEP or a national body to develop a system of objectives, or a process for defining local objectives, which takes appropriate account of educational, cultural, and ethnic diversity? Perhaps more important, if a few NAEP leaders do not see the objectives as viable expressions of some imagined unitary American values, what are the consequences of their taking a traditional testing and measurement position that the *exercises themselves* should be viewed as objectives? How many of the Assessment's exercises can really withstand scrutiny as specific things that students should be taught or know how to do?

Two additional related comments must be made. First, from NAEP's internal point of view, if a majority of its leadership really believes that the delineation of subject areas was wise, that the objectives and subobjectives are derived from a valid process, and that the exercises are good measures of the objectives, then it should support their dissemination without worrying about whether or not some teachers and school systems will teach from the test. The question of how many exercises should be released has little, if any, negative bearing on this judgment, because some may teach from 50 percent of the exercises, which might produce a more undesirable slant in curricula than would a release of all the assessed exercises or the entire pool. Stated differently, if NAEP really has faith that what it measures are desirable educational achievements, then what would be the harm if students actually learned to perform well on such measures? Thus, in a roundabout way the Assessment's objectives and exercises could in the long run become one of the many causes of the very educational achievement which the Assessment measures, but from USOE's point of view, at least, this would not thwart its primary efforts—to measure and improve educational progress.

A second and final remark is necessary on the 100 percent disclosure plan. Unfortunately, given the inadequacies of many of the exercises, their loose fit with the objectives and subobjectives, and the limited amount of hypothesis-generating data that comes out of the sampling and packaging system, it is doubtful that even doubling the numbers of released exercises will really increase the utility of the results for serious educational researchers. This is especially true since the released and unreleased exercises are quite comparable as described in the quotation above from the *General Information Yearbook*. This comparability suggests that most of the inadequacies that have shown up in the released exercises are likely to show up in approximately the same proportions among the unreleased exercises. This reservation is not intended to negate the idea of the 100 percent release, however, which would not only save NAEP a variety of selection problems, but would also help mitigate other inadequacies of the partial release system, and might provide extra data that would indirectly help states and local schools develop both their accountability systems and curricula.

REPORTING THE RESULTS: DESCRIPTION VERSUS EXPLANATION AND PREDICTION

The issue of whether NAEP's reporting categories are descriptive or explanatory and predictive has become increasingly problematic. As discussed in Chapter 6, Tyler and Tukey saw the Assessment as measuring national levels of educational achievement and identifying pockets of excellence, average performance, and low performance. While they expected to use various measurement categories to find out *where* these pockets were, they did not expect to use these same categories to explain *why* the pockets were where they were, or to predict where they would be in the future.

Despite Tyler's and Tukey's early and continuing humility in this regard, and despite clear technical and political limits on the utility of explanatory analyses, various important developments in recent years have further clouded these inherently hazy distinctions.

As of 1970, NAEP's position on the issue of interpretation of the results was ambivalent, but candidly so:

> It has long been apparent that National Assessment must develop multiple reports, of differing types and natures. Detailed, voluminous reports of every exercise selected for reporting in a given year must be prepared. These will be the basic National Assessment reports. Such reports, however, do not lend themselves to immediate or "obvious" conclusions. Someone, hopefully many different "someones," must pore over and sort out the results in a fashion that is most meaningful. Whether or not this latter step is one that National Assessment itself should attempt, or whether it should be left to the scientist, to the classroom teacher, to the school board member is a moot question. Some people feel that National Assessment should provide information only, leaving all interpretation up to the user of the results. Others feel that some attempt at interpretation is necessary, if only to posit various hypotheses that are tenable, unless one wishes to run the risk of gross misinterpretations. This issue has not been settled yet. As is often the case a middle ground may well be found.[6]

There are two particularly important aspects of the above statement. The first is that one can conceive of many types of interpretations that might flow from the NAEP results, not just those that would be made along the dimension of description versus explanation and prediction. The second is that NAEP, as in so many other instances, is candid about the dilemmas it faces, but expects to resolve them adequately through middle-ground compromises and often fails to do so.

NAEP's wording indicates that it knows its reports do not lend themselves to immediate or "obvious" conclusions. This is partly due to the many inadequacies of the data and the reporting system as discussed throughout earlier sections of this report. But it is also due to other factors.

First, there has been an unanticipated diminution of interest in NAEP's

---

[6] *What Is National Assessment?* (Denver: ECS, 1968; reprinted, 1970), pp. 37–38.

measurement of outcomes since the Assessment was conceived in 1963. The effect of the several major surveys of educational achievement and inequality (as mentioned in Chapter 6) has been to make most of NAEP's findings quite unsurprising. If released between 1963 and 1965, many of NAEP's subsequent findings comparing performance between and among groups would have generated great excitement, but after Coleman and a large variety of more impressionistic books on educational inequality, NAEP's major achievement findings had become relatively common knowledge. (Though this is not true of the Citizenship results and of various process-oriented exercises in the other subject areas, NAEP has not seen fit to invite interpretations by major sociologists and political scientists, perhaps partly because the validity of so many of the exercises is questionable.)

But, then, even when NAEP does come up with findings that are somewhat different from those of well-known studies, there is general agreement that the NAEP data is too soft to accomplish anything but perhaps raise some new broad questions. An example of this problem appears in an interpretive article in the March 1972 issue of *American Education:*

> The specific data show black students, those in the inner city, and those whose parents have the least education all tending toward catching up with national performance in science as they increase in age.
>
> For example, black nine-year-olds had a median of 14.5 percent fewer exercises correct than the median for nine-year-olds in the nation as a whole, but black seventeen-year-olds turned in a showing only 11.8 percent below national performance.
>
> Those familiar with the results of nationally standardized achievement tests released by big-city school systems are likely to find this startling. The typical pattern from national achievement testing is one of widening gaps between the progress of black and other students living in economically depressed city areas and those who live in more favorable circumstances.
>
> Does the contrary trend in the National Assessment data mean these black students and others are learning more than previously believed?
>
> Several of the nation's distinguished social scientists who were asked to comment on this trend suggested that the sampling and statistical procedures now being used by National Assessment are inadequate as a basis for drawing definite conclusions. Robert J. Havighurst, professor of education at the University of Chicago, noted, for example, that there is no way of telling for sure whether the tests for each age group were equally difficult. In addition, by age seventeen many less able students may have dropped out of

school, and Assessment officials admittedly have been less successful than they had hoped in including dropouts in the seventeen-
year-olds' sample. Therefore the improvement of black seventeen-
year-olds could be merely a reflection of their higher dropout rate.
Havighurst and others concluded, however, that it is probably
safe to say that from ages nine to thirteen the performance of
these groups does not decline.

Even if this evidence is only suggestive, it is still contrary to
expectations set by national achievement test data.[7]

This is a simple illustration of the general problem we considered in Chapter 6 in the discussion of whether NAEP should begin measuring more input
data. NAEP continues to face the problem. *Weaknesses in the educational findings
have helped to diminish interest in interpreting the Assessment's achievement results, and
concomitantly they have increased the extent to which emphasis is placed by NAEP and
others on the Assessment's findings with regard to subgroups of the population, as well as
the extent to which the distinction between description and explanation has become important. Instead of the emphasis being on what the Assessment's implications are for education
and particular subject areas, it has largely focused on the comparative performance of
subgroups and why they perform differently.*

Still another factor concerning historical context has complicated these
developments. The re-emergence of the classic debate regarding genetic differences and their effects on intelligence and educational achievement has
significantly altered the societal context in which NAEP's reporting categories are interpreted. As Keppel assumed at the outset, the Assessment's reporting by racial background might have been expected to lead to recognition of inequality of opportunity and then to major educational or social
reforms; while some clearly interpret the results in this same framework today, the social and political climate is such that there are many who would
interpret low black performance as an inevitability and would argue that the
schools cannot be held responsible for the unsuccessful education of poor
black children.

NAEP enters this "explanatory" realm in its milder forms by publishing
outside interpretations such as the following one from the supervising principal of Pocantico Hills, New York:

---

[7] Hope Justus, "Findings in National Assessment Science Survey," *American
Education,* vol. 8, no. 2, p. 9, March 1972.

Someone asked if on the basis of this report it was possible to say whether Johnny can read and I'd say the answer is yes and no. If Johnny is Susie and she lives in the Northeast and she comes from an affluent suburb and her parents are well-educated, the chances are that she probably can read. If Johnny is a he, if he lives somewhere in the vast Southeast and he's Black and he lives inside a big city and he suffers from the disadvantages that many Americans do—poverty and ill health—he probably can't read very well despite whatever he has going for him.

That may be jumping to conclusions but I say that because I think this is part of the problem that is revealed in the report— and dramatically so—that it's more than just the schools and more than simply teachers and teaching of reading. I think it's a problem in American society that we're putting our dollars in places other than places we might put them. . . . I think we have to look into the homes of those who can't read, into their neighborhoods and into the kinds of problems they deal with on a twenty-four-hour-a-day basis, seven days a week and that are insurmountable and that make the teaching of reading into something in which they have no interest.

I think this report provides us with the information everyone's been clamoring for about where the problem is. Now, more importantly, what do we do about it.[8]

At still other times the interpretation of NAEP results moves much more directly toward causal inferences, or statements reinforcing the opinions of those inclined toward fatalistic positions because of the IQ debate.

The Hope Justus article quoted earlier contains these remarks:

This color division presents results in a fashion indicating, for example, that at age thirteen more black children than non-black exhibit a curiosity and questioning attitude about the world around them. *It suggests that along some lines of questioning color seems to make little or no difference:* About equal percentages of black and non-black thirteen-year-olds know that giraffes have long necks as a result of natural selection. Likewise, both groups show up about equal in having acquired some common bits of misinformation. . . . [Emphasis added.][9]

While raising the suggestion that color per se makes a difference in some

---

[8] Dr. Richard Montesi (supervising principal, Pocantico Hills, New York; lecturer, University of Connecticut; and former classroom teacher) in *National Assessment Newsletter,* vol. 5, p. 4, June–July 1972.

[9] Justus, op. cit., p. 7.

exercise results, Justus goes on to offer these patronizing (and perhaps malicious, in the case of the giraffe example) items of evidence about occasional instances when blacks do equally well or better. Though the article ends with the presentation of an environmentalist position that suggests much might be done to enhance the educational achievement of blacks, the section just preceding the end summarizes the "limitations" of blacks, and also provides a gross contrast with affluent whites.

> With regard to the kinds of exercises in which various groups perform best and poorest, the results established the clearest patterns for blacks and affluent suburban youngsters. They show that blacks generally do best on exercises dependent on daily experience and common knowledge and on certain straightforward tasks that require them to do something with relatively simple pieces of equipment.
>
> For example, about 96 percent of both black and non-black nine-year-olds can do an exercise that requires them to balance one weight by hanging a second weight on a beam balance. And again, the percentage of black thirteen-year-olds who know that teeth are brushed to keep them from decaying is about the same as that in other groups.
>
> Black performance lags the most on exercises that require use and interpretation of complicated data, use of sophisticated equipment, and knowledge of difficult scientific words or facts remote from daily life. That manipulation of abstractions proves particularly difficult for blacks shows up clearly in their differing performances under the four science objectives. Exercises intended to find out whether students possess the skills and abilities necessary to engage in the processes of science were precisely the ones on which they displayed their poorest showing.
>
> For example, only half as many black thirteen-year-olds as thirteen-year-olds in other classifications can use a graph and tabular data to determine the daily food needs of a dog. In contrast, youngsters attending the most affluent suburban schools tended to make their strongest showing in comparison with the rest of the nation in just this area—application of relatively abstract principles and the use of textbook knowledge probably learned in the classroom.[10]

NAEP has been trying to deal with the changing societal context to some extent, and to take steps to minimize misinterpretation. But as NAEP itself predicted in the 1970 statement quoted earlier, it has attempted to resolve the

---

[10] Ibid., p. 10.

problem of description versus explanation by finding some middle ground. The result to date has been a muddled policy.

At the very beginning of the detailed report on Science Results as described by sex, region, and size of community, NAEP undertakes to clarify its position:

> There is a kind of interpretation that should never be made on the basis of the sort of figures given in this report. The fact that figures reflect Southeast performance or Big City performance does not mean that the performances thus reflected have arisen precisely from living in the Southeast or in a Big City, or from the attitudes, techniques, facilities and staffs of the school system involved.
>
> In particular, just what happens in a region involves other things than that region's schools. Larger fractions of the children in some regions belong to a particular size-of-community group. Thus effects due only to size of community can appear to be regional differences. Larger or smaller fractions of the parents in some regions have particular amounts of education. Thus effects due only to parental education can appear to be regional differences. And so on. Migration from one region or size of community to another can further complicate the picture. There are such difficulties, some of which we know how to adjust for, and some of which we do not.
>
> It is important for us to distinguish between an interest in causes and an interest in what the present situation is. To guide readers who want to think about causes, numbers usually have to be found by looking at (or considering) combinations of several classifications. Such numbers will be more appropriate for thinking about causes than the sort of number given in the present report, although they may still be far from perfect. (Such numbers will be given in a later report.) To guide readers who want to compare today's situations, as they stand, say region versus region or one size of community versus another, it is appropriate to look at regions separately or at sizes of communities separately, which has been done in this present report. This distinction between causes and present situations is important. Readers should be careful to understand it and then keep it in mind.[11]

Here NAEP asks the reader to be especially alert to the distinction between description and the understanding of causes. Yet at the same time NAEP itself continues to misunderstand or misrepresent that distinction. It makes

---

[11] *Report 4, 1969–1970 Assessment* (Denver: ECS, 1972).

the unnecessary point that *total* causality should never be derived from a single classification. The example used—that region by itself cannot be taken as *the* cause of differences in educational achievement—is depressingly obvious and oversimplified. But more seriously, the overall presentation and the example encourage loose inferences that most classifications or combinations of classifications below the regional level do have simple and direct—and easily discernible—cause and effect relations with educational achievement; for instance, the sentence "Thus effects *due only to size of community* can appear to be regional differences." (Emphasis added.) It is startling that NAEP would suggest that it knows, or will soon know, to what extent educational achievement effects are *due only* to community size. No research group has developed data or analysis techniques sophisticated enough really to answer such a question.

To make matters even more confusing, the statement of the Report's limitations then goes on to say that one really cannot expect to learn too much about causes in terms of single classifications, when compared with what one can learn from combinations of several classifications. NAEP notes that the information obtained from such combinations may still be far from perfect, but goes on to promise that they will be published in a forthcoming report.

This discussion might seem unnecessarily prolonged and detailed, but it is necessary. NAEP's statements, and more importantly its policies on the issues at hand, are quite significant and must be clearly understood. In the statement quoted above, it is clear that NAEP, in 1971, decided to try to ride the thin edge of this political and intellectual razor blade: It simply states that understanding causes is one thing and describing the present situation is another, but then it goes on to imply that it will eventually do both.

Clearly this dilemma has been an explicit problem for NAEP, and a year later, in the Introduction to the *General Information Yearbook,* 02-GIY, the statement of limitations was largely rewritten to come closer to saying what NAEP is actually capable of doing:

> When the data show that a group has achieved either above or below the nation as a whole, one must exercise *great caution* in attributing causation to these obtained differences. National Assessment is not intended to provide reasons for differences; its purpose is to describe such differences if they exist. Many factors may affect an individual's ability to give acceptable responses to exercises in the assessed subject areas. Consider, for example, a hypothetical group whose achievement is well above the national average. Most members of the group may attend schools which

have excellent physical facilities and high quality faculties, belong to high socio-economic families, have parents with a high level of education, come from homes with many reading materials and so on. All these factors could contribute to the group's high level of achievement while membership in the group itself may contribute very little or nothing.

The name of a group is merely a categorical label. When we look at the data for a given group, therefore, we cannot say that any difference in achievement between that group and the nation as a whole is attributable solely to membership in that group. In other words, a group must not be construed as necessarily being *the* cause or even being *a* cause for the comparatively high or low achievement of that group as compared to the nation as a whole.

Often a disproportionately large percentage of the members of a group of interest are also members of particular groups defined by other factors. All these factors may contribute to the group's high (or low) level of achievement. The data obtained from these groups do not allow one to evaluate the effectiveness of the educational process on these groups apart from the advantageous (or debilitating) factors. A statistical procedure called balancing adjusts for the disproportionate distribution of group members in other categories or groups for which there are adequate data available. This procedure gives the achievement data for the group in question that would have been obtained had the members of the group been distributed proportionately across these other categories or groups. National Assessment data, balanced for disproportionate representation, are presented in a special research volume. Again *great caution* must be exercised in interpreting the balanced data. The balanced data still reflect many extraneous factors not assessed by National Assessment and, therefore, are still not "pure" measures of the impact of membership in the group in question. Even with balanced data, a group must not be construed as necessarily being *the* cause or even as being *a* cause for the differential achievement between that group and the nation as a whole.[12]

In this case, NAEP clearly declares its intentions and capacities: "National Assessment is not intended to provide reasons for differences; its purpose is to describe such differences if they exist." It then describes its plans to balance the data, to control particular variables, and to report performance levels for combined classifications that are underrepresented in the sample. So far, the intent is still clear, as is the fact that if NAEP has interesting results to report,

---

[12] *General Information Yearbook*, 02-GIY, pp. v–vi.

the balancing and combining of classifications will help to describe relatively precisely the relationships among the classifications and the exercise results. But then, once again, NAEP slips back into extended remarks which blur its own distinction between description and explanation. In Chapter XII of the *General Information Yearbook*, 02-GIY, NAEP describes the balancing system in more detail:

THE MERITS AND WEAKNESSES OF ADJUSTMENT
(INCLUDING BALANCING)

The educational administrator wants to make comparisons between groups, to find out who is learning more and who less in hopes of being able to improve performance in the lagging groups. Indeed, he would like to go further and find out what factors to change and how much changes in these factors would strengthen the educational achievement of the students affected. For example, when we find that boys know less about the reproductive system of both sexes than do girls, this raises at once the question of strengthening the education of boys. Inevitably the desire is to subdivide the country into finer and finer groups so as to make comparisons between subgroups that have "everything alike" except the variable being studied.

In other words, we search for causes of the differences. Unfortunately, we cannot have "everything alike" in social problems and rarely in physical problems either, and so we are not actually able to carry out the precise programs. But half a loaf may be better than none, and so we may carry out that part of the program that seems feasible. We subdivide by important variables and make comparisons in performance among groups.

One thing that happens is that as we introduce several variables the number of subdivisions grows like a product. For example, if we have 5 variables with 2, 3, 5, 7, and 4 categories respectively, we have $2 \times 3 \times 5 \times 7 \times 4 = 840$ subgroups, and a sample of 8,400 people would give an average of only 10 per subgroup. Naturally many subgroups would be empty and many fuller than 10, but it will still be hard, if not impossible, to make comparisons among subgroups, for most will contain too few people.

We might try to avoid these sparse cells by only looking at factors one at a time.

However, children in the extreme affluent suburb tend, more than children in the extreme inner city, to have better educated parents. Because of this lack of balance, part of the difference between these two groups may be considered as growing out of the difference in parental education.

It is natural to ask, "What would the difference between these extreme types of community have been if the distribution of parental education, sex, color and region had been the same for both types of community referred to above?" Were it possible to rearrange the world to equate these distributions for each type of community, the effects upon our nation and its schools would be profound. Such rearrangement is not possible. It is usually appropriate to think of such balanced results as reflecting the differences we would see in the absence of masquerading by the other four factors. We can be reasonably sure the balanced results do a much better job than the unadjusted results of reflecting such differences.

Still another question concerns the combination of factors. The performance of a given group may be found to differ, depending upon subgroupings on other variables. Thus, the effect associated with extreme affluent suburbs may be different in the Northeast and the Southeast. Or the effect associated with sex may be somewhat different for Blacks and Whites. Such interactive differences may be of importance; balancing does not adjust for them.

It is natural to ask whether this or any such method of analysis can help us. To some extent they can aid, to some extent not. We cannot make up for cases we don't have but we may be able to supply approximate analyses that will come near to answering such a question as what is the effect of region of the country on performance when you control for size-and-type of community and several other variables. If the effect of region is substantially reduced by the analytical adjustment, we may be inclined to think that region is not in itself the cause of the raw differences as much as the other variables. One role of adjustment then is to help us make approximate comparisons and summaries that we cannot make by directly subdividing all the variables.

Elsewhere (see Foreword and chapter 8) we have many cautionary remarks about the dangers of misinterpreting the causative powers of given background variables, for they may be poorly measured and they may not mean what they say. For an example, from the field of warfare, in World War II the more fighter opposition bombers had, the closer to the target were the bombs. Why? Fighters didn't come up when the weather obscured the target. Such proxy variables, especially when their correct interpretation may be the absolute reverse of their obvious effect puts us in grave danger of making mistakes. We do not go further into that here.

Nothing but experimentation, if that, can serve to demonstrate what the actual effect of changes will be. We are, however, trying to get hints and insights from the data we have. Furthermore, if someone does have a causative model involving the variables National Assessment measures, he does have a chance to check it against these results.

We see then that the purpose of the analysis and adjustment is to help the data reveal information that they cannot give in their raw form. Aside from the dangers of misinterpretation, we have the political arguments for and against adjustment. First, against: if adjustment for background variables seems to reduce the differences between a group of the population and the national average, it has been argued that this tends to minimize the disadvantage of the group and, it is further argued, that adjustment should not be made. The direction of the effect of an adjustment is not necessarily one-way; adjustments can increase differences as well as decrease them. Those arguing against adjustment in the reduction case would presumably argue for it in the case of increased discrepancies.

A second argument favors adjustment. It argues that we must adjust for important variables (presuming that the adjustment will reduce effects) so that we show the potential of the disadvantaged group.

Clearly the people making the first and second argument want the same thing, to improve the position of the disadvantaged group, and of course, this is a national goal. Steps toward achieving such goals do depend on searching for causes and methods of improvement, on finding weak spots in a system and so on. We should, therefore, look at our data in every way we can for hints about how the system works and how to improve it. Analysis and adjustments are tools for doing this. The question is not whether to adjust or not, but, "What are the useful ways?" and "What do the variables mean?" "What further variables do we need to measure?" and "How shall we interpret the results?"

NAEP's philosophy of "half a loaf may be better than none" has no innate virtues to recommend it over a more direct and realistic statement that NAEP's purpose and its only really feasible potential—conceptually, economically, and politically—is that of description. *Balancing can be employed for the sake of more sophisticated description; but again it should not be confused as in the above quoted paragraphs with balancing for the sake of causal analysis.*

NAEP seems unable to say—in an era of great interest in causal relationships between inputs and outputs—that it does not have the data or the techniques necessary to accomplish conclusive and fruitful work in this area. Here we refer back to the observation of the Gilbert and Mosteller memorandum in Chapter 6. It is clear that NAEP is very unlikely to make pathbreaking progress in terms of identifying manipulable variables (especially school variables) that will lead to precise policy implications for either the federal government, state departments of education, or local school districts. One way for the Assessment to move toward fulfilling its own objectives and the society's expectations is by making those objectives and expectations much more patently realistic. Recognizing that an admission of more circumscribed utility might jeopardize federal support for the Assessment, it still seems obvious that NAEP's energy spent trying to do things it cannot do is really energy wasted, and that sooner or later society, and Congress in particular, is sure to understand what the Assessment can and cannot produce. NAEP itself should be among the first to recognize its own limitations, clarify its real potential, and concentrate its energies on fulfilling it. This and other related questions on the Assessment's utility are examined in more detail in the next chapter.

9

CONCLUSION:
PAST AND FUTURE
USES OF THE ASSESSMENT

There are many ways to ask the question, "What has the National Assessment accomplished?" One might inquire as to what uses can be made of its results. Are the results worth the more than *$25 million* that has been spent to obtain them? In coming years will they justify federal expenditures of several million dollars per year? In our judgment these and other important questions about what the Assessment has accomplished can be answered judiciously and gainfully only by taking a broader view. We must return to the typology of the Assessment's early objectives, as presented in Chapter 2, and consider which of these objectives have been achieved relatively successfully and which have not. In addition, we must consider any new objectives that have been added to NAEP's definition of its purposes.

Given the extensive evidence in Chapters 3 through 8 regarding the Assessment's many serious conceptual, technical, and procedural deficiencies, our consideration of a broader view of what has been accomplished might seem to be little more than an exercise in courtesy. But it is not. Trying to understand the Assessment's worth and its achievements requires taking into account all of its objectives. In the long run, even if the National Assessment ceases to exist, the attainment of some of its less publicized objectives may exercise major influence on American education, regardless of its performance on its more widely known objectives.

Below we review the original major objectives, in the reverse order of their presentation in Chapter 2. Reversing the order seems helpful because it allows us to move upwards from the most operational to the most emphasized and major objectives.

    E.   Operational Objectives

        12. To create an independent committee to manage the development of the Assessment.

        13. To develop widespread acceptance among the educational establishment so that the Assessment could gain access to school systems.

        14. To develop widespread political support so that the federal government would take over the funding of the Assessment, while at the same time assuring that representatives of state and local governments would not be too uneasy about the project being federally funded.

        15. To develop lists of educational objectives that would "fairly reflect the aims of American education" and serve as guides for the exercise writers.

As we have seen, the Assessment succeeded in achieving the first three of these important operational goals. Given the complexities of educational politics, attainment of objectives 13 and 14 is no minor feat. The expenditure of time, energy, and money involved was quite substantial, but the resulting success was essential to pursuit of any of the other objectives.

The detailed analysis of the Assessment's subject-matter objectives in Chapter 4 brings attention to serious shortcomings in the attempt to fulfill objective 15, when it is broadly defined. But if this objective is more narrowly construed, some significant successes are apparent. Considering the broader definition first, the consensual style of developing the subject-matter objectives may appear to "fairly reflect the aims of American education," but, as we have seen, in general the objectives reflect merely the least-common-denominator objectives that most people can agree on, to the neglect of any of the *deeply felt* aims held by various individuals and groups. When viewed in a narrower sense, however, objective 15 has produced some unexpected consequences of considerable positive significance. While most of the subject-matter objectives are quite conventional, those in the fields of Reading, Music, and Career and Occupational Development represent substantial improvements which could have propitious effects on educational planning at the local, state, and national levels. Though some of the original Assessment leaders viewed the delineation of subject-matter objectives merely as a device to help the exercise writers, in a few instances the objectives have turned out to be useful in their own right. As we show later, the dissemination of NAEP's objectives booklets to state departments of education and local school districts has now come to be seen as a NAEP *objective* in and of itself, at least by some NAEP leaders.

    D. Major Low-Profile Objectives

        9. To lead a movement away from relying solely on norm-referenced testing which discriminates among individuals and toward some form of objective- or criterion-referenced tests that assess how much an individual or group actually knows about a particular area of knowledge.

      10. To lead a movement away from current testing which relies largely on measuring knowledge in ways that overemphasize memorization and that underemphasize actual skills, understandings, and attitudes.

      11. To encourage new modes of testing that are better fitted to the kinds of information being gathered and the particular characteristics of the respondents.

The evidence in Chapter 5 indicates that NAEP employed an extremely narrow definition of criterion referencing, that it overlooked the implications of the basic theoretical concepts underlying criterion referencing, and that it did not really produce criterion-referenced exercises of any significance. Similarly, though with certain interesting exceptions, NAEP was generally unable to develop valid and reliable process exercises that could advance the measurement of skills, understandings, and attitudes.

But substantial evidence shows that, mixed with these procedural failures, NAEP's interest and ambitions in these directions—and its development of some successful new modes of testing—have exerted a potentially very significant impact on educational testing in general. In other words, while NAEP did not have the capacity to advance these new fields, it did help to convince many groups of the current limitations of relying so heavily on norm-referenced tests and narrowly defined cognitive measures. Interest is now widespread in finding more constructive and comprehensive measures of individual educational development. It is likely, however, that serious advances in this field will flow from small and stringently defined projects intended to accomplish these specific purposes, rather than from a more unwieldy and less economical operation such as the National Assessment. Of course, developing the measures without developing extensive interest in employing them would be unproductive, and so the fact that NAEP has encouraged such interest is of major note.

An additional low-profile objective of the National Assessment has been to evaluate the performance of young adults (twenty-six to thirty-five), a group that has never been tested in so comprehensive a way before. NAEP has succeeded in sampling and reaching this group, although as yet the data or the interpretations of it have not yielded especially interesting findings. Furthermore, NAEP has not taken advantage of this unusual opportunity to raise fundamental questions about how much of what is taught in school is forgotten by ages twenty-six to thirty-five. If retention of school-taught facts is quite low, perhaps the most basic premises of formal schooling should be seriously reconsidered.

C. Subordinate Objectives
   7. To promote concern about more meaningfully defining the nation's educational objectives.
   8. To provide comparative data to stimulate competition among the states and local communities (without encouraging invidious comparisons).

In considering objective 7, it is important to note again that the Assessment's objective booklets are attracting sizable interest from states and local districts that are planning assessments, from curriculum developers, and from some lay groups. On first examination, given the trend toward widely diffused and disparate uses of these objectives, and the Assessment's relatively facile consensual model of defining national educational objectives, it appears that NAEP has failed with regard to objective 7; and in fact, if one evaluates this in the terms on which NAEP expected to achieve it, by meaningfully defining national educational objectives, one must conclude that these efforts *have* failed.

But since the United States has no unified national school system, the task of defining nationwide educational objectives is manifestly difficult. It involves highly complex educational, cultural, and political questions: Who, if anyone, has the right or capacity to define national objectives? Should the objectives include only what actually is done in the schools, or should they be the stated *goals* of the schools, or should they be advanced normative objectives which some experts decide ought to be the goals of the nation's schools? The answer to this last query is crucial since different answers raise still other important issues. If the objectives are linked to the existing practice or goals of the schools, they have conservative tendencies, providing national sanction of the present. By contrast, if they are well ahead of existing practice and existing goals, students in many school systems are likely to perform especially poorly and it may well appear that state and local control is being eroded, even though some may believe that the new objectives are crucial if education is to become meaningful. Further, how can the development of national subject-matter objectives be reconciled with the development of diverse learning environments or any newly developing respect for educational and cultural pluralism?

Most of the proposals for determining national education objectives are basically centralized and consensual in their nature. For instance, John Goodlad suggests, "We need a national body of leading citizens whose primary purpose is to give continued attention to the formulation of educational aims. . . ."[1]

Philip Smith has proposed a similarly centralized group, but in this case comprised of leading professionals:

> . . . the problem of objectives for American schooling is a problem calling for highly competent professional resolution. . . . The determination of objectives that will give curricular force and other operational meaning to the central purpose in the years ahead calls for sophisticated theoretical, technical, and administrative decisions.[2]

This second proposal is closer to the quasiparticipatory model which the National Assessment used, letting contractors establish lists of objectives and then letting schoolpeople and prominent lay people review them. As we demonstrate in the next chapter, however, NAEP's consensual style of resolving conflicting educational objectives has its definite limitations if its findings are to guide policy decisions which in turn are meant to lead toward attainment of those objectives.

There remains the subtle possibility, nonetheless, that NAEP's present failure in this regard could lead to major progress. We will raise this point later, but for the moment we should note that the explicit lack of definitions of the nation's educational goals could in itself ultimately alter forms of governance and encourage more meaningful determination of these goals.

Judging NAEP's performance on objective 8—providing comparative data to stimulate competition among the states and local communities—is particularly exacting. Our opinion, as formulated in Chapter 6, is that NAEP's

---

[1] John Goodlad, *School Curriculum Reform in the United States* (New York: The Fund for the Advancement of Education, 1964), p. 81.

[2] "Objectives for American Education," in Stanley Blam and Gordon Swanson (eds.), *Educational Planning in the United States* (Itasca, Ill.: Peacock, 1969), p. 9.

primary backers did not have strong or consistent convictions that the National Assessment should collect data by states and local communities. When viewed in this way, one can maintain that NAEP has not failed at objective 8; instead, the evidence is that NAEP has played a fairly major role in encouraging states to set up assessment systems for comparing local school districts. The NAEP sampling model, the objectives booklets, some of the exercises, and some of the reporting techniques are being adopted (and adapted) by various states, and by some local districts.

If one views objective 8 in a more normative sense, though, it can be argued that NAEP's long-run utility to the nation in general, and to the Congress and USOE in particular, is severely restricted by its failure to collect *uniform* comparative data from all the states and a variety of representative local districts. But as suggested earlier, this interpretation too can be turned around to imply that having regional data might in some ways give the federal government an advantage by allowing it to develop goals and programs that need not be administered through either existing state departments of education or local school districts.

B.   Major Long-Term Objectives
   4.   To continue collecting the national data at regular intervals so that comparisons could be made over time concerning national levels of achievement, performance in various subject areas, and performance in various subgroups, vis-a-vis themselves and other subgroups. This would provide a census of educational progress in America.
   5.   To forestall the development of "less effective or misdirected" attempts at assessment. Some backers of the Assessment disapproved of plans for a California assessment and the national proposals of Admiral Hyman Rickover, both of which were less interested in reducing inequality than in separating elites from the average population so "excellence" could be pursued efficiently.
   6.   To make international comparisons possible once sampling and testing problems could be resolved.

Objective 5, "to forestall the development of 'less effective or misdirected' attempts at assessment," is also difficult, and is directly related to the foregoing discussion concerning objective 8. NAEP has certainly failed on objective 5 if one assumes the intent was to eliminate, or almost completely eliminate, "less effective or misdirected" attempts at assessment. Despite the National Assessment's many grave deficiencies, some of the state and local assessments being developed are clearly inferior in their conception, design, and implementation. In fact, if one major set of assessment recommendations from the ETS Center for Statewide Educational Assessment is any indication, the situation is likely to get worse in the future.[3]

If objective 5 was to eliminate such inferior models of assessment, then one might assume that the resolve in objective 8 was to collect uniform data for states and many local communities. It appears from the transcripts and related memoranda that NAEP's leaders may not have noticed the importance of the relationship between these two objectives.

On the other hand, if one takes objective 5 more literally, and more nominally, the intent was merely to forestall inferior and misdirected assessments. In this case, if NAEP's model, materials, or methods are better than someone else's, then NAEP is succeeding every time a state or locality adopts some aspect of the National Assessment program. Of course, this argument may be spurious. Given transference of scattered parts of the whole, maladaptation might be just as likely as functional adaptation.

Objective 6—to make international comparisons possible—cannot be judged because there has been no real attempt to achieve it. It is worth noting, however, that the IEA studies of educational achievement being conducted in twenty-two countries would seem to eliminate the need for America to prescribe the development of an international system.

It is also too soon to comment upon the achievement of objective 4—the development of a long-term census of educational progress in America. If the Assessment has any major potential for the future it is clearly in this area. But important questions remain to be asked about what the probable utility of such a census would be, especially given the present low returns and high costs. After the evidence presented in Chapters 3 through 8 it is difficult to support even the potential utility of such a census unless the present Assessment's conception and methods are radically revised. At this point we can return to the question, "What uses can be made of the Assessment results?"

We have seen that the Assessment has accomplished, or partly accomplished, several of its objectives. But now in considering its overall utility, we must distinguish between these objectives and its three *Major Short-Term Objectives*. Some of the objectives that have been achieved were largely operation-

---

[3] Nancy L. Bruno, Paul B. Campbell, and William H. Schabacker, *Statewide Assessment: Methods and Concerns* (Princeton, N.J.: Educational Testing Service, 1972).

al—including setting up the administrative organization and gaining widespread public and political support for establishing the Assessment. These could be regarded as major objectives only until the time they were achieved. Other objectives that have been partly attained—including altering concepts of testing, producing some advanced subject-matter objectives, and facilitating the development of state and local assessments—are effective largely through indirect influence; that is, rather than producing specific results, the Assessment has exercised an influence generally on various components of American education. In each of these instances, the Assessment may have been quite important but must be rated only as one factor among many.

NAEP'S MOST CRITICAL OBJECTIVES

In the long run, neither the operational objectives nor the influential objectives merit current levels of public support ($6 million per year) for the Assessment. While it clearly deserves credit for progressing toward its objectives, ultimately the Assessment will have to perform well on its three major short-term objectives, redefine them substantially, or find some other major objectives to pursue. The original and continuing major commitments of the National Assessment are:

A. Major Short-Term Objectives
   1. To obtain *meaningful* national data on the strengths and weaknesses of American education (by locating deficiencies and inequalities in particular subject areas and particular subgroups of the population).
   2. To provide this data to Congress, the lay public, and educational decision makers so that they could make more informed decisions on new programs, bond issues, new curricula, steps to reduce inequalities, and so on.
   3. To provide this data to researchers working on various educational problems concerning teaching and learning, either to answer some research questions or to identify specific problems which would generate research hypotheses.

No attempt will be made here to restate the detailed evidence of Chapters 3 through 8 which indicates that to date the Assessment is generally failing in all three of its major short-term objectives. We summarize by noting some of the many factors responsible for this failure, each of which has been considered in detail earlier. They include the limitations of the selection of subject areas, the delineation of subject-matter objectives and subobjectives, the development of exercises, the measurement of descriptive background characteristics, and the combined use of the matrix sampling, the packaging system, and short testing times. More generally, the results have been adversely affected by the technical limits of social science, the politics of federal-state-local educational relations, economic constraints, time constraints, the particular intentions of the Assessment's original leaders, poor management planning, mediocre service by many of the major contracting groups, and by the appearance of the Coleman Report and several subsequent reports detailing major aspects of educational achievement, documenting inequalities, and advancing standards for hard evidence beyond the standards employed by the Assessment. Finally, beyond all these, there are additional defects inherent in the way in which the results are reported.

These limitations leave the Assessment with: (1) virtually no capacity to answer research questions and even very little capacity to generate significant research hypotheses that could not have been generated more precisely and less expensively by smaller studies; (2) virtually no capacity to provide the federal government, the lay public, or most educational policymakers with results that are directly useful for decision making; and (3) most surprising of all, virtually no really significant and supportable new findings with regard to the strengths and weaknesses of American education.

NAEP'S RESPONSES TO THE LIMITED UTILITY OF ITS RESULTS

NAEP has become keenly aware of the limited validity and utility of its results. To date, beyond attempting incrementally to correct for some of the problems mentioned earlier, NAEP has offered six major responses to the matter of lack of utility.

First, it has begun to put more emphasis on the importance of the indirectly influential objectives considered earlier in this chapter. Second, it has begun to publish somewhat more qualified statements about what it expects to accomplish with its results. Third, it has begun disseminating its subject-matter objectives as if they were significant results unto themselves, which in some cases they are. Fourth, it has published a large number of articles trying to explain how the Assessment results might possibly be used. Fifth, it has asked for patience, claiming that the first round is only a benchmark and that interesting findings and changes will not show up until two or three cycles have been completed. And finally, it has created a Department of Applications and begun to pursue some new objectives. The second, fourth, and last of these responses are discussed in greater detail below.

A variety of articles by NAEP staff members and friends of NAEP have begun to be more humble about what can be expected of the Assessment. Without explicitly abandoning the objectives of providing directly useful data to policymakers and researchers, attempts are being made to reduce the expectations for the Assessment without reducing support for it. To date, such efforts contain numerous contradictions. In the October 1971 issue of *Phi Delta Kappan,* the former staff director of NAEP and the then assistant to the director for exercise development coauthored the following disclaimer, in an article ironically titled "How Will National Assessment Change American Education?"

> A recurring concern, both among those who support national assessment and those who have reservations about it, is the ultimate utility of the results. How will they affect education in this country? This is a very difficult question. While national assessment is designed to provide general information, it is not designed to produce answers to specific educational questions.
>
> Certainly the originators of national assessment expected the project to contribute to improved educational decision making. Certainly they felt that better answers can be produced by decision makers if they have more information. Their thesis was that someone needed to begin, systematically, to gather information (not answers) about educational outcomes in this country.
>
> These originators were men and women of sufficient vision to see innumerable possibilities for the use of assessment-type information: for legislators faced with hard decisions, e.g., whether to allocate extra monies for instruction in reading if it means refusing requests for other educational needs; for school board members faced with the question of how to deal with educational needs of disadvantaged groups or minority groups; for curriculum specialists and teachers faced with decisions of how best to allocate class time to educational materials related to specific goals.
>
> But national assessment was designed to be just one information-gathering project, to fill one information void. Well-designed state assessments, local school district assessments, and special research studies seeking answers to specific educational questions would all be necessary to complete the picture.[4]

---

[4] Frank B. Womer and Marjorie M. Mastie, *Phi Delta Kappan,* vol. 53, no. 2, p. 118.

Despite these judicious remarks, later in the very same article we find the authors suggesting various debatable ways in which members of different interest groups might make direct use of the Assessment results. Numerous articles of this sort have been published by NAEP between 1969 and the present. In general, they seem counterproductive because they unwittingly point up how commonplace the findings are, how imprecise they are, how indirectly they relate to any particular constituencies or needs, or how the same kinds of information could be obtained more readily, usefully, and economically in other ways.

Sometimes the suggested uses for the results are incredibly unimaginative—or, perhaps, quite imaginative, but also incredible. The following appeared in a special issue of *COMPACT* magazine devoted entirely to the National Assessment. Published in February 1972, the article from which this excerpt comes appears side by side with others, some of which lower and others of which raise expectations for the Assessment. This particular essay is entitled "Industry—An Unnoticed Consumer." It begins by claiming, "The importance of National Assessment to curriculum-makers, textbook publishers, teachers and other educators is obvious." It then goes on to describe the implications of the Assessment for American industry:

> Industry will react favorably, for example, in considering assessment results in terms of plant location and employment practices. When an industry considers a certain geographic area for an industrial development, it will be concerned with the educational competence of the people in that area. Important to any industry would be information as to the educational make-up of a community: schooling, general knowledge derived from experience and whether members of that community show a desire for continuous self-education after leaving school. Where but from National Assessment results can this particular information be obtained?
>
> Industries planning to hire locally will want to know the levels of knowledge and skills of their potential employees. One of the important industrial problems now is the development of continuing education programs for people working in plants. To plan adequate and useful continuing education programs, an industry must first find out what employees already know and can do.
>
> If the industry plans to bring employees in from another part of the country, it will be concerned about whether they will be willing to move. A great consideration for any family faced with a move to a new location is the local school systems available for their children. Fortunately for industry, a look at the cumulative data from National Assessment reports will give some indication

as to the nature of school systems in different geographic regions plus information on the overall make-up of communities.[5]

In fact, the National Assessment can provide none of the specific data suggested in these passages.

At the same time that NAEP has stepped up its efforts to think of possible uses for the Assessment results, it has also taken steps to find other uses for itself and thus to assure continuing widespread support. In October 1971, a Department of Utilization and Applications was formed within NAEP. While this department overlapped with the existing NAEP Public Relations Department to some extent, its top priorities were quite different. While there was to be continuing interest in disseminating Assessment results, this new department's main purpose was *to begin disseminating the Assessment model, rather than the results.*

The department budget for the first year was approximately $150,000, and for the second year approximately $450,000. The chief functions include running workshops to inform states and local school districts of how they might make use of the Assessment models, either in terms of the processes for determining subject-matter objectives or in terms of using NAEP exercises, or the NAEP sampling, packaging, or reporting systems, and so on. The department works directly with individual state offices of education and also with local school districts.

This change is important for two reasons. From our interviews at NAEP it seemed apparent that the new emphasis on disseminating the model instead of the results would draw priorities and resources away from the really substantive revisions which are necessary to make the Assessment's results more useful in the long run. Second, it seemed clear that there were strong political implications in the creation of the new department and the emphasis being given to it. In part it was established because USOE was under pressure from Congress to indicate how the Assessment would be useful, and USOE, in turn, applied that pressure to NAEP. The departmental change gave NAEP a chance to deemphasize its shortcomings and to start building a new set of constituents who could then testify as to its utility before USOE and Congress. In fact, the Assessment's model and materials may well be more useful at the state or local level than at the national level. But since NAEP and ECS are controlling this process, there is great emphasis on allowing the states leeway to develop their own assessments, which are bound to vary considerably in quality just as they are bound to collect noncomparable data.

---

[5] John K. Wolfe, *COMPACT,* February 1972, p. 7.

RECOMMENDATIONS: THE FUTURE OF THE NATIONAL ASSESSMENT OF EDUCATIONAL PROGRESS

What should be done with the National Assessment of Educational Progress? It has accomplished its original operational goals and has been one major source of influence on various aspects of American education. But it is generally failing in its three major objectives: the collection of *meaningful* data on the strengths and weaknesses of American education; the provision of directly usable information to decision makers, including politicians, educators, and lay people; and the solution of research problems, or at least the specific generation of important research hypotheses.

(1) We recommend strong but constructive skepticism regarding the Assessment's future. One proposal for action, coming from NAEP's leaders, is the same as it has been since the fall of 1963: Everyone should wait patiently because the "first cycle is only the benchmark and we really can't know what results we'll have until the second or third cycle."

Among the numerous difficulties with waiting longer is the high cost involved. If it takes three cycles to know whether anything interesting has turned up, and the cycles are five years each, at an average annual budget of over $6 million, some $90 million will be spent waiting to see.

But leaving cost aside for the moment, the plea for patience must be examined more closely in its own right. It is easy to recognize that it was hard to think through everything the Assessment might produce when the idea first came up in 1963, but difficult to understand the origins of the argument that the first cycle is "just a benchmark" and that it will be the comparisons over time that will be really interesting. After all, the Assessment's work involves testing four age groups (including young adults), in ten subject areas, at three different levels of difficulty, in the four categories of knowledge, skills, understandings, and attitudes. Furthermore, the subject areas include Citizenship and a broadly defined area called Career and Occupational Development, both very interesting areas which are seldom tested across such a spectrum of the population.

Our impression of all this is that the Assessment potentially constitutes one of the most significant acts of self-consciousness ever undertaken by a nation. Though many of its aspects might have been more broadly defined, the Assessment even now covers society's educational status more comprehensively than any other such venture. Because of this, it seems to us that the first round might be very exciting in terms of what it tells about the society.

Concomitantly, we feel relatively certain that most of the changes over a five-year cycle will be small, only reinforcing the significance of the baseline data. Furthermore, we would suggest that more attention be paid to the first cycle by sociologists, historians, and political scientists—looking at it as a measure of the overall literacy of the society; this type of analysis is essential, in part because the individual results are so difficult to interpret precisely. Moreover, major changes in results from one cycle to the next are likely to do no more than stir debate as to whether the change is a result of schooling, or some societal factor, or some flaw in the testing situation. We have looked through exercise after exercise, positing upward and downward changes and then asking, "So what?"

In a way, it seems that at this point the proposal to wait patiently is partly a defense to cover up for the anxieties at NAEP about how the Assessment results can really be useful. In fact, NAEP itself is *not* waiting patiently; quite to the contrary, it has been busy "cutting and pasting" in an effort to eliminate some of the most elementary deficiencies of the first testing. Being patient may in the end be excellent advice, but in the meantime drastic changes must be made, both in the societal expectations for the Assessment and in its own sense of purpose.

(2) It should be made very clear that the Assessment is not a national "school accountability" system. It cannot directly measure the *outcomes of schooling;* nor can it measure the *effectiveness* of any particular input of any school, curriculum, federal program, or state school system, etc. If it could measure *outcomes, causal factors,* and *effectiveness* it would obviously be extremely useful for both research and policy purposes, but it cannot, as we have demonstrated in Chapter 6.

(3) It also should be made clear that the Assessment is not a short-term research or decision-making tool. We are convinced by the evidence in Chapters 3 through 8 that the National Assessment is not, and cannot economically be, an effective mechanism for the solution of educational research problems, for the direct generation of research hypotheses, or for the provision of information that will be of significant and immediate use to educational policymakers or the lay public. We have not been able to think of any educational research problems or major policy matters that could be most directly and precisely clarified through the mechanism of the National Assessment. It is enlightening in this context to return for a moment to the original planning meeting of December 19, 1963. John Flanagan has just finished proposing that the Assessment should try to measure aspirations regarding the kinds of courses students want or whether they want to go to college.

CHAIRMAN GARDNER: Well, I think, John, those are extremely interesting items. I think they'd be a little hard—or the kind of things you might want to try out on a smaller scale before you plunged in on a national sample, don't you think?

MR. TUKEY: Is there anything in this for which this isn't true? (Laughter.)

MR. HOLLAND: That's my answer! (Laughter.)[6]

The matter of whether the Assessment is an appropriate instrument for the conduct of serious research or data gathering for policymakers has become quite grave since that first meeting. During our second session of interviews at NAEP headquarters in Denver, in August 1972, a representative of the National Center for Educational Statistics (NCEST), the monitoring office within USOE, was no less than startled to find that Tyler confirmed our limited view of what the Assessment could accomplish in the short term, while NAEP's administrative officials, James Hazlett and Stanley Ahmann, remained silent on the issue.

At some point in the near future the Assessment may have to be more candid about these research and policy limitations, although we recognize that an admission that even with a lot more work the Assessment is likely to become a useful long-term census and little more may jeopardize funding. The risks are high either way, but we believe that a careful lowering of expectations, coupled with a great deal of timely excitement about how America is mature enough to be able to afford a longer-term attempt at educational self-consciousness, might leave the "census-like" Assessment intact.

If NAEP is unable to back away from its commitments to generate specific data for research hypotheses, the most direct way in which to increase its utility in this regard may be to expand the testing periods and the packages so that individuals can be tested for meaningful relationships among their performances in different subject areas, across difficulty levels, and across the categories of knowledge, skills, understandings, and attitudes. It should be emphasized, however, that refining such measures would undoubtedly be pursued more economically in the context of a more specialized effort.

(4) Next, serious notice should be taken of the implications of the Assessment's switch of priorities toward disseminating the Assessment model. If NAEP is to become a federally subsidized clearinghouse to help states and

---

[6] *Proceedings of the National Testing Project Conference,* December 18–19, 1963, Carnegie files, p. 130.

local districts with developing their own assessments, the decision should be clearly thought out.

Various states have developed their own assessments, some of which are inferior to NAEP's, and many more states are now setting up assessment or accountability systems. Thus, the federal government is not getting uniform data, but perhaps more important is the fact that it is thereby encouraging the growth of an accountability movement that will produce new bureaucracies in most state departments of education. Should a time come when the federal government requires uniform data collection in education, these new bureaucracies will most likely oppose changes in their idiosyncratic evaluation systems.

Given the trends of the last one hundred years, it seems likely that the federal role in education will continue to grow. But the distinct possibility at the moment is that between thirty-five and forty of the states will develop their own assessments in the next few years. From existing state costs we estimate that the total cost among these states would be more than $25 million per year by 1978, and that even then many of the assessments would be of limited applicability and almost none would provide truly comparable interstate data.

In 1972, USOE proposed establishment of "A Common Core of Data Program" (CCD). This would provide for the collection of standardized data in all the states, while at the same time providing federal money for states to do additional data-systems development. Beginning in 1972, small amounts have been spent for planning activities. Major requests for funds have not yet been granted by Congress.

One possible way of handling the federal subsidy aspect of the dissemination of the model to the states and local communities is to put some or all of this aspect of NAEP into the private economy, so that it receives fees for services and competes with ETS and other assessment consulting firms.

(5) Whether or not any of the above suggestions are accepted, it is beyond debate that the Assessment materials should be markedly improved. The general tendency of our suggestions in Chapters 3 to 8 is toward more complex concepts and measures of knowledge, skills, understandings, and attitudes. One possibility is that instead of working toward criterion referencing individual exercises, the Assessment might work out a way to criterion reference several objectives and subobjectives, or even an entire subject area. Definitions of proficiency could be formulated and among any cluster of objectives and subobjectives there might be found various combinations of ways in which respondents could demonstrate proficiency.

(6) If this broader concept of criterion referencing were extended to a more complex level, the Assessment could really serve a crucial societal function by working out a three- or four-level definition of *functional literacy,* and then developing tests to measure progress toward the various levels. The Assessment could thereby move away from measuring specific subject areas and use its Citizenship and Career and Occupational Development objectives as a base for the development of definitions of functional literacy. This would provide an excellent opportunity to study the young adult population carefully to see how much school-taught material is retained and how much is needed to function effectively in various situations.

(7) Consideration should be given to the costs and benefits of widening the Assessment cycle to ten years, if it is found after the second cycle that mostly minor changes are being measured. The quality of NAEP's undertaking, including the exercises and their interpretation, might be significantly improved if there were fewer time constraints. Furthermore, some economies would emerge in widening the testing cycle.

In sum, given the multitude of its deficiencies, if the Assessment does not take these or similar major steps to encourage more realistic expectations, and at the same time to make its procedures more sophisticated and more directly useful, it will continue to suffer from an internal identity crisis, as well as from severe external pressures to prove that its annual federal appropriation is warranted.

10

EPILOGUE:
SOCIAL INDICATORS AND
THE REFORM OF EDUCATION

Cast out from the Eden of understanding, the human
quest has been for a common tongue and a unity of
knowledge, for a set of "first principles" which, in the
epistemology of learning, would underlie the modes of
experience and the categories of reason and so shape a set
of invariant truths. The library of Babel [Jorge Luis
Borges] mocks this hubris: like endless space, it is all there
and is not all there; and, like Gödel's theorem, knowing it
is a contradiction makes it not a contradiction. In the end,
said the poet, is the beginning. This is the curvilinear
paradox, and necessary humility, in the effort to measure
knowledge.

—Daniel Bell, "Knowledge and Technology," in Eleanor
Sheldon and Wilbert Moore (eds.), *Indicators of Social Change*

Analysis of social statistics—such as those gathered by the
National Assessment—cannot be restricted to specific conceptual and operational matters alone but must consider the development of social indicators as
a reflection of general structural change in America. It is frequently observed
that America is becoming a postindustrial society, characterized, in Daniel
Bell's analysis, by the creation of a service economy, the preeminence of the

professional and technical class, the centrality of theoretical knowledge as the source of societal innovation and policy formulation, and the evolution of a new intellectual technology. Over 50 percent of the United States labor force is now employed in the service sector (which includes the personal services, as well as trade, finance, transport, health, recreation, research, education, and government), and services make up more than 50 percent of the national product.[1]

Arguments for the development of social indicators usually rest on the theory that the transition to a service economy will create particular strains in the market system. In Western industrial society, the market has long been the forum for the allocation of value, in which first the "invisible hand" and later national monetary and fiscal policy ensured that decisions by individual economic actors sustained the economy's workings. In the postindustrial society, collective decision making increasingly may replace the market in the allocation of value.

Microeconomic theory teaches that a perfectly competitive market economy is optimal (in the Pareto sense) whenever private costs equal social costs and private benefits equal social benefits. The economy will either under- or overproduce certain goods if these conditions are not met. There is substantial agreement among welfare economists that, for education, health, transportation, and other social services, equality of private and social costs or benefits is not achieved. The social benefits of college education, for example, are possibly greater than the sum of the private benefits to each college-educated individual. For services such as education and health—often called collective goods—perfect competition in unregulated markets will not allocate resources optimally. The composite of the decisions of individual economic actors will differ substantially from decisions that might be made collectively by the population.[2]

Social indicators are expected to improve both individual and collective decision making by illuminating social benefits and costs—for example, the

---

[1] See Daniel Bell, *The Coming of the Post-Industrial Society* (New York: Basic Books, 1973), and Robert L. Heilbroner, "Economic Problems of a Postindustrial Society," *Dissent,* Spring 1973, pp. 163–176. For a compelling argument that collective decision making based on professional judgments and new intellectual technology may not be an issue in a more humane social order, see Henri Rabasseire, "On Post-Human Society," *Dissent,* Winter 1974, pp. 108–112.

[2] See, for example, Mancur Olson, Jr., "The Plan and Purpose of a Social Report," *The Public Interest,* no. 15, Spring 1969, pp. 85–97.

functional literacy of the population, its health, the incidence of crime, or the level of pollution. It often is imagined that social indicators might produce a balance sheet useful in clarifying policy choices or delineating performances in areas of defined social need.[3]

A considerable range in the complexity of data gathering has been evidenced in proposals for social indicators. The simplest possibility of all is the one-time measurement of a single item—for example, the present birth rate, literacy level, or size of population. Here, one simply seeks to discover the present value of some variable. A somewhat more sophisticated exercise is the collection of time-series data. For example, the U.S. census provides population trends for a two hundred year period. A third possibility is the construction of an accounting system in which the collected data forms an interrelated network. For example, the national income and product accounts indicate the total amount spent on final output by all participants in the economy, the total income earned by participants for productive services, and the sum of the output produced by all producing units.[4] Finally, data can be collected which play an important role in a theory of some social process. For example, the price index, unemployment rate, and investment, government, and consumption expenditures are all important elements of neo-Keynesian economic analysis.[5]

Whatever data are collected, characteristics of large organizations inevitably influence the ways data are used. First, it is far more likely that an organization will develop indicators of progress toward long-standing goals than toward those recently established. Second, indicators which are positive, i.e., which show progress, are more likely to be used than those which are negative. Third, those variables which are easy to measure or which are needed for administrative purposes will be obtained before those less observable or not so greatly required for administration. Fourth, indicators seem to

---

[3] These particular objectives for social accounting were suggested by the National Commission on Technology, Automation and Economic Progress. See Raymond Bauer, ed., *Social Indicators* (Cambridge, Mass.: M.I.T., 1966), pp. xiv–xv; and Daniel Bell, "The Idea of a Social Report," *The Public Interest*, no. 15, Spring 1969, p. 78.

[4] For a description of the national income and product accounts, see any good macroeconomics text. One excellent presentation is available in Warren Smith, *Macroeconomics* (Homewood, Ill.: Irwin, 1970), pp. 23–89.

[5] For a particularly elaborate proposal for a social accounting system, see Bertram M. Gross, "The State of the Nation: Social Systems Accounting," in Bauer, op. cit., pp. 154–272.

manifest cultural lags; i.e., indicators fail to keep abreast of the techniques of statistical measurement, new indicators are not developed to meet new needs for information, and indicators fail to change in the manner needed to reflect alterations in the phenomena for which they are an index. Fifth, indicators are most likely to be developed in a policy area in which there is a large interest group providing pressure. This may or may not mean that such a policy area merits statistical concern, or that areas for which there is little public notice necessarily merit small concern.[6]

Consideration of organizational constraints may expand and improve the use of data. For example, as Albert Biderman suggests, paying attention to the way knowledge is used might help identify:

(1) Institutional, political and other barriers that are responsible for gaps in data about crucial social phenomena. These findings may point toward ways of increasing the correspondence of available measures of aspects of the society with their perceived importance and desired state.
(2) Barriers to the comprehension and use of data in planning and administration.
(3) Sources of distortion and bias in the recording and reporting of social data.
(4) Neglected pertinences of data to social values.[7]

Study of the way knowledge is used might also call attention to the nonscientific roles data can play. Biderman suggests that data can be employed

(1) as the bases of claims against resources according to allocative devices established by law or custom, (2) as ammunition for the various parties to the adversary procedures of interorganizational politics, (3) as the cohesion of organizational alliances, (4) as symbols for the persuasion of publics, and (5) as new grounds for national and institutional creeds.[8]

Organizational structure and practice, then, have a strong influence on both the kinds of social statistics gathered and the ways in which they are used. Any attempt to use social statistics for collective decision making therefore would seem to require an organization with relatively clear and distinct

---

[6] Albert D. Biderman, "Social Indicators and Goals," in Bauer, op. cit., pp. 68–153. Biderman's essay includes an excellent case study of federal crime statistics.
[7] Ibid., p. 73.
[8] Ibid., p. 102.

goals and practices—features not usually characteristic of education or other social services.[9]

Further, if we assume that the primary (although perhaps not single) purpose of social data gathering is to provide empirical evidence for scientific analysis of public policy, then the logical position of such data within the social sciences must be made clear. That is, if it is to be employed in the service of science, it must be collected in accordance with the imperatives of the science involved. Data do not speak for themselves—use of theory and empirical evidence are closely linked. Only when evidence is collected with a specific hypothesis in mind, in the hope of either supporting or refuting the hypothesis, can appropriate controls be developed to exclude irrelevant events which would otherwise mask the phenomena to be observed.[10]

It is unlikely, then, that item-by-item collection of general social statistics will provide information for rigorous hypothesis testing, unless the data is collected with a theory in mind.

It is possible that generally collected data may provide some aid in the *generation* of hypotheses. This may be particularly true if the data describe items which are quantified in ordinary usage (such as age, number, size, dollar value). But variables to be measured are constructs—they are not given by nature, but must be defined by the experimenter. Hence, even within a seemingly well-defined policy area such as health care, there is no guarantee that the variables chosen for a general census would be those useful in theory-based analysis.

---

[9] For discussions of the broad aims of social action programs, see Robert S. Weiss and Martin Rein, "The Evaluation of Broad-Aim Programs: Experimental Design, Its Difficulties, and an Alternative," *Administrative Science Quarterly*, no. 15, p. 97, 1970; and Stephen Bailey and Edith Mosher, *ESEA: The Office of Education Administers a Law* (Syracuse: Syracuse University Press, 1968).

[10] One can argue further that, in order for empirical evidence to be useful in human activity, it must be collected as part of an ongoing life practice of criticism and hypothesis testing. For an analysis of this thread in Marxism, existentialism, pragmatism, and analytic philosophy, see Richard J. Bernstein, *Praxis and Action: Contemporary Philosophies of Human Activity* (Philadelphia: University of Pennsylvania Press, 1971). For the more narrow view that "data do not speak for themselves," see Ernest Nagel, *The Structure of Science* (New York: Harcourt, Brace & World, 1961).

Science also can be understood as an effort to interpret the world, to create symbolic frameworks through which the world appears to "make sense." In this view, the methodological concern is not in arranging experimental controls for hypothesis testing but is in understanding evidence within a broader conceptual structure. See Peter Winch, *The Idea of a Social Science and Its Relation to Philosophy* (London: Routledge, 1958).

It becomes apparent that certain problems are attendant upon the collection of scientifically useful census data. The essential point is that unless such data is gathered by a community which shares fundamental assumptions about the phenomena observed, it is unlikely that the data can have scientific utility. But in reference to any important public policy matter for which it is hoped such data will have value, there is surely no single community of assumptions.

Biderman lists six technical obstacles to developing an adequate and respected system of indicators: invalidity, inaccuracy, conflicting indicators, lack of data, incompatible models, and value consensus.[11] As we have suggested, these obstacles can be explained as consequences of the attempt to develop empirical evidence in the absence of shared theory.

The transition to a service economy may well bring, then, not a new social balance sheet to supplement the GNP, but rather a heightened recognition of fundamental conflicts and contradictions in social policy. The ideal of a balance sheet for collective decision making rests on the possibility of an authentic consensus, which, at least in education, rarely exists.

But conflict, beyond appearing inescapable, may actually be an advantage. Paul Feyerabend [12] has suggested that pluralism is essential for the advancement of knowledge: *It is only in the competition between alternative theories, each one held with a tenacity by some community, that tests of hypotheses are strengthened and refuting facts are uncovered.* This principle of competition might also be applied to social statistics (and to smaller evaluations, as is noted below). Rather than a single set of agreed-upon indicators in a field such as health or education, the federal government might collect data urged by a number of different communities, each having its own assumptions and values. Presumably, over time the competition between theories (as well as the competition for resources) would lead to the demise of certain indicators in a field and the growth of others.

It must be admitted that for the single well-developed example of social statistics, the economic indicators, there is but one theoretical frame, neo-Keynesian analysis. There is no real competitiveness in the economic indicators. Nevertheless, there is presently considerable debate concerning definitions of "unemployment," "investment" (for example, in human as well as

---

[11] Biderman, op. cit., pp. 79–86.

[12] "Outline of a Pluralistic Theory of Knowledge and Action," in Stanford Anderson (ed.), *Planning for Diversity and Choice* (Cambridge, Mass.: M.I.T., 1968), pp. 275–284. For a discussion of this view, see Bernstein, op. cit., pp. 281–299.

physical capital), "national product," and other elements of the economic data base. One wonders whether, as the consensus on the meaning of these fundamental terms erodes, the scientific-policy use of economic statistics will decline.

SOCIAL INDICATORS IN AMERICAN EDUCATION

We can conclude from this discussion that *the assumptions underlying an organizations's system of social accounting will reflect the assumptions underlying the organizations's understanding of its own activity: The scientific utility of a system of indicators is in the most fundamental sense a function of the correctness of the organization's understanding of its goals and structure.*

An organization that would establish a social accounting system must first come to understand its aims and the way in which it is structured to attain them. Second, it must devise a system of measures to ascertain its effectiveness in achieving its goals. Finally, on the basis of its theoretical understanding of its structure, it can change policies in the service of realizing more effective performance. The development of organizational consciousness, the first stage of social accounting, inevitably uncovers intrinsic contradictions in an organization's structure. Awareness of these may or may not lead to a new theoretical synthesis and the political action required for structural change and growth.

In considering the Assessment from this point of view, the organization in question *is not* the National Assessment of Educational Progress, but rather the entire American educational system. Despite the long-term trend toward more collective decision making, and despite the movement toward more decision making at the federal level, it is obvious that insofar as one can speak of American education as an organization at all, its understanding of its own goals and structure is highly ambiguous. *Predictably then, the educational system has created a social accounting system—the National Assessment of Educational Progress—in its own fragmented and jumbled image. And just as predictably, failing to grasp the salience of the diverse practices and goals of American education, the National Assessment has been plagued by all the dilemmas of invalidity, inaccuracy, conflicting indicators, lack of data, incompatible models, and continuing lack of value consensus.* While NAEP received most of these dilemmas as a direct legacy from the American educational system, it then made numerous decisions—as described throughout this study—which exacerbated them. In addition, various factors considered earlier have placed NAEP pretty squarely in the tradition of other large institu-

tions collecting social statistics, and, as mentioned by Biderman above, this
means overemphasis of long-standing goals, overmeasurement of easily measured phenomena, and lagging behind the most sophisticated techniques of
statistical measurement.

The Assessment's style of resolving basic conflicts ensured that no consistent view of American education would emerge, and, at the same time, that
a functional pluralism could not develop. Rather than encouraging either
one or several consistent views of the educational process, the Assessment
promised to stay as close as possible to present administrative practice in
education (i.e., knowledge was by and large to be construed as falling within
subject-matter areas, progress would be measured by exercises, and outcomes
which "the schools are not trying to teach" would be neglected). In reality, as
noted in Chapters 3 and 4 and elsewhere, the Assessment strayed from this
promise, both wittingly and unwittingly, and the result was a still more inconsistent view of the goals of American education. Theories of cognitive
development of some standing in the research community, such as Jean
Piaget's and Jerome Bruner's work, were neglected—partly because these are
still in the process of being validated in experimental situations, and partly
because no developmental theory of any kind has ever been accepted seriously by the United States educational establishment. The Assessment's determination, an inevitability given the varied sources of NAEP's support, is that
theory is important only after it has entered the public trust. Furthermore, no
effort was made to create a consistent system of measures by developing at
least minimal, complexly defined, functional literacy standards.

As we have remarked, when social statistics are gathered by a community
with a weak set of shared assumptions, the statistics fall into various traps,
and therefore have little precise theoretical or programmatic use. However,
as was also mentioned earlier, this does not mean such statistics are not used
at all. Instead of being employed scientifically, they are used like any other
political resource.

We have commented that agreement on fundamental issues is difficult to
obtain in American education and was not obtained by the Assessment; facile
consensus, rather than resolution of a pluralism of competing values, ruled its
process. We must expect, then, few uses of Assessment results in the development of rational decision making.

We might ask under what circumstances it is conceivable that systematically usable educational social statistics might be gathered. In the field of
education, one hope is that a new *general theory* will be published which cap-
tures the spirit of the times. One can only guess, of course, whether a tract in

this field can be written having the relatively clear policy implications of a Keynes.

Another hope, doubtlessly more likely and certainly more modest, follows the example of client-oriented therapy more nearly than that of economics. Individuals and organizations may come to realize that acts imply consequences and that real choices are possible. If this were the supposition of large numbers of people and organizations, information, especially greater self-knowledge, would become a more valued resource in the process of growth and reform.

EVALUATION: WHEN IS SELF-KNOWLEDGE ACTED UPON?

We have concluded that the National Assessment will have very limited applicability as a source of either specific research hypotheses or specific policy guidelines. Beyond that, our analysis of the prerequisites of an effective large-scale system of social accounting demonstrates that no such system lies within reach in the field of education. We have also expressed our pessimism about the near-term development of a general theory, which might serve as a basis for an effective system of educational/social indicators. And finally, we have suggested that in the short term the most likely approach to educational change is through enlarging the use of increasingly refined self-knowledge by particular educational institutions.

Given these macro-level realities, and given the hope of change occurring more often at the local or institutional level, it is helpful to consider various conditions that seem to affect the institutional use of evaluations and self-knowledge.

We deal only incidentally with the many psychological and social factors that cause people in educational systems and other organizational settings to rigidify and reify their own attitudes and behavior patterns; the literatures of psychology, sociology, organizational development, change theory, and learning theory have made manifest beyond the point of reasonable doubt that these factors are common characteristics of people in institutional settings. Therefore, for present purposes, we take human weakness and inefficiency (which can sometimes be viewed as strength and sensitivity) as givens. The emphasis here will be on describing conditions which help surmount or circumvent these factors when necessary. In other words, the question here is not the broader one of how to make all people in educational organizations continuously crave change and utilize critical evaluations, but rather how to create conditions which induce or force people to overcome habitual resistance to change and critical evaluations.

What cannot be considered to be a given, as we have seen in the foregoing analysis of the National Assessment, is the availability of high-quality evaluative information. Decision makers in organizations might be faulted for not craving information, but it is more difficult to blame them for not using the highly imperfect information which is accessible to them. In general, Wilensky[13] and others tend to give the benefit of the doubt to the quality of the information and to see decision makers as refusing to act on the basis of adequate information. That is, the quality of information gathering has far outpaced its utilization. A much more extreme case of attempting to assume high-quality information is found in Gary M. Andrew's and Ronald E. Moir's volume, *Information-Decision Systems in Education*,[14] a 1970 publication which emits the evangelical tone of the nineteenth-century itinerant mountebank—a tone not very different from that of too many twentieth-century salesmen for PPBS or other educational management information systems. Analysis of the problem of underutilization of information is retarded by such efforts to separate the issue of quality of information from the issue of use. This is not a case of total disagreement with Wilensky; it is more a matter of emphasis. Indeed, the best support for the contention that the quality and utility of information are inextricably bound together is Wilensky's own excellent definition of high-quality information. It is much more than merely pragmatic and well organized. It is

> . . . *clear* because it is understandable to those who must use it; *timely* because it gets to them when they need it; *reliable* because diverse observers using the same procedures see it in the same way; *valid* because it is cast in the form of concepts and measures that capture reality (the tests include logical consistency, successful prediction, congruence with established knowledge or independent sources); *adequate* because the account is full (the context of the act, event, or life of the person or group is described); and *wide-ranging* because the major policy alternatives promising a high probability of attaining organizational goals are posed or new goals are suggested.[15]

---

[13] Harold L. Wilensky, *Organizational Intelligence: Knowledge and Policy in Government and Industry* (New York: Basic Books, 1967).

[14] Itasca, Ill.: Peacock, 1970.

[15] Wilensky, op. cit., p. ix.

Arthur B. Toan, Jr., a partner in Price Waterhouse and Co., agrees on the need for timeliness, reliability, and clarity, and adds two additional criteria that seem reasonable. First, information must be of a significant or vital nature to the organization involved. Second, evaluations should be accompanied by appropriate bases for comparison. In the latter context, Toan suggests five useful possibilities: comparisons against the past, the present, a plan for the future, an ideal, and competitors.[16]

The main point here should be quite obvious: When have school systems been offered information meeting criteria such as these set down by Wilensky and Toan?

Certainly there are available great quantities of neglected information of *good* quality, but can use really be expected until either information is of *high* quality or there is very strong incentive for innovation? Experience in other fields indicates that, lacking high quality information, predictable use is unlikely. For instance, problems with the quality of information have been documented and analyzed with regard to sociological research and its use and nonuse in such diverse fields as medicine, business management, education, and American foreign policy.[17]

The quality of planning and evaluation in education has been especially weak, so that if it improves, it will be necessary to reeducate decision makers to this circumstance. As we know, information on major education issues such as class size, per pupil expenditures, teacher experience and qualifications, and school size has been highly contradictory and largely incorrect. In more general terms:

> Evaluation is sufficiently untidy that it usually is possible to redo a study in such a fashion that the data is qualified if not refuted. This practice is, admittedly, a somewhat rare occurrence—but the fact that it is possible prompts leadership to take evaluation evidence which is destructive to the prevailing system less seriously than it might.[18]

Indeed, there is substantial evidence that even in the business world, with its

---

[16] Albert B. Toan, Jr., *Using Information to Manage* (New York: Ronald, 1968), pp. 6–7, 11.

[17] See Martin D. Hyman on medicine, Abraham Zaleznik and Anne Jardim on management, Neal Gross and Joshua Fishman on educational establishments, and W. Phillips Davison on foreign policy, all in Paul F. Lazarsfeld, William H. Sewell, and Harold L. Wilensky (eds.), *The Uses of Sociology* (New York: Basic Books, 1967).

[18] Martin W. Essex, *Educational Evaluation,* 1969, p. 76.

relative precision, it is highly probable that competing information systems will produce different evaluations and implications for policy.[19]

As a matter of emphasis then, it seems important for change agents seeking to develop accountability and evaluation systems to keep the issues of quality and comprehensiveness of information in the forefront. Furthermore, they should seek to inform decisions that will be made in the face of inevitable uncertainties. Many branches of the business world have already adjusted to this provision of uncertainty, which is clearly more ingrained in schools and other service-oriented organizations whose specific goals and output measuring capacities are less specific.[20]

H. N. Broom[21] and Ijiri, Jaedicke, and Knight[22] discuss decision making under conditions of uncertainty, or what the latter authors call—perhaps unfairly, because they imply some pathological state—"ill-structured environments." Broom states:

> The decision-making model most common to the business and managerial field is that involving uncertainty in various degrees, but usually not total ignorance. Uncertainty may exist when some objective experience is available but not enough. . . . The case tends to approach risk, but decision-making under risk assumes that a probability distribution is known. As the amount of objective experience decreases, the decision-maker must rely more upon the personal feelings or judgment concerning the selection of various strategies. Significant problems in the field are to determine (1) when the objective experience becomes so small that it should be replaced by a subjective probability analysis, or an assumption of ignorance, (2) what techniques can be used to combine effectively subjective probability information, and (3) in gen-

---

[19] See Edward H. Caplan, "Behavioral Assumptions of Management Accounting," pp. 406–409, and Yuji Ijiri, Robert K. Jaedicke, and Kenneth E. Knight, "The Effects of Accounting Alternatives on Management Decisions," p. 422, both in Alfred Rappaport (ed.), *Information for Decision Making* (Englewood Cliffs, N.J.: Prentice-Hall, 1970).

[20] For discussion of problems of evaluation arising from ambiguous goal structures in the field of mental health, see "Evaluation in Mental Health" (Washington: HEW, 1955), p. 6. In the field of delinquency see Helen Witmer and Edith Tufts, "The Effectiveness of Delinquency Prevention Programs," Social Security Administration, Children's Bureau, No. 350 (Washington: HEW, 1954), pp. 1–2.

[21] H. N. Broom, *Business Policy and Strategic Action* (Englewood Cliffs, N.J.: Prentice-Hall, 1970), p. 60.

[22] Op. cit., p. 430.

eral, we need a confidence measure for subjective probability distributions.[23]

In other words, designers of educational accountability and evaluation systems, in planning the gathering and presentation of information, should take into full account the subjectivity of most decision making and prepare their information so that it will link positively with the situational politics and psychology which are bound to be major components in the decision-making process.

Noting the importance of obtaining high-quality information, even though flawless information is not available, and assuming that for some time to come decisions in educational institutions will be arrived at through subjective processes, we have reviewed various case studies and analyses enumerating a variety of factors that first affect the quality of information collected by an organization and then, once the information has been given, increase or decrease utilization. Most of these factors can be viewed as manipulable policy tools to be used in enhancing the use of evaluative information.

Among the most important of these factors are the degree of prior agreement on the need for change; the degree of urgency or (internal or external) pressure for change; the quality of leadership; the extent to which evaluative information is deliberated, once gathered; the scope and significance of the recommendations; the size, structure, and degree of specialization of the organization; the degree of value consensus; the degree of population homogeneity; the use of "insiders" and/or "outsiders" in performing evaluations; the *quality* and *intensity* of insider participation in evaluations; the use of competitive evaluation reports; the sociostructural ramifications of evaluation recommendations; the salience of profit motives or other reward systems; the degree of overcentralization or overdecentralization; the degree of openness or secrecy in the performance of the evaluation; and the use of neutral professionals as fact finders.[24]

---

[23] Broom, op. cit., p. 60.

[24] Among the major studies reviewed were Dwight R. Ladd, *Change in Educational Policy* (New York: McGraw-Hill, 1970); Alfred Marrow and John R. P. French, Jr., "Changing a Stereotype in Industry," *Journal of Social Issues,* vol. 2, no. 1, pp. 33–37, 1945; Howard E. Freeman, "Conceptual Approaches to Assessing Impacts of Large-Scale Intervention Programs," *American Statistical Association Proceedings,* 1964, pp. 193–194; Philip H. Thurston, *Systems and Procedures Responsibility* (Boston: Harvard Business School, Division of Research, 1959); Toan, op. cit.; Karl Mannheim, "Roots of the Crisis in Evaluation," in *Diagnosis of Our Time: Wartime Essays of a Sociologist* (Routledge, 1943), pp. 15–30; Elting E. Morison, "A Case Study of Innnovation," in

THE NEED TO BE SITUATION-SPECIFIC

Consideration of these numerous conditions and approaches that increase and decrease the utilization of evaluations leads to a predictable but generally neglected conclusion. There are many factors that tend to distort and block the use of evaluations by organizations and, short of radical transformation of the overall milieu, these factors will be found in highly varied combinations from one organization to another. There also are many approaches to increasing utilization of evaluative information, but any particular one of these is useful only in a given situation in which particular factors are causing distortion and blockage. The implications for federal-state-local and private evaluation policies are apparent. Within the existing pseudo-decentralized framework, any evaluation scheme which assumes that conditions blocking and favoring change are the same—or even largely similar—in each of many different organizations and institutions will not succeed in bringing about basic changes. This would apply for a large school system which attempted to evaluate and change the local schools comprising it, as well as for a state evaluating local school districts, a foundation evaluating different project sites, or the federal government evaluating states or local districts.

Instead of taking for granted that rationality will prevail, or that analogous political factors are germane in each of many situations, these institutions must begin designing evaluations on the explicit assumption that each local or state educational institution has peculiar organizational, cultural, or psychological idiosyncrasies that make acceptance of criticism and change more or less difficult. Whether federal, state, local, or private officials are ordering or conducting the particular evaluations, they must recognize they will need situation-specific approaches if they really expect to induce higher utilization of the evaluation results. This will mean highly systematic consideration of the kinds of issues discussed in this chapter, as well as more sophisticated training for evaluators in the art of teaching—inducing change and altering attitudes and behaviors. In fact, once such situation-specific work has begun in earnest, it will become clear that the task is not as difficult as intimated above. Every situation will continue to have its idiosyncratic aspects, but more often than not the situation's key characteristics will fit one of several

---

Warren Bennis, Kenneth Benne, and Robert Chin (eds.), *The Planning of Change* (New York: Holt, 1961); Daniel Katz and Robert Kahn, *The Social Psychology of Organizations* (New York: Wiley, 1966); Wilensky, op. cit.; Anthony Downs, *Inside Bureaucracy* (Boston: Little, Brown, 1967), chap. 13.

recurring patterns, for which evaluators should eventually be able to develop particularly effective patterned approaches. The point is that an understanding of the patterns of the differences among organizations (in terms of their receptivity to change) *will be more precise and effective if it emerges from an initial assumption of pervasive uniqueness, rather than from the present assumptions that a few approaches should work in every case.*

These observations are applicable at each level at which evaluation of educational programs and organizations might occur. But they seem especially relevant now at the federal and state levels, where so much investment is being made in accountability systems designed to improve the delivery of educational services at the local level.

It is important to return to the National Assessment here, to note that it has been one of several potent forces serving as a new impetus for an institutional creed; that is, the social accounting movement in education is spreading all across the country at a rapid pace, often in imitation of the Assessment's style. Insofar as any refined accountability or evaluation systems at the federal or state levels might become effective in securing basic changes in education, ultimately they will have to rely on precise knowledge of the diverse goals and situations in a variety of local systems.

But, a major subtlety in all of this deserves final mention. As we earlier noted in detail, the Assessment's consensual style obscures the fundamental conflicts in the goals and structure of American schooling and makes any fundamental resolution impossible. This indicates that the data collected will be of little immediate use in more closely approximating the nation's labyrinthine educational goals. *Instead, the ultimate major function of the National Assessment may be to focus attention on the contradictions, and the failings, of the overall organization of schooling in America.* If this is so, the long-term effect will probably be to reinforce the trend toward greater educational decision-making power at the federal level.

This change might veer in the direction of greater uniformity in schooling, whereby the goals of public education become limited to the transmission of certain widely agreed-upon skills; or change might take the direction of a new freedom whereby equality and basic training for functional literacy remain as goals but are defined in terms of an increasingly diverse range of respected educational outcomes, many of which might be determined at the local level.

PART TWO

RESPONSE OF
THE NATIONAL ASSESSMENT
OF EDUCATIONAL PROGRESS

The following reply to Mr. Greenbaum's 1973 report was written in early 1975. Because Mr. Greenbaum did not update his material, we felt it would be unfair to make more than minor additions to our response. Readers should know, however, that changes at National Assessment render obsolete some of the descriptive information and criticism in this report. For complete information about the current National Assessment, please write to National Assessment Project, Suite 700, 1860 Lincoln Street, Denver, Colorado, 80203.

Roy H. Forbes
Director

1

GOALS AND ACCOMPLISHMENTS OF THE NATIONAL ASSESSMENT, 1969–1975

Several years ago, members of the Carnegie Corporation decided to review a number of the programs and projects to which they had contributed developmental funds. Consequently, they commissioned Mr. William Greenbaum, of Harvard University, to review the National Assessment of Educational Progress (NAEP). His study, entitled *Measuring Educational Progress: A Study of the National Assessment,* is published in Part One of this book.

The staff of the National Assessment of Educational Progress was invited to respond to Mr. Greenbaum's review. The following paper, largely under the editorship and authorship of Dr. Rexford Brown of the National Assessment staff, represents the National Assessment of Educational Progress view of its goals, accomplishments, and efficacy over the years.

Contributions to the following chapters in Part Two of this book were made by many individuals. Prominent among those who made substantial suggestions, however, were the members of the National Assessment of Educational Progress Analysis Advisory Committee: Dr. Frederick Mosteller, Harvard University (present chairman); Dr. John Tukey, Princeton University (past chairman); Dr. Lincoln Moses, Stanford University; Dr. James Davis, Director of the National Opinion Research Center; Dr. Janet Elashoff, Center for Advanced Study in Behavioral Science; Dr. John Gilbert, Harvard Computing Center; and Dr. William Coffman, University of Iowa.

National Assessment is a dynamic project based upon prolonged and thoughtful planning by prominent scientists such as Dr. Ralph Tyler and Dr. John Tukey. The fact that it has remained true to its original charge and at the same time responded to the changing times is repeatedly demonstrated in the following analysis of the project and its plans for the future.

More than 63,000,000 Americans are directly involved in the educational process today. In 1974–75 more than $120 billion will be spent by educational institutions, making this enterprise the nation's largest. Since the first meetings were called in 1963 to discuss the nationwide assessment that became the National Assessment of Educational Progress (NAEP), the expenditure per pupil in average daily attendance in American public schools has more than doubled, rising from $419 to almost $1,000. The federal government's yearly contribution to the support of education has increased sixfold—from $2.1 billion to almost $13 billion in the same period.

These staggering numbers suggest both how critically important it is to gather national-level data about educational achievement and how enormously difficult the task is bound to be.

The National Assessment of Educational Progress is the only attempt that has ever been made to appraise systematically this gigantic American commitment. The cost of this farsighted attempt to determine the effectiveness of the educational enterprise represents 3/100 of 1 percent of the annual federal investment and 4/1,000 of 1 percent of the total yearly investment in American education.

The consequences of investing such a minuscule proportion of the federal outlay in an effort to find out what $120 billion is buying the American taxpayer have already been manifold. And the future promises even greater returns on the investment. When a school board member wants to know how many seventeen-year-olds can read at a certain level today or how many more can comprehend at a certain level than could a few years ago; when a legislator wants to know what level of political awareness is typical for thirteen- or seventeen-year-olds; when a researcher wants to characterize American attitudes toward music or art or literature; when a government agency or foundation wants to know whether there is a need for a Right to Write program or a National Mathematics Foundation or a major commitment of funds to particular career-directed or vocational programs, or whether the nation needs a major investment in programs designed to increase participation in the fine arts—there is currently only one hope that the necessary information exists or is forthcoming: the National Assessment of Educational Progress.

The following pages set forth a rationale for the Assessment and describe its major goals and accomplishments. It is hoped that, after finishing this brief introduction, the interested reader will turn to some of the many detailed reports of Assessment findings for a more concrete appreciation of the scope and importance of this project.

J. Stanley Ahmann
Project Director, 1971–1975

2

CHOICES FACED BY
NAEP'S PLANNERS

The primary goal of the National Assessment of Educational Progress is to provide educators and those who allocate funds for education with concrete information about educational achievement.

The assessment idea grew out of the realization, in the early sixties, that such information did not exist and would be needed if the federal investment in education continued to run into the billions of dollars. Given the decision to gather such information, it was necessary for the planners to choose among alternative types of information, various means of gathering it, and numerous ways of analyzing it. The choices made in those early years determined the character of the National Assessment's developmental problems but also laid the groundwork for its great potential as an educational resource. Had other choices been made, the Assessment would have faced other problems and would now serve other purposes.

Accordingly, any evaluation of the Assessment must begin with a consideration of the choices facing Dr. Ralph Tyler, Dr. John Tukey, Dr. John Gardner, and the many other early planners of this unprecedented project, as well as the choices the Assessment confronts today as it continues to strive for improvements.

To begin with, who was to be served by a national assessment? The answer, from the very start, was educational policymakers at the national level—people who must decide, for instance, if more federal money should be invested in raising the national level of literacy, or if the federal government should allocate more money for vocational programs (and if so, which ones?), or if there should be a National Endowment for Humanities (and if so, what areas in the humanities need strengthening through government support of what programs?), and so on. Ideally, the audience should consist of individuals in executive branches of federal, state, and local governments; members of Congress; legislators; school board members; and every citizen who votes. A national assessment would *not* be established primarily for educational researchers—this in spite of the fact that many of the founders were themselves established researchers who would have relished an opportunity to test hypotheses on a national scale. This early decision, made in the interest of practicality, narrowed somewhat the audience for the assessment. Although the assessment data *do* have research potential and have, in fact, contributed to educational research, they were not developed primarily for that purpose.

The second planning question then became: What kind of information would be useful to these policymakers, given that such a project would always face limited funding? The answer was very conservative: the project's efforts would be "census-like," analagous to measuring the national incidence of unemployment, its changes from time to time, and its distribution among regions, sexes, and various social groups. Such a project could point to educational deficiencies and inequities and monitor changes in them; however, any effort to gather enough data to *explain* fully those deficiencies and inequities would be too large an undertaking. The national need for more research could best be met with smaller-scale studies, often of a different kind.

Census-like data, the planners knew even then, would not be very dramatic. People expecting quick and simple answers to fundamental questions (*Why* can't Johnny read?) would be disappointed with initial assessment results. But there was an urgent need then—and it is still urgent today—to document and measure the magnitude of educational deficiencies and inequities as an important step in forging policy changes that might shape the future. As efforts are made to improve achievement in certain areas, we need to know which efforts work and which do not. During the Assessment's first seven active years, the consequences of this early choice have been obvious and sometimes negative: Expectations for the Assessment have often been unrealistic and a certain amount of disappointment inevitable. In some respects, the raising of expectations was an unavoidable consequence of the young project's struggle for creditability, recognition, and funding. In other respects, the public's hopes for immediate solutions to what some perceive as a dismal educational situation have placed heavy burdens on most educational projects and agencies. The country's expectations for educational change are, in general, exceedingly high, and legislative and professional hopes for the outcomes of educational research are often in advance of its performance, perhaps of its capabilities.

The next problem confronting assessment planners (and still faced periodically by today's Assessment staff) was what to assess. Should the effort be keyed to traditional subject-matter areas or should it be devoted to the measurement of global skills and attitudes that transcend learning-area divisions? Given the major goals of the assessment and the decision about primary audience, the latter course did not seem practical in the early sixties. Nor does it seem so today.

To begin with, the measurement of such things as creativity, curiosity, self-concept, critical thinking, problem-solving skills, and moral attitudes is by no means an easy task. The technology for a measurement enterprise concerned with these "intangibles" of education was not very developed in the mid-sixties and would have been very expensive to marshall. Furthermore, the issue of invasion of privacy always intrudes into such studies; a national investigation of these matters has already provoked extreme controversy, as we know from responses to aspects of the Emergency School Aid Act (ESAA) program. As William Greenbaum points out, "Perhaps such a conception would be seen as fanciful and luxurious at any time in history—including the present. Certainly in the early sixties it would have been considered impractical in light of what were then perceived as the urgent needs of American education" (page 23).

The other course of action—to test in traditional areas for which the school has clearly accepted responsibility—offers an information base that is easily translated to specific programs, school concerns, and academic areas susceptible to manipulation. Moreover, selection of learning areas does not preclude—and was never meant to preclude—the assessment of "intangibles" insofar as adequate measurement tools are available. All the National Assessments survey attitudes, and many of them probe for such things as curiosity, creativity, and self-concept. The Citizenship and Career and Occupation assessments involve many of these "intangibles" as well. If someone wants to know if American education is producing "free and responsible" citizens—and this is one of those global goals the Assessment has been urged to tackle—he or she has an enormous amount of relevant data in currently available Assessment results.

But is there professional consensus about the goals and content of traditional school disciplines like reading, literature, mathematics, or social studies?

To begin with, there *is* a consensus among professionals about many fundamental matters. Many disagreements among learning-area specialists concern not *what* they are trying to accomplish but *how* best to accomplish it. Many other disagreements center around *emphasis,* i.e., how much attention should be paid to particular goals. For instance, some English teachers believe an objective of literature instruction should be cultivation of a taste for "excellent" literature; this may be their primary goal. Others argue that "excellent" cannot be defined and that no two teachers would endorse the same list of "great" works; these teachers may well have some other primary goal. But both kinds of teachers want their students to read works of literature, and, thus, they share a common objective, however different their conceptions of literary art or their sense of the importance of this particular goal. It is certain that all literature teachers want their students to read, all want them to respond to literature in various ways, and all want them to value it in some way or at least recognize that someone might well value literary art highly. A "literature" teacher who does *not* want his or her students to read, does not want them to respond to literary art in some way—emotionally, interpretively, evaluatively, whatever—and does not want them to recognize its value (if not for them, then for someone else) is not teaching literature in a sense that would be generally recognized.

Given these three rather abstract but fundamental goals that unite literature teachers, it is possible to create literature objectives that encompass the entire spectrum of classroom approaches and literary tastes but nonetheless define the essence of literary instruction and permit diverse opinions about what is important. Such objectives are very difficult to create successfully. Sometimes the assessment effort has not led to their creation, but often it has. Where it has succeeded it has developed true consensus objectives acceptable to professionals and lay people alike. They *are not* "bland," any more than the United States Constitution—a somewhat abstract document, arrived at through a laborious series of compromises—is bland. Nor are they too abstract to serve both as information-gathering guides for the creation of NAEP exercises and as guides for the development of objectives at the state, district, or classroom level.

The next step in the creation of a national assessment was the most important one of all: Items had to be created to determine how many people were meeting the objectives that scholars, teachers, and concerned citizens had agreed were important. The items had to be sound, they had to relate directly to the objectives, and they had to produce the information that educators and educational policymakers need. This step has been a most difficult one to take successfully over the years, but on the whole, the Assessment is now managing it well.

That it was difficult to find useful assessment items in the early years should surprise no one who knows what the "state of the art" was in the mid-sixties. The major test developers had built a strong reputation for success in the normative testing of a very few cognitive skills. The Assessment's need for measurements in the affective domain, for testing in areas such as art and music, for descriptive and diagnostic scoring systems, and for innovative assessment items of all sorts simply exceeded the capabilities of the testing industry of the day. Add to that the Assessment's difficulties in getting exercise development and review procedures implemented when time and money were short and it is not surprising that some of the thousands of items developed for the early assessments were of dubious quality. Fortunately, the quality and utility of the exercise pools as a whole, combined with that of the Assessment's scoring schemes and analyses, outweigh the distracting effects of the poor items which found their way into a few of the early assessments.

No shortcoming has received more attention from the Assessment staff than the mixed quality of assessment items, as the later discussion of NAEP goals illustrates. Since the Assessment is a long-term operation, much effort has been devoted to development of procedures for ensuring that the Assessment's high standards for exercise quality are being met. Suffice it to say at this point that the exercises used each year are better than the last, thanks to a rigorous new quality-control procedure and NAEP's considerable influence upon its contractors in the measurement community. As William Greenbaum points out, NAEP "did help to convince many groups of the current limitations of relying so heavily on norm-referenced tests and narrowly defined cognitive measures. Interest is now widespread in finding more constructive and comprehensive measures of individual educational development" (page 162). NAEP is harnessing that interest today, and the consequence will be higher quality in exercises, greater usability of results.

The original NAEP design called for objectives and assessment exercises addressed to the objectives, with a view toward reporting percentages of people who are meeting specific objectives. This approach has sometimes been referred to as a criterion-referenced measurement (CRM) approach, but, as that term has acquired more specific definition, it no longer applies. The assessment is *objectives*-referenced. No attempt has ever been made to define achievement levels in a criterion-referenced fashion—that is, to say "80 percent of the nine-year-olds should meet this objective 90 percent of the time." What percentage of America's teen-agers "should" be able to sing, or paint a picture, or respond emotionally to a poem or understand evolution? The truth is, no one knows for sure what a reasonable percentage of success should be, partly because concrete achievement data have never been available—those are the data NAEP is attempting to collect in the first place! And one of their primary uses may well be to assist CRM-test developers in estimating realistic criteria for learning tasks.

In short, the Assessment planners never aspired to the creation of a criterion-referenced test as such tests have come to be defined today. They chose to leave the establishment of performance levels to the readers and interpreters of the reports of Assessment findings. And so it is today: Each reader of a report can decide for himself whether 65 percent on a given exercise is too low, about what one should expect of the age level under existing conditions, or surprisingly high. Each reader can mull over the implications of the percentages selecting various wrong answers or responding in various undesirable but interesting ways to particular questions. In addition, the Assessment encourages professional groups to analyze the exercises, establish criteria, compare the criteria to the actual results, and discuss the curricular and pedagogical implications of any disparities they find. This seems like a reasonable way to apply NAEP data to specific needs, and it keeps the responsibility for establishing criteria in the hands of those most capable of doing it well—the learning-area professionals who have at hand the means to correct inadequacies and respond to potential weaknesses.

All the decisions discussed above and further decisions about data analysis have had direct consequences for National Assessment reports. Clearly, the reports have had to be descriptive, rather than prescriptive. The Assessment could only be an information-gathering project, not a direct educational-change agent. The early hope was that professional groups, legislatures, researchers, and others would examine the data, discuss their implications, and recommend changes where warranted. Accordingly, the first reports were very cautious, very dry descriptive statistical reports. No inferences were drawn about what caused the results to be what they were, and no recommendations were made for corrective action.

Although several groups did express interest in the early reports, audience response was generally disappointing. It became clear that people were not going to use the data just because they were available. The Assessment would have to become far more aggressive in disseminating its results and promoting their interpretation. Accordingly, there have been major changes in Assessment reports over the years, and a considerable effort has been made to enlist professional groups (e.g., the National Council for the Social Studies, National Science Teachers Association, National Council of Teachers of English, National Council of Teachers of Mathematics, Music Educators National Conference) in interpretive efforts. These efforts, coupled with a new reporting strategy that aims at several different audiences, have greatly improved the Assessment's visibility and utility, as we will see in the discussion of more specific NAEP goals.

Given the ultimate goal of the National Assessment, it is apparent that a number of its major features followed as a matter of course. Each feature— the primary audience, the content of the assessment, the objectives, the types of exercises, the analyses and reports—was considered in the context of practical alternatives and such factors as funding, the state of the art of measurement, and political realities. There were choices to be made along the way, and they were made in full awareness of the alternatives and the consequences. However, the Assessment is always prepared to reconsider choices if developments warrant change, and it is always looking ahead for ways to expand its utility, as we shall see in the discussion of specific goals. The Assessment is a flexible project, both responsive to the times and true to its original mandate; it is growing, refining its procedures, and interacting profitably with such audiences as legislators, curriculum specialists, classroom teachers, and parents concerned about American education. For a project of such scope and importance, it is off to a very impressive first half-decade.

3

GOALS OF THE ASSESSMENT AND PROGRESS TOWARD ACHIEVING THEM

GOAL 1: TO DETECT AND REPORT CHANGES IN THE EDUCATIONAL ATTAINMENTS OF YOUNG AMERICANS

The "baseline" period is over now for National Assessment and the change era has begun. In 1975, NAEP reported a slight decline in science achievement since 1969, stimulating national discussion about the importance of science education and the implications of a less scientifically literate electorate. The NAEP Writing Mechanics report, released later in the year, revealed declines in overall writing skill among seventeen-year-olds and thirteen-year-olds but a surprising positive trend for nine-year-olds. This information, too, sparked national discussion of writing's importance to this society and prompted a number of studies designed to isolate major writing problems and find cures. Working with the Right to Read Program, NAEP also published the results showing an unexpected increase in the number of Americans able to read at a basic, functional level. 1976 will see reports of changes in Reading (both at the functional level and beyond), Social Studies, and Citizenship. Every year thereafter will bring more unique data about changes in American education as NAEP sets about doing what it was primarily established to do.

National Assessment's unprecedented attempt to measure educational change has forced it to sail in uncharted waters. How much of a change in attainment should one expect to see in a four- or five-year period? If it is small, will it be detectable? What kinds of sampling, weighting, and analysis will best enable NAEP to detect changes of one or two points? What statistical and analytical operations will make us confident that the change is real and not a reflection of disproportionality of populations or subtle changes in test administration or sampling variability?

The Assessment staff, along with a special analysis group headed by Dr. John Tukey, have given highest priority to the solution of these thorny problems. They have developed procedures to ensure that NAEP's percentage estimates are as "sharp" as any that can be obtained anywhere, and they have developed a procedure to balance out "masquerading" due to differences between proportions of various groups represented in samples selected in any two assessment years. Numerous other innovations, e.g., new applications of methods for estimating standard errors, improvements on the NAEP balancing technique, and other approaches too technical to list here, are documented in *Frontiers of Educational Measurement Systems,* edited by William E. Coffman.[1] Suffice it to say that the technical accomplishments of the Assessment in this area have been considerable, and its innovative plans for the refinement of change measures are sure to have a major impact upon the entire field of educational measurement. Nowhere are the standards for "hard" data being advanced with more diligence and more potential importance for the future than within the National Assessment program.

The Assessment realizes that if the measurement and reporting of change are to be its highest priorities, it must continually improve its procedures to insure the accuracy and increase the utility of those measurements. Accordingly, it is engaged in a number of refining activities.

It has addressed the complex question of changing objectives. The problem the Assessment faces is this: If objectives remain the same over two or three assessment cycles, they may lose their relevance to educators; if they keep changing, the Assessment cannot report progress or decline in achievement of particular objectives. The first step in the solution of the problem is to create "meta-objectives"—that is, objectives that truly reflect the essential aims of

---

[1] Robert Larson et al., "A Look at the Analysis of National Assessment Data," presented by J. Stanley Ahmann in William E. Coffman (ed.), *Frontiers of Educational Measurement and Information Systems—1973* (Boston: Houghton Mifflin, 1973), pp. 89–111.

learning-area instruction at any time in history. The new Literature objectives, mentioned earlier, are a step in this direction. The next step is to "weight" the objectives so that a particular assessment will emphasize those objectives most relevant to the profession at a given time. As emphasis in the profession changes over the years, so will emphasis within the assessment objectives change to keep pace and ensure relevance of results. Today, the Assessment routinely requests hundreds of subject-matter consultants and lay people to weight the objectives and subobjectives for their relevance and importance. The staff plans to refine this procedure even more in the next several years.

Aware that exercises must have exceptional integrity if they are to be used to measure change over five- or ten-year periods, the Assessment has directed considerable attention to the refinement of exercise review and quality-control procedures. Today there are four times as many item reviews as there were in the first two years, and items are scrutinized from every conceivable angle by subject-matter experts, professionals in child development, measurement specialists, and experienced staff. In addition, exercise writers are required to explain in writing what a particular exercise is measuring, how it relates to an objective or subobjective, what we can infer about those who select the correct answer, what we can infer about those who select particular wrong answers, what should be reported and more. No exercise will pass without such a rationale, and all items sent back for revision are reviewed again. Throughout this elaborate and costly process, writers and reviewers are constantly made aware of the special requirements imposed by our first-priority goal—to measure changes over time.

There are other changes in the NAEP model that could improve efficiency in measuring change but would alter the Assessment's impact in other ways. All such changes are given serious consideration as the organization strives to respond to the many demands made upon it; when such changes appear to be in order, the Assessment, like any growing and responsive organization, will make them.

GOAL 2: TO GATHER IMPORTANT KINDS OF INFORMATION ABOUT THE CONCRETE ACHIEVEMENTS OF YOUNG AMERICANS

This second goal is qualified, of course, by obvious constraints upon the Assessment project: It gathers information only about nine-, thirteen-, and seventeen-year-olds and young adults; it gathers only the kinds of information one can obtain in assessment situations; and it gathers only so much testing information as it has time and money to gather. But it intends to obtain a valuable (and heretofore unavailable) kind of information which, when coupled with other kinds of data about education—enrollment figures, cost per pupil ratios, standardized results, small-scale studies, etc.—can assist people in spotting deficiencies and, in general, seeing where American education might be headed.

Such a goal poses numerous questions: Should the Assessment stay with ten learning areas or should it have more or fewer? Should results be analyzed with the current five variables or should the Assessment employ other background factors which might correlate more highly with achievement and allow more hypothesis testing? Should Assessment coverage in particular learning areas be broader or deeper—that is, should the Assessment address particular subobjectives in sufficient depth for research, or should it attempt to measure all objectives equally?

Some of these questions have been dealt with briefly in the earlier discussion of NAEP's overriding goal. However, they deserve more comment and should be examined in the light of the Assessment's accomplishments to date.

To begin with, NAEP has not quite completed its initial mandate to reassess in ten learning areas. There have only been three reassessments so far, and it will be many years before all ten areas have been covered twice. This, in itself, represents a tremendous undertaking and, considering that it takes five years to develop an assessment, it seems unlikely that NAEP could broaden its area coverage if only for logistical reasons. In fact, it has already consolidated Social Studies and Citizenship and combined Literature, Art, and Music into a Fine Arts assessment in order to use resources more efficiently.

But what should not be ignored in any discussion of potential changes of coverage is *how much information has already been collected.* Before one suggests new endeavors for the Assessment, one should appreciate the enormous amount of information at hand about achievement in Science, Writing, Citizenship, Reading, Literature, Social Studies, Music, Mathematics, Career and Occupational Development, and Art. Most of these data have been analyzed in only a few of many possible ways. The Assessment performs several basic analyses, writes two or three reports about an area, and then hopes others will approach the materials from different perspectives. Some professional organizations have, indeed, written interpretive studies of the results or turned them over to their research committees; with data tapes now available to researchers in some learning areas, it is likely that much more will be done with existing information in the near future.

Consolidation of learning-area assessments does not limit assessment coverage; in fact, it opens the door to other possibilities. National Assessment is already cooperating with the Right to Read program in a special reading assessment. Plans for the near future include other special probes for particular kinds of information, a feasibility study for a functional literacy assessment, and creation of an "index of basic skills" assessment. All such efforts would increase the immediate utility of assessment results and provide national-level planners with kinds of information they desperately need today.

Should NAEP use other variables than it now uses? There is no easy answer to this apparently simple, but, in fact, very difficult question. As a first step in answering it, however, NAEP contracted with Westat, Inc., to conduct a thorough review of the literature of background variables. The results of that review appear in a NAEP monograph entitled *Associations between Educational Outcomes and Background Variables*. The Assessment staff is now considering the implications of that review for its policy toward background factors, not with a view toward *explaining* what causes educational inequities (the review makes it clear that no existing variables can be used causally), but with a view toward creating "cleaner" variables that do not overlap as much as the current ones do and that are compatible with factors used in other educational studies. Other variables could conceivably assist NAEP in presenting better descriptive data; there is no intention to *explain* educational achievement. Nevertheless, given variables that do help explain educational achievement, NAEP would be wise to measure some of them because they could be used to strengthen the analysis and the interpretations. For example, performance on an algebra problem may depend a good deal on the amount of algebra studied. A profitable analysis, consequently, might view not only the raw data, but comparisons of groups after adjustment for differential amounts of algebra studied. Thus, there are many ways of explaining results, and stronger variables may well help educators better interpret the findings.

The issue of assessment breadth versus depth is another one that the Assessment has wrestled with for years. Were sufficient funds available, the Assessment still could not examine all subobjectives in great depth, simply because the measurement tools for certain things are not available. Some educational objectives will always be slighted, especially under the current and projected budgets. In part, the effort to "weight" objectives has been a response to this dilemma. In effect, the Assessment is saying to the educators and scholars who weigh objectives, "If we could not do everything you desire, what things should be given highest priority?" The hope is that what we do measure we will measure well.

But there are some auxiliary questions about breadth and depth that beg for clarification: What *is* depth and what constitutes "breadth"? Depth can simply be quantitative: i.e., we need x number of items in order to be able to discuss achievement of a subobjective or objective. Clearly, x will vary with the complexity of the task involved. But those x items should not be all of the same type, nor should they all approach the skill being measured from the same angle; furthermore, they cannot all be easy, or all difficult.

In an attempt to resolve this problem, the Assessment has been investigating new exercise-development techniques. Most notable among these is an attempt to examine exercise depth in the light of current theories about cognitive and affective development. Given that there will be, say, forty exercises in the content domain of biology, we would like those exercises to be distributed over the range of cognitive and affective levels articulated in Bloom's and Krathwohl's taxonomies of educational objectives.[2]

The Assessment's financial situation would limit the number of content domains; however, within the domains tested there would be considerable strength for generalizing about performance.

It is often suggested that another answer to the breadth versus depth problem is to create enormous numbers of exercises and then choose exercises in a series of stratified random selections. All indications are that the creation of a sufficiently large and comprehensive number of exercises is not economically feasible.

Yet another response to the desire for comprehensive, usable data is to find out what people wanted in a particular assessment and did not get, and to structure the next assessment to ensure that they get it. The project is designed with a "feedback loop" to increase its efficiency and utility as it grows. Information about problems arising in a given assessment is passed along to the people creating the next one in time to make improvements. Questions about what to report are asked at the *beginning* of an assessment cycle, not at the end. In that way we can be assured that an exercise was created with certain specific purposes in mind, the scoring criteria were created in harmony with these purposes, and the data analyses will be directly applicable to a

---

[2] B. S. Bloom et al. (eds.), *Taxonomy of Educational Objectives: Cognitive and Affective Domains* (McKay: New York, 1969) and D. R. Krathwohl et al., *Taxonomy of Educational Objectives,* Handbook 2, The Affective Domain (McKay: New York, 1964).

certain reporting strategy. This is not at all an easy matter to coordinate, but it is being done with increasing effectiveness every year.

Another way of increasing effectiveness and utility of data is to work closely with people involved in similar enterprises. National Assessment and the International Association for the Evaluation of Educational Achievement (IEA) have both profited from exchanges of information about common problems. Contacts with the Organization for Economic Cooperation and Development (OECD) have also been fruitful. And the yearly NAEP workshop for state assessment personnel—often cited as an example of NAEP influence upon states—is just as profitable to NAEP as it is to others.

What are some plans for the future that will assist National Assessment in meeting this goal? Not the least of them is a resolve to continue refining many of the efforts just mentioned, several of which are only in exploratory stages. Others include the development of new data analyses, efforts to make NAEP variables more compatible with other variables, efforts to place NAEP results into a larger context of educational indicators, increased interaction with other projects, and more aggressive attempts to assist others in the further use of existing NAEP data.

GOAL 3: TO CONDUCT SPECIAL PROBES INTO SELECTED AREAS OF EDUCATIONAL ATTAINMENT

National Assessment's system for sampling national populations allows for some "piggybacking" of small probes upon regular assessments without over-burdening the field staff. Accordingly, the Assessment for two years assisted the Right to Read program by conducting a functional literacy "mini-assessment." The intent was to discover how many seventeen-year-olds are unable to read at a level sufficient for productive employment and citizenship. This project involved the administration of two extra booklets of specially selected NAEP reading exercises to some 5,200 seventeen-year-olds. The Assessment scored the exercises, drafted reports of results, and passed them along to the Right to Read staff for their use. Functional literacy indices were reported for the usual NAEP variable groups and for seventeen-year-olds both in and out of school.

Another such special enterprise may well to be to create an "index of basic skills" assessment. During the 1974–75 assessment there was a research study using two packages of "basic skills" exercises directed toward gathering information about the logistics of such an assessment; meanwhile, the staff has been working with consultants to determine what skills are fundamental to active and productive participation in American society, and what exercises might best detect the presence or absence of those skills. Later there will be a full-scale feasibility study.

Although the exact design of this study is dependent upon many factors (level of funding, development of objectives and new exercises, and preliminary indications from the 1974–75 effort), it is presently anticipated that the Index of Basic Skills would be assessed within the next few years. While the Index could provide data on the performance of basic skills, the addition of new background variables would allow NAEP to explore the variables producing or affecting the performance. NAEP is also considering the possibility of investigating the performance levels of thirteen-year-olds and adults on the Index of Basic Skills (IBS).

On the basis of the preliminary studies, the Assessment will determine whether or not it is possible to establish an Index of Basic Skills, whether or not such an Index provides unique and needed information about the performance and abilities of seventeen-year-olds, and whether or not this information can be used and applied. If the Index of Basic Skills is able to satisfy these three conditions, National Assessment plans to proceed with the full-scale development of the Index.

Another special probe planned for the 1975–76 assessment year is in the area of "basic" mathematics. For several years there has been considerable attention devoted to defining those aspects of mathematics that should be mastered by all citizens if they hope to function effectively in American society.[3] In response to the need for concrete information about existing levels of achievement in basic mathematics skills, NAEP will conduct this special study.

The development of the basic mathematics assessment is based on work that had previously been done in mathematics by the National Assessment. In 1972–73, mathematics was thoroughly assessed at ages nine, thirteen, seventeen, and at the young adult level. Exercises used in the special basic math assessment were selected from the exercises used during the 1972–73 assessment.

There are ten content areas involved in the study: numbers and number

---

[3] See, for instance, Max S. Bell, "What Does 'Everyman' Really Need from School Mathematics?" *Mathematics Teacher*, March 1974, pp. 196–202.

concepts, numbers and their operations, arithmetic computation, sets, measurement and estimation, mathematical sentences, geometry, statistics and graphs, personal and consumer math, and attitudes. For each of these areas the assessment will determine how many people can (1) recall or recognize facts, definitions, and symbols, (2) perform mathematical manipulations, (3) understand appropriate mathematical concepts and processes, (4) solve appropriate word problems, and (5) demonstrate an appreciation of the need for skill in the area. This matrix of ten different areas and five approaches to each will yield a number of specific and relevant reports about strengths and weaknesses in fundamental mathematical skills.

Yet another special probe currently being developed combines reading, writing, listening, and speaking skills into a communications assessment. Like the IBS, it is being developed in stages and will work its way into the schedule as it proves itself.

Other special probes are possible whenever there appears to be a need for them and the staff time and resources are available.

GOAL 4: TO PROVIDE ANALYSES AND REPORTS UNDERSTANDABLE TO, INTERPRETABLE BY, AND RESPONSIVE TO THE NEEDS OF A VARIETY OF AUDIENCES

As of the fall of 1974, National Assessment has published fifty reports about results in nine learning areas. In the early years of National Assessment, staff effort was largely consumed by the problems of contract monitoring, sampling, data analysis, and objectives and exercise development; little time, money, or staff were available for consideration of NAEP's end product, its reports. In fact, NAEP staff did not fully assume responsibility for the communication of its results until the second assessment year (the Analysis Advisory Committee was largely responsible for Year 01 reporting), when reports in Literature and Reading were produced by the Research and Analysis Department. Recent years have seen a major shifting of attention to the area of report writing and dissemination and a relaxation of NAEP's original policy of not producing interpretive reports.

To begin with, report writing was moved to the Utilization/Applications Department in May 1973. This shift was impelled by the necessity to get NAEP information to different audiences in different ways. Though Research and Analysis will continue to produce technical documents for researchers, replicators, etc., Utilization/Applications' responsibility is to present assessment results in less technical, more appealing, and selectively focused ways to educators, legislators, and many lay audiences.

The first reports written in Utilization/Applications met that responsibility. *Political Knowledge and Attitudes* drew from the Social Studies assessment those results that could contribute concrete information to the current debate about America's political health; *Contemporary Social Issues* cast new light on America's social awareness in an easy-to-read, interesting, and nontechnical presentation of data. The *Musical Performance* report generated more publicity and audience response than any previous report; its follow-up, *A Perspective on the First Music Assessment*, was the first NAEP report to present results in the context of professional discussion of research, curriculum, and teaching issues. Professional comment also accompanied reading results in *Recipes, Wrappers, Reasoning and Rate: A Digest of the First Reading Assessment*, and *Writing Mechanics, 1969–1974*. Response to these reports has been enthusiastic, indicating that NAEP is moving in the right direction.

To further ensure the utility and relevance of its reports, NAEP consults often with subject-matter experts in order to determine what reports would best serve the profession at a particular time. For instance, in August of 1973, members of the National Council of Teachers of Mathematics examined the math exercises, suggested ways of combing results for greater utility, and speculated about potential reports, some of which could be written by NAEP, some by NCTM people. This meeting led to an NCTM proposal to write interpretive reports and articles about the Mathematics assessment, coordinating their effort with the NAEP reporting effort in order to ensure that several different audiences are served in different ways. The NCTM did, indeed, write a series of articles about the Mathematics assessment and its implications published in *Arithmetic Teacher*, a journal that reaches thousands of elementary classroom teachers, supervisors, and teacher educators. The focus of these articles has been on direct application of specific results to curriculum and pedagogical approaches. National Assessment publishes reports on achievement in such areas as computation and consumer math. Not only do the reports detail percentages of students who arrive at correct answers, they note percentages of students making particular kinds of errors and percentages working out problems in particular ways. These error analyses and computational studies will have direct bearing upon teaching techniques and curriculum reform. NCTM writers are also drafting articles about competence in probability estimation, buying, reading tables, use of geometry concepts in problem solving, calculating area, and other topics for publication in *Mathematics Teacher,* a journal aimed primarily at secondary school teachers. In addition, some NCTM writers have drafted a manuscript detailing the Mathematics assessment's implications for research. All these reports and articles—plus the mathematics overview, a report about math in the inner city, complete technical documentation reports, the usual newspaper coverage, presentations at professional meetings, short "fact sheets" for legislators, and an intensified dissemination effort—will ensure wide coverage for the results and greater impact of NAEP upon the educational community and the public at large.

GOAL 5: TO ENCOURAGE OTHERS
TO APPLY NAEP DATA
TO THE SOLUTION
OF EDUCATIONAL PROBLEMS

The planners of a national assessment assumed that if such a project gathered important information, people would naturally seek it out and apply it. This has not proven to be true, apparently because there are so many different kinds of information about education available that interested people do not know where to start. The various programs developed to centralize the information and coordinate demands for it have yet to master the situation, and until they do it is necessary for projects like NAEP to be more aggressive about dissemination of results. Aware that its results become more meaningful after they are studied by learning-area professionals and translated into action of some sort, the Assessment staff has intensified efforts to help people follow through on the results.

To date, NAEP has contracted with several national professional organizations and worked closely with many others in order to foster interpretive studies of Assessment results. The National Science Teachers Association studied the results of the first Science assessment and speculated about the implications of the results for classroom teachers. The National Council for the Social Studies examined the Social Studies results, set tentative expectancy levels for achievement, commissioned an interpretive report, and devoted the May 1974 issue of *Social Education* to National Assessment and its findings. The National Council of Teachers of English developed a monograph that carries the results of the Writing, Reading, and Literature assessments to its 100,000 members. The National Council of Teachers of Mathematics is actively working with NAEP on the interpretation and dissemination of Mathematics assessment results as was noted in the discussion of Goal 4. And the Music Educators National Conference has worked closely with NAEP in the preparation and dissemination of its Music reports, one of which—*A Perspective on the First Music Assessment*—presents the interpretive observations of prominent music educators.

In an effort to encourage somewhat different but equally important groups to examine assessment data, NAEP has contacted such groups as the Association of American Publishers, the Council of Great City Schools, the American Association of School Administrators, the ERIC Clearinghouse for Teacher Education, the American Bar Association Special Committee on Youth and Citizenship Education, the U.S. Chamber of Commerce, and other groups with a stake in the quality and progress of American education.

Interpretive reports written by members of professional educational organizations should not be the only ones the Assessment fosters. In the future, the staff plans to experiment with alternative approaches, such as the commissioning of nationally known educational leaders to write articles or papers, the establishment of regular invitational workshops for the generation of interpretations, or preparation of an "interpretation" manual or kit that would assist anyone who wanted to interpret results in some way.

When reassessment of a particular area reveals significant changes in achievement, the Assessment reports immediately to organizations responsible for curriculum and instruction in that area. This takes the form of a letter or executive summary signed by the Executive Director of the Education Commission of the States and addressed to the leaders of such organizations as the National Science Foundation, the U.S. Office of Education, the American Association for the Advancement of Science, and so on.

Increased quality of exercises, greater sophistication in analysis technique, involvement of future audiences in the development of assessment materials and plans, and expansion of both educational and noneducational contacts— these measures have already greatly accelerated interest in interpretation of results. There is every reason to believe that interest in this important last step will continue to grow over the years.

GOAL 6: TO ASSIST THOSE WHO WISH TO APPLY NATIONAL ASSESSMENT TECHNOLOGY AT STATE AND LOCAL LEVELS

An extensive outline of National Assessment's efforts to meet this goal would be too lengthy for this paper. We can do no better for the moment than to summarize in the following sections the contents of ECS Report No. 48, *National Assessment Achievements,* which outlines some of the major activities.

Aiding State Efforts

NAEP has provided consulting services, technical assistance, assessment materials, and/or data to thirty-seven states interested in developing their own state education evaluation programs. The nature of the service the project provides ranges from exploratory and planning sessions with state education officials, governors, and legislators to supplying special materials for state use.

In addition to assistance to individual state education agencies, NAEP annually sponsors a series of workshops on assessment methods which offer state officials an overview of the techniques and materials of large-scale assessment pioneered by the National Assessment. The workshops also afford state officials the opportunity to share experiences in this relatively new field.

To help states develop greater expertise, NAEP also assisted six states in forming a new organization—the National Council for the Advancement of Educational Assessment—which explores mutual assessment problems on a continuing basis. Charter members of the new group include representatives from California, Florida, New Jersey, New York, Pennsylvania, and Texas.

Some states need no more than technical assistance with the methods of large-scale assessment. Others find that the full range of materials, data, and services of the project can be economically adapted to fit their needs.

Connecticut, following its first statewide assessment in reading, was able to make direct comparisons between state, regional, and national levels of performance. Connecticut used this information to plan more effective use of state education resources. One outcome of that evaluation and planning effort was a new stress on urban reading programs. Connecticut began using NAEP exercises in a statewide science assessment in the fall of 1974.

The Maine Assessment of Educational Progress was conducted with NAEP materials from several learning areas. Analysis of Reading results revealed that Franco-American students in Maine performed considerably below other children of the same age. Using the NAEP/MAEP data to substantiate this educational inequity, the Maine Public Broadcasting Network applied for ESAA funds to support a series of television programs designed to enrich the educational opportunities of Franco-American youngsters. They recieved a $250,000 grant to conduct such a program for two years.

Iowa used NAEP objectives and exercises in 1971 and 1972 to assess a statewide sample of students in three academic areas—science, reading, and literature. The Iowa assessment was designed to find out how well state education objectives were being met. Iowa also uses NAEP materials in its continuing assessment services to local school districts. The state helps local school officials tailor Assessment methods to local program evaluation needs.

NAEP and Local School Districts

Since its inception, NAEP has received hundreds of requests from local school districts that wish to take advantage of the findings of the project and the methods it has developed in their own evaluation and curriculum reform efforts. Many districts have adopted NAEP materials.

One of the most thorough applications of the NAEP approach in a local district is the student writing demonstration project of Montgomery County, Md., public schools. School officials in this suburban Washington area were interested in comparing the writing skills of their thirteen- and seventeen-year-olds to other suburban children. By using NAEP materials and drawing on NAEP's assistance, they were able to carry out a districtwide mini-assessment of writing that revealed their youngsters were performing above national suburban levels in all but a few instances.

At this point, at least fifty school districts that are either participating in a state assessment effort or have demonstrated the staff and funding capability for carrying out an effective program have received direct assistance from the NAEP staff. Since the NAEP staff is small, assistance to other districts has necessarily been limited to providing materials and written monographs about the project's methods, results, and design.

Following is a brief description of four "model" school districts that demonstrate the kinds of impact the project has on local school programs.

San Bernardino, California   In 1972, the San Bernardino school system undertook a major evaluation of its curriculum offerings and goals. The $300,000 project compared local curriculum objectives with the educational objectives developed for NAEP by panels of scholars, educators, and interested citizens. The result was a total revision of local curriculum offerings and a new statement of educational goals. The San Bernardino effort illustrates the typical approach: adaptation of NAEP educational objectives to suit local values and needs rather than wholesale adoption.

Lincoln, Nebraska   Lincoln school officials recently asked themselves: What should we be teaching? It was an attempt to take a fresh hard look at the education needs of their students. When they found their answers, they looked to NAEP for help in finding out how well they were achieving those educational goals. Although the local school district developed its own answers to the critical question of what should be taught, they found that a number of NAEP exercises reflected local district objectives. By selecting those exercises to use in their local evaluation program, Lincoln school officials were able to compare local student performance with national performance levels. Lincoln officials also took note of an added bonus: Because the district was able to duplicate the exercises and methods used by NAEP, they saved both time and money.

The evaluation program showed that Lincoln students' overall achievement is superior or equal to national levels with a few specific exceptions. And it is to these few exceptions that Lincoln teachers are now giving added emphasis in the instructional program.

Shawnee Mission, Kansas   The Shawnee Mission school district encourages innovation but wants to make sure that innovation pays off in better student achievement. After school officials launched a new interdisciplinary curriculum project on American studies in 1973–74, they sought help from NAEP in developing means of evaluating its success. By incorporating social studies exercises used in the national surveys, the district hopes to gauge the comparative effectiveness of their new curriculum approach.

Milwaukee, Wisconsin   Milwaukee education officials wanted to know how well students had mastered science subjects. To find out, the city used NAEP Science exercises in a systemwide evaluation of science achievement in 1971. Milwaukee is using the information it gathered to plan curriculum approaches that will be effective in upgrading students' science achievement.

Other school districts that have begun planning or are using the NAEP approach or materials in local evaluation programs include:

Jefferson County Public Schools, Colorado
Atlanta Public Schools, Georgia
Bellingham Public Schools, Washington
Cheyenne Mountain School, Colorado
Herricks, Long Island, Public School, New York
Monterey Peninsula, California
Memomonee Falls, Wisconsin
Overseas Dependents Schools
Kamehameha Schools, Hawaii
Montgomery County, Maryland
Greeley Public Schools, Colorado

Bloomington Public Schools, Minnesota
Fairfax Public Schools, California
Rockville Centre, New York
Philadelphia Public Schools, Pennsylvania
Chicago Public Schools, Illinois
Columbia Public Schools, Missouri

GOAL 7: TO CONTINUE TO DEVELOP, TEST, AND REFINE THE TECHNOLOGIES NECESSARY FOR GATHERING AND ANALYZING NATIONAL ASSESSMENT ACHIEVEMENT DATA; AND TO CONTINUE RESEARCH STUDIES NECESSARY FOR THE RESOLUTION OF EXISTING PROBLEMS

Simply put, this goal affirms the Assessment's commitment to improving itself in every way possible. No critics of the project are more demanding than the National Assessment staff members themselves. Some of their plans for improvement have already been mentioned earlier in some detail. Briefly, they include:

1. Continued refinement of the exercises and objectives development processes, with emphasis upon increasingly effective use of weighting, creation of stable "meta-objectives," employment of Bloom's *Taxonomy* in exercise pool evaluation, increasing the number of reviews by a factor of four, and more efficient use of staff resources
2. Continued investigation of the validity of NAEP exercises and the reliability of NAEP scoring techniques
3. Continued study of the sources of systematic nonsampling errors in assessment data. Since systematic bias can crop up anywhere in the assessment process—from packaging of exercises to types of analysis—this continual monitoring of itself is a major NAEP activity
4. Development of sampling, packaging, and analysis techniques for generating interaction data
5. Improvement of the national try-out system to make it more efficient and make better use of try-out data
6. Continued exploration of sampling design changes and their implications
7. Improvement of NAEP's capacity to respond quickly to new ideas and problems without compromising its primary goals
8. Refinement of a management information program designed to assist the Assessment's efficiency and effectiveness
9. Integration of an adventurous research program that will continue its study of such things as:

(*a*)   The influence of exercise format upon results
(*b*)   The problems that hinder direct relationships between exercises and objectives
(*c*)   The influence of package organization upon results
(*d*)   The presence or absence of a fatigue factor in results
(*e*)   The advantages and liabilities of various long-range sampling plans
(*f*)   Determination of the effects of refusals and nonresponses, both by individuals and large districts or cities
(*g*)   Alternative incentive strategies
(*h*)   Sources of between- and within-scorer variability and general problems with scorer bias
(*i*)   Alternative ways of aggregating data within learning areas, across learning areas, and across years
(*j*)   Improved data adjustments
(*k*)   Exploration of possible multivariate approaches to data analysis
(*l*)   Alternative reporting and dissemination strategies based on studies of user needs and more

It is important to note that all this vigorous activity is not aimed at changing the Assessment in radical ways in response to unrealistic expectations or a new definition of its purpose. These are efforts to improve the Assessment's effectiveness in carrying out its original complex mission. Naturally, as the organization refines its procedures and increases its efficiency it will remain alert to developments in measurement and education that it can or should respond or contribute to.

This concludes a very brief description of the accomplishments and aspirations of the National Assessment project. Clearly it is an ambitious undertaking; if it achieves its goals in the coming years, it will have a lasting and positive impact upon American education.

4

CONCLUSION:
COMMENTS ON THE
NATIONAL ASSESSMENT,
1974

SOME COMMENTS ON "RECIPES, WRAPPERS, REASONING AND RATE"

"Well organized, good data base, offers broad research information, useful publication, am sharing with appropriate staff members."

Dr. L. Harlan Ford
Assistant Commissioner of Education
Texas Education Agency
Austin, Texas

"The information provided through 'Recipes, Wrappers, Reasoning and Rate' is indeed interesting and most revealing. The content is made more meaningful through several readings and possible dialogue with colleagues of mutual interest and responsibilities.

Many of the items reported in the preparation can be used in certain programs sponsored by this State Department and implemented at the local level."

George W. Burton
Assistant Superintendent for Administrative Field Services
State Department of Education
Richmond, Virginia

"An interesting report which I intend to use with various groups particularly to extend the speculation of the panel as to the interpretation of the data. At least the report supplies benchmarks for additional research and program development."

Leo Fay
Director, Division of Teacher Education, Indiana University
Bloomington, Indiana

"Thank you for your note about the appearance of 'Recipes, Wrappers, Reasoning and Rate.' As you can see from the attached newsletter, we have already noted its attractiveness and usefulness and have called it to the attention of our members. It is much more comprehensible than the technical report and should help them see the total picture."

Ralph C. Staiger
Executive Director, International Reading Association
Newark, Delaware

"*Excellent*—very understandable—nice job of putting the data together—very useful."

A. Sterl Artley
Professor of Education, University of Missouri
Columbia, Missouri

"Very helpful to our faculty and students. Please keep us on your mailing list."

Dr. A. Garr Cranney
Director, Reading Center, University of Florida
Gainesville, Florida

SOME COMMENTS ON "POLITICAL KNOWLEDGE AND ATTITUDES," 1971–72

"I have found the booklets interesting and I am turning them over to the social studies division of the department of the school district of Philadelphia. I particularly found helpful the questions to students in the booklet on Political Knowledge."

David I. Grunfeld
Chairman, Philadelphia Bar Association

Young Lawyers Section
High School Law Course Committee

"Excellent publication. It will be of tremendous help in shaping the course we teach on 'Contemporary Legal Problems' at our high school."

Dr. Charles M. Wetterer
Principal, Cold Spring Harbor High School
Cold Spring Harbor, New York

"Provides excellent data for those of us who have the responsibility for developing a social studies curriculum."

Anthony J. Petrillo
Coordinator, Social Studies
Jefferson County School District
Lakewood, Colorado

"I had earlier sent for and received the 'Political Knowledge . . .' monograph and have found it an excellent basic source for me and my writings and for my graduate and undergraduate students."

Melvin Arnoff
Professor, Kent State University
Kent, Ohio

"I found 'Political Knowledge and Attitudes, 1971–72' a most useful and informative booklet. I am showing it to everyone in my classes and in our office."

Gail R. Kirk
Consultant, Law-Focused Education
University of Washington
Seattle, Washington

"I hope to distribute 'Political Knowledge and Attitudes' to participants in the Colorado Legal Education Program."

Mary Jane Turner
Staff Associate, Social Science Education Consortium
Boulder, Colorado

SOME COMMENTS ON "A PERSPECTIVE
OF THE FIRST MUSIC ASSESSMENT"

"I have always found NAEP publications most helpful and hope that I may continue to receive them. You are performing a very important and needed service for all of us seriously concerned about education."

Peter R. Greer
Associate Director, National Humanities Faculty
Concord, Massachusetts

"Highly important to all music educators. I hope the results have been widely disseminated."

Thomas Brown
Associate Professor of Music, Creative Arts Center
West Virginia University
Morgantown, West Virginia

"An interesting report . . . somewhat less shocking than the results written up in the newsletter. Certainly points up the fact that music educators need to take a hard look at goals, philosophies, etc."

Sara Holroyd
Associate Professor of Music Education and Director of Choruses
School of Music, University of Kentucky
Lexington, Kentucky

"A worthy and much needed project—seems to be progressing well. Appreciate NAEP getting the profession's input via the representative and reputable groups cited in this report. Obviously (to me, at least) we have more directions to go before the assessment program can attain high validity. I refer particularly to the matters of understanding music in a human (social, political, religious, economic, psychological, biological) context; and to using music."

Paul A. Haack
Associate Professor, Music Education and Music Therapy
University of Kansas
Lawrence, Kansas

"Information was well organized and conveyed meaningful statements as to selected aspects of the music assessment. The copy is being shared with the state supervisor of music."

Randall L. Broyles
Assistant State Superintendent, Department of Public Instruction
Dover, Delaware

"Impressive! It looks like a study every music educator should be throughly familiar with.

I should like to include comments on this publication, and the succeeding related publications, in our official publication, *MUSART,* beginning with the fall 1974 issue. If there is additional material you would like us to consider, we should be glad to receive copies—but our deadline for the next issue is *soon!*"

Sister Jane Marie Perrot
Executive Director, National Catholic Music Education Association
Hyattsville, Maryland

"A very good beginning—provocative of further study."

Oscar Brand
Vice President, Songwriters Hall of Fame
Great Neck, New York

SOME COMMENTS ON "SOCIAL STUDIES: AN OVERVIEW"

"Terrific—I intend to relay portions of report to teachers in my department so that weaknesses shown in report can be corrected in our school."

Ermil Jones
Chairman, Social Studies Department,
Belleville High School
Belleville, Michigan

"This is one of the most beneficial publications I have ever received. It will be very helpful in assessing our program and making recommendations."

Ms. Harriet Parrish
Social Studies Coordinator
Winston-Salem/Forsyth County Schools
Winston-Salem, North Carolina

"I have briefly read the report and find it most helpful and interesting. It will provide us with some guidelines from which to work as we develop our curriculum and courses at the regional high school where I teach and am Department Coordinator."

Priscilla Blanchette
Social Studies Department Coordinator
RHAM Jr. Senior High School
Hebron, Connecticut

"Interesting results and reporting. Results have profound implications for educational planning."

Dr. Lee H. Smith
Department Chairman and Project Director
St. Louis Park High School
Minnetonka, Minnesota

"It is valuable reading because it will serve as a guide and criterion for our own curriculum development in the social studies. I am particularly pleased with how clearly the data and conclusions are presented. I will be discussing the report with our social studies supervisor."

Alex J. Kramer
Director of Curriculum, Moon Area Schools
Coraopolis, Pennsylvania

"I have found 'Social Studies: An Overview' to be interesting and informative. I am sure that as we progress with our state assessment efforts that this type of reporting style and content will prove most useful."

H. Michael Hartoonian
Social Studies Specialist,
State of Wisconsin Department of Public Instruction
Madison, Wisconsin

NATIONAL ASSESSMENT POLICY COMMITTEE

(Chairman of Policy Committee)
Mr. Robert McBride, President
National Association of School
   Boards of Education

Dr. George Brain
Dean, College of Education

Washington State University
Pullman, Washington

Mr. William R. Conway
Education Committee
Florida House of Representatives

Dr. Lyman V. Ginger
Superintendent of Public Instruction
State Department of Education
Frankfort, Kentucky

Dr. George Kozmetsky
Dean, Graduate School of Business
University of Texas

Ms. Joyce E. Lewis
Maine House of Representatives
  Education Committee

Dr. Bill Lillard
Superintendent of Schools
Oklahoma City, Oklahoma

Dr. Frederick Mosteller
Chairman, Department of Statistics
Harvard University

Dr. Julian Samora
Professor, University of Notre Dame
South Bend, Indiana

Ms. Eleanor P. Sheppard
Chairman, Education Committe
Virginia House of Representatives

Dr. Stephen Wright
Vice President, College Entrance
  Examination Board

Ex officio

Dr. Ralph W. Tyler
Science Research Associates
Chicago, Illinois

NATIONAL ASSESSMENT ANALYSIS ADVISORY COMMITTEE

Dr. Frederick Mosteller, Chairman since 1973. Professor of Mathematical Statistics, Harvard University (1970–   ).

Dr. John W. Tukey, Chairman 1965–1973. Professor of Statistics, Princeton University (1965–   ).

Dr. Robert Abelson, Professor of Psychology, Yale University (1965–1972).

Dr. David Brillinger, Professor of Statistics, University of California at Berkeley (1973–   ).

Dr. William E. Coffman, Professor of Education, University of Iowa (1970–   ).

Dr. Lee J. Cronbach, Professor of Psychology and Education, Stanford University (1965–1969).

Dr. James A. Davis, Director of National Opinion Research Center, Chicago, Illinois (1973–   ).

Dr. Janet Elashoff, Statistical Advisor, Center for Advanced Study in the Behavioral Sciences, Palo Alto, California (1973–   ).

Dr. John P. Gilbert, Staff Statistician at the Harvard University Computer Center (1970–   ).

Dr. Lyle V. Jones, Professor of Psychology, L. L. Thurstone Psychometric Laboratory, Dean of the Graduate School, University of North Carolina (1965–   ).

Dr. Lincoln Moses, Professor of Statistics, Dean of the Graduate School, Stanford University (1974–   ).

Dr. Ralph W. Tyler, Science Research Associates, Chicago, Illinois (1965–1969).

SELECTED BIBLIOGRAPHY

Alkin, M. C.: "The Development of Evaluation Theory," *Evaluation Comment,* Center for the Study of Evaluation of Instructional Programs, Los Angeles, October 1969.

Anderson, Stanford (ed.): *Planning for Diversity and Choice* (Cambridge, Mass.: M.I.T., 1968).

Andrew, Gary M., and Ronald E. Moir: *Information-Decision Systems in Education* (Itasca, Ill.: Peacock, 1970).

Bacher, Françoise: "Some Inquiries into the Problems of Real Assessment (Docimology)," in Joseph Lauwerys and David Scanlon (eds.), *The World Yearbook of Education 1969—Examinations* (London: Evans Brothers, 1969).

Bauer, Raymond A.: *Social Indicators* (Cambridge, Mass.: M.I.T., 1966).

Bell, Daniel, and Mancur Olson, Jr.: "Toward a Social Report," *The Public Interest,* vol. 15, Spring 1969.

———— (ed.): *Toward the Year 2000: Work in Progress* (Boston: Beacon Press, 1967).

Berlak, Harold: "Values, Goals, Public Policy and Educational Evaluation," *Review of Educational Research,* vol. 40, no. 2, American Educational Research Association, Washington, D.C., 1970.

Bernstein, Richard J.: *Praxis and Action: Contemporary Philosophies of Human Activity* (Philadelphia: University of Pennsylvania Press, 1971).

Bloom, Benjamin S.: "Learning for Mastery," *Evaluation Comment,* vol. 1,

Center for the Study of Evaluation of Instructional Programs, Los Angeles, May 1968.

————: *Stability and Change in Human Characteristics* (New York: Wiley, 1964).

————: *Toward a Theory of Testing Which Includes Measurement—Evaluation—Assessment*, Occasional Report No. 9, Center for the Study of Evaluation of Instructional Programs, Los Angeles, 1968.

———— and D. R. Krathwohl: *Taxonomy of Educational Objectives*, Handbook 1, The Cognitive Domain (New York: McKay, 1956).

Brady, William T.: "The Management of Innovation" in William T. Greenwood (ed.), *Decision Theory and Information Systems* (Cincinnati: South-Western Publishing, 1969).

Broom, H. N.: *Business Policy and Strategic Action: Text, Cases, and Management Game* (Englewood Cliffs, N.J.: Prentice-Hall, 1970).

Caplan, Edwin H.: "Impact of Information on Decision Making" in Alfred Rappaport (ed.), *Information for Decision Making* (Englewood Cliffs, N.J.: Prentice-Hall, 1970).

Caswell, Hollis L.: *City School Surveys: An Interpretation and Appraisal* (New York: Teachers College, 1929).

Central Advisory Council for Education: *Children and Their Primary Schools*, vol. I: Report; vol. II: Research and Surveys (London: Her Majesty's Stationery Office, 1967).

Cohen, David: "Politics and Research: Evaluation of Social Action Programs," *Review of Educational Research*, April 1970.

————: *Social Accounting in Education: Reflections on Supply and Demand*, Harvard University, Cambridge, Mass., 1969. (Mimeographed.)

Coleman, James S.: *Equality of Educational Opportunity* (Washington, D.C.: U.S. Government Printing Office, 1966).

Cox, Roy: "Reliability and Validity of Examinations" in Joseph Lauwerys and David Scanlon (eds.), *The World Yearbook of Education 1969—Examinations* (London: Evans Brothers, 1969).

Deutsch, Karl W.: *The Nerves of Government* (New York: Free Press, 1968).

Donald, A. G.: *Management, Information and Systems* (New York: Pergamon, 1967).

Duffy, N. F., and P. M. Taylor: "The Implementation of a Decision," in William T. Greenwood (ed.), *Decision Theory and Information Systems* (Cincinnati, Ohio: South-Western Publishing, 1969).

Dyer, Henry S.: "Statewide Evaluation—What Are the Priorities?" *Phi Delta Kappan*, June 1970.

Elam, Stanley, and Gordon J. Swanson (eds.): *Educational Planning in the United States* (Itasca, Ill.: Peacock, 1969).

Etzioni, Amitai: *The Active Society* (New York: Free Press, 1966).

Flanagan, John C., et al.: *The American High School Student*, Final Report, University of Pittsburgh, Project TALENT Office, 1964.

Habermas, Jurgen: *Knowledge and Human Interests* (Boston: Beacon Press, 1971).

Husen, Torsten: "International Impact of Evaluation," in *68th Yearbook of Education, Part II, Educational Evaluation: New Roles, New Means*, National Society for the Study of Education, Chicago, 1968.

——— et al.: *International Study of Achievement in Mathmatics: Phase I, A Comparison of 12 Countries* (New York: Wiley, 1967).

Ijiri, Yuri, Robert K. Jaedicke, and Kenneth E. Knight: "The Effects of Accounting Alternatives on Management Decisions," in Alfred Rappaport (ed.), *Information for Decision Making* (Englewood Cliffs, N.J.: Prentice-Hall, 1970).

Katzman, Martin T., and Ronald S. Rosen: "The Science and Politics of National Educational Assessment," *Teachers College Record*, vol. 71, May 1970.

Kravetz, Nathan: *The Evaluation of Educational System Outputs: An Exploratory Study* (Paris: International Institute for Educational Planning, 1970).

Kuhn, Thomas S.: *The Structure of Scientific Revolutions* (Chicago: The University of Chicago Press, 1962).

Ladd, Dwight R.: *Change in Educational Policy: Self Studies in Selected Colleges and Universities* (New York: McGraw-Hill, 1970).

Majur, Joseph L.: "Educational Objectives: An Integral Part of Evaluation," in *Educational Evaluation*, official proceedings of a conference sponsored by the Ohio Department of Education, prepared by Joseph L. Davis and Martin W. Essex, State Superintendent of Public Instruction, Columbus, Ohio, 1969.

Morell, R. W.: *Management: Ends and Means* (San Francisco: Chandler, 1969).

Pepper, Stephen C.: *World Hypotheses* (Berkeley, Calif.: University of California Press, 1961).

Rubin, Louis J.: "Leadership and the Use and Misuse of Evaluation Evidence," in *Educational Evaluation*, official proceedings of a conference sponsored by the Ohio Department of Education, prepared by Joseph L. Davis and Martin W. Essex, State Superintendent of Public Instruction, Columbus, Ohio, 1969.

Sheldon, Eleanor Bernert, and Wilbert E. Moore: *Indicators of Social Change* (New York: Russell Sage, 1968).

Skager, Rodney W.: "Cognitive Skills: A Consideration in Evaluating Instructional Effects," *Evaluation Comment,* vol. 1, Center for the Study of Evaluation of Instruction Programs, Los Angeles, January 1968.

————: "Objective Based Evaluation: Macro-Evaluation," *Evaluation Comment,* vol. 2, Center for the Study of Evaluation of Instructional Programs, Los Angeles, June 1970.

Thurston, Philip H.: "Who Should Control Information Systems?" in Richard A. Kaimann and Robert W. Marker (eds.), *Educational Data Processing: New Dimensions and Prospects* (Boston: Houghton Mifflin, 1967).

Wilensky, Harold L.: *Organizational Intelligence: Knowledge and Policy in Government and Industry* (New York: Basic Books, 1967).

Williams, Lawrence K.: "The Human Side of a Systems Change," in Richard A. Kaimann and Robert K. Marker (eds.), *Educational Data Processing: New Dimensions and Prospects* (Boston: Houghton Mifflin, 1967).

INDEX